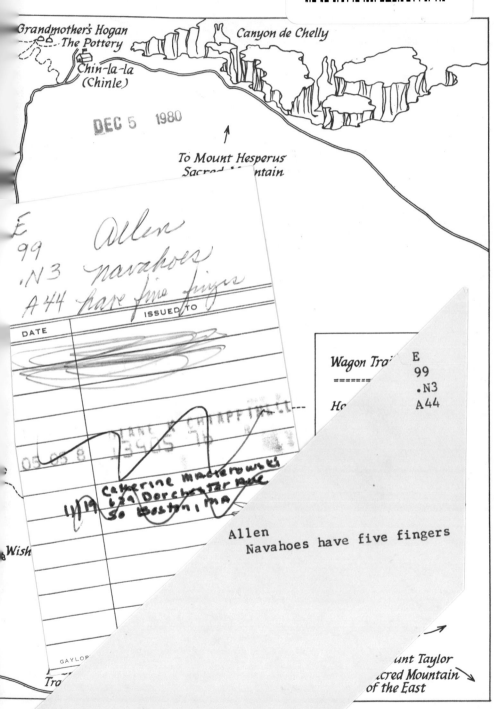

MAY 5

Grandmother's Hogan
The Pottery
Chin-la-la
(Chinle)

Canyon de Chelly

To Mount Hesperus
Sacred Mountain

E
99
.N3
A44

Allen
navahoes
have five fingers

ISSUED TO

DATE

Wagon Train E
======= 99
.N3
Ho A44

Catherine Mac...
639 Dorchester Ave
So. Boston, MA

11/19

Wish

Allen
     Navahoes have five fingers

GAYLOR

Tra

unt Taylor
cred Mountain
of the East

NAVAHOS HAVE FIVE FINGERS

NAVAHOS HAVE FIVE FINGERS

By T. D. Allen

UNIVERSITY OF OKLAHOMA PRESS : NORMAN

By T. D. ALLEN

Doctor in Buckskin (New York, 1951)

Troubled Border (New York, 1954)

Ambush at Buffalo Wallow (Greenwich, Conn., 1956)

Miss Alice and the Cunning Comanche (New York, 1960)

Prisoners of the Polar Ice (Philadelphia, 1962)

Tall as Great Standing Rock (Philadelphia, 1963)

Navahos Have Five Fingers (Norman, 1963)

(With Emerson Blackhorse Mitchell) *Miracle Hill* (Norman, 1967)

INTERNATIONAL STANDARD BOOK NUMBER: 0–8061–0575–5

LIBRARY OF CONGRESS CATALOG CARD NUMBER: 63–17167

Contents

Illustrations

Preface

FREEDOM FEVER is epidemic throughout the world. It even rages through a "foreign" country spang in the middle of the United States, where we are accustomed to think of Freedom as *en*demic, not *epi*demic. Here, close at hand, is a world situation. Here we, husband and wife, initiated our Peace Corps in Little. Here results can be observed.

We started taking side excursions inland from the Santa Fe Railroad and off Highway 66 twenty-five years ago. Our curiosity and interest focused early on the Navahos—The People, in their language and self image. During the years, as we made frequent brief visits to their reservation, we came to know schoolteachers, missionaries, traders, and Bureau of Indian Affairs personnel. We made friends, also, with a few English-speaking Navahos. Finally, during the spring and summer in 1955 and 1956, we were given an opportunity to become reservation residents with a kind of informal official status.

Our meetings with The People were similar to those anyone might have, given the same foot in the door. We were white people, outsiders. We were provided a comfortable place to live and a pickup truck. (Many who have studied the Navahos have been forced to live in great discomfort, under unhealthful circumstances.)

We are not anthropologists although we have read virtually all of the voluminous ethnic studies made among these Indians. Neither are we traders or missionaries or public health nurses or schoolteachers or engineers or miners or bootleggers. Many representatives of these professions have had experiences on the reservation that outshine ours by a Navaho mile.

Although we were provided with some slight excuse for being there, for the most part we met The People as plain, undesigning other people. We arrived as strangers and lived deep on the reservation. We spoke through signs and interpreters. We became involved with "singers," and suffered with The People through accidents and diarrhea. They put up with our trial-and-error home remedies, and with our slow races against the stork. They played jokes on us. We took notes on them. We learned to use laughter as our common language.

We are telling, as objectively as we can, what happened when our habits and attitudes rubbed against theirs. Now that the Navahos are suddenly scaling the physical and cultural barriers that for hundreds of years have fenced them in, we'd like to add our two-cents' worth to the cause of understanding.

Miss Virginia Boardman, R. N., is the one who went away, bless her, and occasioned the need for someone to stay at Tselani during her absence. Dr. Joseph A. Poncel is the General Superintendent of Ganado Mission and the good friend who suggested that we stand by while "Ginny" was away. Mrs. Poncel (Thelma) frequently fed us or put us up for the night after we'd made a hurried run to the hospital with a patient. She also read our manuscript and said, "I like it."

Robert W. Young (Assistant to the General Superintendent of the Navaho Agency of the Bureau of Indian Affairs, Department of the Interior) read the manuscript and caught some of our mistakes. How we envy him his skill and experience with the Navaho language!

Dr. Duncan Spining and Dr. David Dolese trusted us to help where we could and to bring real medical problems to them. Sage Memorial Hospital at Ganado let us observe a few births so we wouldn't be paralyzed with fear in case we might not make it to the hospital on time and might need to assist at a delivery en route.

Arthur Dodd, Principal of Ganado High School, also a musician and camera artist, generously provided the photographs reproduced in this book.

Mrs. June Baker, Junior Boys' housemother at Ganado, shared with us her love for her boys, her sense of humor, and "punishment" papers she sometimes required for laughing after "lights out" or for pinching during church.

All of these friends know far more than we do about the Navahos, but they are (or were) too busy working among them to stop and write a book.

The Health Center at Tselani was closed at the end of 1962 because Public Health Service had become adequate to serve the needs of the people in the area. The Board of National Missions of the United Presbyterian Church in the U. S. A.—by establishing and maintaining Ganado Mission since 1901 and its various outstations which included the Tselani Health Center—deserves much credit for its medical, educational, and evangelistic work on the Reservation, and even more credit, perhaps, for knowing when to turn over various of its endeavors to special agencies as they come of age.

Many of our Navaho friends don't entrust their "real" or "war" names even to each other for fear of wearing them out by overuse. We have respected their anxiety in this regard and have given them nicknames, as they themselves do, or we have assigned them other Navaho names, again as they do, often without warning or explanation. We have also disguised them with "make-up," since most of them are far too diffident among strangers to be pleased at finding themselves on bare-faced display in a book. Even so, we're indebted and grateful to the young ladies who interpreted for us and accepted us as human beings.

We are husband and wife, and we write as a team. First person accounts are new to us and somewhat too intimate for our taste, but we are describing real experiences with real people and don't want to pretend even by fictionally resorting to the third person. Using "I" to mean only half the team is merely our device for avoiding awkward and frequent identifications. We were both in this together and are both doing the telling.

TERRY AND DON ALLEN

"Words and Music"
Carmel-by-the-Sea, California

NAVAHOS HAVE FIVE FINGERS

CHAPTER ONE

Don't Take Any Wooden Indians

CIGAR STORE INDIANS were, at one time, common in this country. Now these wooden figures have become collectors' items. Other stereotypes inspired by Indians are not, unfortunately, rare. "Indians are stolid." "Indians are lazy." "Indians are unreliable." "The only good Indian is a dead Indian."

These and a hundred other generalizations are commonly spouted and commonly accepted, and many of us continue to treat any and all Indians as if we were dealing with carved wooden images. We are either too solicitous and helpful, as if they were rarities to be sought out and wrapped in cotton batting until they can be turned to a profit; or we are indifferent, as if they were sidewalk dummies in peeling paint to be stared at and promptly forgotten.

The two of us were struck, many years ago, by the discrepancies between the handsome wooden Indian guarding the Harvey House at Albuquerque and the women selling pottery and beads on the station platform and the men in Levis and rolled-brim hats lounging nearby. The live models never seemed to fit the wooden pattern, or the other way around.

We soon discovered, through reading and by personal contacts, what you may have found out long ago for yourself: namely, that

3

braves in breechcloths and feathered headdress, staging a war dance for tourists, bear little resemblance to the warriors who harried Kit Carson in Civil War days. We learned that they also bear little resemblance to themselves as they go about their everyday business of making a living, of propagating and rearing their families, of spending Saturday nights or Monday mornings in Albuquerque, Gallup, or Winslow.

Then in 1955 came the opportunity to live at a remote outstation of the Ganado Mission in the heart of the Navaho Reservation. Through the spring and summer of that year and of the year following we had the privilege of daily contacts with The People— the self-styled designation of that proud and aloof tribe. We arrived in time at a startling and revolutionary conclusion. Namely, that Navahos have five fingers.

The Navaho language—contrary to the prevalent notion that it is primitive, illogical, and so limited in vocabulary as to, in turn, limit The People's ability to think—is actually as versatile as lemon juice.

We use lemon juice in sweet or sour salad dressings, for rinsing hair, for heightening the flavor of fish and meat, or for removing stains and odors. The Navahos use a basic vocabulary in the same way. Their words serve as ingredients in recipes, and with them, they produce layer-cake expressions that provide ample means for accurate and imaginative communication.

For example, *bila' 'ashdla'ii* means literally, the one that has five fingers. Blended by usage, the words mean "human being."

So, Navahos are human beings! Not a very profound discovery, you may object. Still, it keeps us from lumping them into categories and from taking them to be wooden Indians.

The kind of human being that any one of us becomes is determined by coded instructions in our genes provided by our parents and grandparents; and by what happens to us after we are born. We discovered early in our nosing around that Navaho Indians are

4

no exception to this rule. The chemical blueprints transmitted by their parents and grandparents determine that they are born individuals. They have individual capacities for accepting and returning, for observing and responding, for enduring, for dreaming, for meeting life as it comes. Their parents and grandparents were not wooden Indians.

As for what happened to The People after they were born, for generations they lived a free, catch-as-catch-can existence in a land delimited by four sacred mountains and smiled upon by their gods. Then they were taken captive by the United States government, marched to a barren military post, and held for four years in concentration camp style.

As a body, the Navahos refused to collaborate with the enemy. (This is a more honorable record of non-collaboration than can be claimed by most peoples.) They scorned the idea of learning the language of their captors. Incessantly the old folks talked of home and freedom. The young men threatened reprisals.

Children born into captivity were nursed on tales of a land of mesas and canyons, a land that belonged to the Navahos by divine decree of the gods.

This proud people, in the eighteen-sixties, sat in their miserable burrows at Fort Sumner and talked of Washington—"Wah-sheen-don" is more nearly the way it clicked off their nimble tongues—and in the nineteen-fifties, yes, even in the nineteen-sixties, "Wah-sheen-don" and "white man" are still often synonymous in their talk and in their resentments.

Even so, at this moment a great fire is burning in the southwestern part of the United States. A black pot bubbles and plops above its hot embers. No slow simmering here. The blending of flavors, if it happens, must happen fast. The melting pot from which we as a nation derive our spicy stew of culture, is at white heat on the Navaho Reservation.

For hundreds of years, our largest Indian tribe has kept to itself,

5

deliberately fenced off inside a corral woven of tradition, fear, and resentment. Now, the Navahos are rushing out to join the rest of us.

Why?

Before Columbus set sail on his big voyage of discovery, several tribes of Indians related by language similarities moved into the American Southwest. Among them were the Navahos. Some years before the Pilgrims introduced white man's piety and culture to the New World, the Spanish conquistadors introduced sheep and horses to the Pueblo Indians along the path of their search for the Seven Cities of Cíbola. The Navahos soon found raiding their neighbors' livestock both profitable and exciting.

Raiding became their way of life. They raided for horses, and became fearless mounted warriors. They raided for sheep, and their women and children became herders. They raided for wives, and brought home Pueblo and Hopi women who taught them to weave. They raided for the sheer fun of raiding and for status among other horse and women owners.

When white men clutching land deeds and the bill of rights in their fists arrived to civilize the Southwest, something had to give. The government built Fort Defiance at the eastern border of Arizona Territory and stationed soldiers there to keep the Indians from harrassing pioneer settlers.

During the Civil War, the government had no troops to spare on its "wild west" territories. Soldiers were withdrawn from Fort Defiance and the Navahos were left free to raid as they pleased. Soon, with good reason, the whole Southwest feared them. Various and desperate military attempts to convert them to peaceful means of making a living met with disaster and derision.

Something had to be done. On September 6, 1863, General James H. Carleton wrote to Adjutant General Lorenzo Thomas at Washington:

"The knowledge of the perfidy of these Navajoes, gained after two centuries of experience is such as to lead us to put no faith in

6

their promises. They have no government to make treaties. They are a patriarchial people. One set of families may make promises but the other set will not heed them. They understand the direct application of force as a law. If its application be removed, that moment they become lawless. This has been tried over and over again at great expense.

"The purpose now is never to relax the application of force with a people that can no more be trusted than you can trust the wolves that run through their mountains, to gather them together, little by little, on to a reservation away from the haunts, hills, and hiding places of their country, and then to be kind to them; there teach their children how to read and write; teach them the arts of peace; teach them the truths of Christianity. Soon they will acquire new habits, new ideas, new modes of life; the old Indians will die off, and carry with them all latent longings for murdering and robbing; and thus, little by little, they will become a happy and contented people, and Navajo wars will be remembered only as something that belongs entirely to the past. Even until they can raise enough to be self-sustaining, you can feed them cheaper than you can fight them."[1]

The Army called on Kit Carson, a man wise in the ways of Indian warfare. He applied scorched-earth tactics. He bribed Utes, Mexicans, Pueblos, and Hopis to help. To receive pay for robbing their archenemy struck them as good strategy.

"Twenty dollars for each horse you steal from the Navahos," Kit Carson promised.

Few of these payments were claimed. Horses were worth more than money. But either way, the Navahos lost their means of running. Grounded and starving, they were easy to round up for confinement and—the country hoped along with General Carleton—for civilizing.

The tribe at this time numbered between nine and twelve thou-

[1] Commissioner of Indian Affairs, *Annual Report,* 1863.

sand. In the late winter of 1864, Kit Carson marched 8,474 Navaho men, women, and children the three hundred miles to Fort Sumner in eastern New Mexico Territory.

There, General Carleton's well-laid plan blew up in his face. Appropriations failed to materialize. Nature sent floods, hail, drought, and caterpillars. The People had no taste for flour and bacon and those hard black beans called "coffee" that never became soft enough to eat no matter how much precious mesquite you burned trying to boil them. More than this, the Navahos were filled with a truly American love of freedom. They resented being fenced in. They considered their captors "the enemy."

Why should they even speak to the enemy? When communication became essential, they'd subject understanding to the vagaries of two interpreters—Navaho to Spanish to English. Insisting on a Spanish-speaking go-between was a way of expressing scorn for the language of "Wah-sheen-don."

They learned, finally, to mix that dusty-tasting white flour with salt, baking powder, and water and slap it into skillet-sized rounds to fry into puffs of bread. They learned to drink the water in which they boiled those hard black beans. Mostly, they did not collaborate with the enemy.

They refused to learn English. After two or three crop failures, they refused to plant seed. Since the government never got around to providing schoolteachers or schools, Navaho children continued to learn, as they had in their own land, the stories of The People's culture and belief, the lore of living by outwitting the white man and other Indians. Always, the Navahos begged to be sent home.

"Oh, our beloved Chin-la-la," they'd wail. "Oh, beloved Black Mountain where the sun is always shining."

Finally, on June 1, 1868, a treaty was made. According to its terms, the Navahos agreed never to go to war against their neighbors. The United States government promised to set aside a small section of the land they had formerly occupied, and let the Navahos

8

return there. The government also agreed to provide each returning man, woman, and child with three sheep and/or goats. A
schoolhouse and teacher were, under terms of the treaty, to be provided by the government for every thirty children of school age.

The Navahos were on their way "home" within a few days. Since
then, they have scrupulously kept their word with regard to going
to war against their neighbors. The size of the reservation has been
enlarged, piece by piece, until it has grown from three and a half
million arid acres to fifteen million arid acres. But because the population has been increasing at a still greater rate, their land base has
long been inadequate to support the people and their livestock. The
schoolhouse-and-teacher part of the agreement, the government
forgot for many years. The Bureau of Indian Affairs finally became
concerned in the nineteen-thirties; but the new schools and in-
creased enrollment, like the land grants, could not keep up with
the galloping birth rate. The People themselves remained indifferent.

Young Navaho warriors did finally go to war again, but not
against their neighbors. They volunteered or were drafted for
World War II. When they returned, they demanded, "What about
those schools we were promised in 1868?" (They also demanded
the right to buy a drink in a bar, to vote, to become first-class citizens
of the country for which their brothers had given their lives.)

With the Navahos themselves demanding schools, Congress
authorized an appropriation of twenty-five million dollars for education, in the Navaho (and Hopi) Rehabilitation Act of 1950, to
be carried out during a ten-year period. Under this, a crash program
was initiated. By the fall of 1954, thirty-seven trailer schools were
dotted around the Reservation. Children began the first grade by
learning the foreign language, English. From that fall on, the
Navahos have been swallowing education like fresh air, in great
gulps.

During those same years the Navahos began to benefit from the mineral wealth of their arid land—millions of dollars from oil and uranium leases. They could have distributed this windfall per capita. Each family share would have been small, but it would have made life easier as long as it lasted. Instead they chose to build for the future, and an important aspect of that future is education.

In 1954 the Tribal Council appropriated $30,000 to initiate a college scholarship program. In 1957 the Council appropriated $5,000,000 as a scholarship trust fund. In 1959 they added another $5,000,000 to this fund, thus assuring an annual income of $400,000 available to high school graduates with not less than one-quarter Navaho blood.

We arrived for our first "sponsored" spring and summer on the Reservation at the dawn of this "education" orgy. It was a significant and revealing period. Older people were trying to decide what they thought about this kind of collaborating with their traditional enemies. Families were disturbed by fears of contamination and by children speaking a language their elders couldn't, and didn't want to, understand.

We were there when The People made a dramatic about-face and burst from their confinement to join the world. We think the Navahos have much to contribute to the general good, and some to the general bad. They have much of both good and bad to receive or reject from the thought and action patterns of the culture into which they are plunging. We all need some background against which to understand these fellow citizens as they become "of us."

This background in our case was furnished by Tselani Health Center, an outstation of the Ganado Mission of the United Presbyterian Church in the U. S. A.

CHAPTER TWO

"Just Keep the Roof on the Place"

THE SUPERINTENDENT of the hospital, boarding high school, church program, and outlying health and evangelistic centers that make up Ganado Mission is a man wise in the ways of the Navahos. "Those people around Tselani are not used to strangers," he said. "With the nurse gone, they won't run to the Health Center for help with every little problem. It will take them at least a month to get over their shyness."

We had stopped at the office at Ganado for our final briefing before going on to Tselani.

Don said, "We can at least open the community room for clinic on Wednesday afternoons when the doctor comes up from here."

"Yes, and in case of emergency," the Superintendent added, "you can call the nurse at Black Mountain. That's only ten miles farther inland, so she can get to you pretty fast. And you can send patients on up to her." He pushed back from his desk and swiveled around to gaze through his office window and out across the Ganado playground. Then he swung back to us. "On the unlikely chance that some of the Navaho boys up there should get bold enough to play at the Health Center under the noses of you two *belliganos*, you can hand out the basketball and take it in at night."

We were more than willing to be the keepers of the basketball.

After all, the Superintendent was a friend of ours and we were here in order to help him out of a spot.

He had groaned to us a month or so earlier, "What the heck am I going to do about Tselani? The nurse has got to get away for a while, but I can't just leave those two houses vacant with nobody to look after them." Then an idea had struck him and he pointed his finger at us. "Why don't you two go up there and stay while the nurse is gone? You've been around here enough to know how to conduct yourselves among The People, and you're always raving about the scenery around Tselani. You'd be doing me a real favor, if you'd just go up there and stay. Do whatever you please—read, write, hike, enjoy yourselves. In return for your rent, you can keep the roof on the place and see that nobody walks off with the butane tank."

Now the Superintendent dictated this version of our duties to his secretary. She typed it, put it in an envelope, and addressed it to the nurse at Tselani Health Center. The Superintendent gave it to us to deliver.

Thirty-five miles, in these days of mechanized transportation, can't be considered far. The thirty-five miles from Ganado to Tselani aren't, however, perfectly adapted to mechanized travel. This road is frequently hub-deep in mud, or washboarded until every bolt in the car threatens to shear off, or bunkered with stretches of bottomless sand. At rare intervals the road is scraped. Then its greatest hazards are its narrow wooden culverts from which boards are invariably broken like missing teeth, and its up-and-down roller-coaster topography. An approaching vehicle is invisible until the moment before impact, and the road isn't wide enough to permit safe converging at the top of the humps.

The traffic hazard on our trip out this day was greatly alleviated by the fact that we met only one car along the entire thirty-five miles. Not knowing at the top of which hummock we'd meet that one car head-on, and not being able to see in advance which teeth were missing from the culverts, kept the crow-straight road across the sagebrush-and-yucca plateau from becoming monotonous. Then, within an hour, we came into arroyos and buttes capped by wind-carved statues. We were nearing our destination.

Tselani is a tin-roofed trading post, a corral, two incongruously comfortable traders' homes, a one-teacher school, and the Health Center. It basks in a kind of hammock between two yellow sandstone mesas. The hammock is slung five hundred feet above the blue-shadowed valley beyond.

We swung to the left through the first gate we came to and promptly got stuck in the sand.

The nurse appeared on the porch of her house when she heard us trying to grind ourselves free. She waved a casual hand and grinned. Then, instead of rushing over either to make us welcome or to help dig us out of the sand, she turned to a boy of nine or ten who was limping across the basketball area on crutches. We watched her grin at the boy and beckon him to follow her into the community room that was a part of her house.

Her casual welcome, we soon discovered, was western hospitality, Reservation style. Those who live among The People for any length of time seem to lose all effusiveness and to take on the apparently off-hand greeting manners of the Navahos. Their pleasure at seeing you is genuine, but their expression of it is likely to be delayed until a kind of rapport of silence has been established.

A Navaho visiting another's hogan would never think of rushing up and knocking on the door. Neither would those in the hogan hurry out with extended hands to greet their guests. Tradition warns that evil spirits may be following the guests, and these *tchindees* must not be led in on friends. They must be fooled into thinking that nobody is at home at the hogan, and that those they were following weren't really going anywhere anyway.

Those Navahos who no longer respect this tradition still observe

13

the custom and it is given the sanction now of "good manners." Naturally, the *belliganos* who live with The People do as The People do until they, too, feel something false in the precipitous, demonstrative greeting.

We were churning backward from our sand trap when the nurse appeared again at the edge of the porch. Her thin arm waggled in our direction, calling us in. Don backed our car onto solid footing and we abandoned it.

We found the combination Ping-pong, clinic, phonograph, school, and church area known as the community room empty except for the nurse and the boy who had arrived on crutches. The boy sat on a cot to the right of the door with one foot soaking in a white enameled washpan. He did not look up as we entered and neither did the nurse.

The nurse said, "Hi," and went ahead tearing strips of adhesive tape and hanging them near at hand on the door of the medicine cabinet. She spoke to us then as if she were going on with a conversation already under way even though it had been more than a year since we'd seen her.

"This foot of John Joe's must be dressed every day for a while. When he comes in, let him soak it for twenty minutes—hot as he can stand." She picked up a large brown bottle. "I put about so much of this in the water. Nothing to it. I've written out the exact procedure for you."

Don and I exchanged wary glances.

The nurse dunked a lollipop stick with a dab of cotton on it in pale liquid and started mopping out a ragged wound on the boy's instep.

"What happened?" Don asked.

The nurse looked up and grinned. "He was pulling his horse's tail," she explained.

This, incidentally, is about as close as we ever came to a direct answer to a direct question on the Navaho Reservation. Reserva-

14

tion residents are expected to keep their eyes open, and they don't go around insulting each other by pointing out the obvious nor by drawing conclusions that the other person is perfectly capable of drawing for himself.

The nurse tilted her grin toward me. "Be sure you clean out all the pus each day," she said. "Then disinfect it and apply a bandage."

"Hey!" I objected. I turned to Don. "Where's that letter we were supposed to deliver?"

The nurse finished cleansing the wound and applied an expert bandage, over which she fitted a clean white sock. She helped John Joe hobble through the door. Finally, she tore open the Superintendent's letter regarding our duties during her absence.

She glanced through the brief paragraph and plopped down on a Primary-size chair. "But this won't do!" she exclaimed. "I know you're not medically trained, but you've had Red Cross First Aid and you've both got horse sense. I've told the people around here that you'll want to help them, any way you can. I'm sure they'll come."

Then she proceeded to run through her idea of what we'd do.

"The men may come with insurance or unemployment compensation papers and ask you to help fill them out," she said. "You'll have to help them or they'll lose their money. You don't need nurse's training for filling out government forms. Two or three will come regularly to have you phone Fort Defiance Hospital and find out how somebody-or-other is. People will come to buy used clothing. They'll bring in babies with diarrhea. You'll have to do something. The treatment is simple, and without it diarrhea is apt to be fatal among these babies. There's no time to shunt them around from place to place, either. First thing you know, they die." She sighed. "You can at least call the nurse at Black Mountain. If nobody does anything here, The People will quit trying to get help and just let the babies die at home while some medicine man 'sings' over them."

"But how can we talk with them?" I asked. "I understood that almost none of the people around here speaks English."

"That's another thing," the nurse said. "My interpreter expects to go right on working while I'm gone, and I can't see why not. She's in my budget and her family depends on her salary. Besides, you're going to need her. She knows a lot of my procedures, and as different things come up, she'll be a big help. Her name is Didibah Singer—Didi, for short. She'll bring her baby sometimes, but it's still on its cradle board. It won't be in the way. Didi's husband will come sometimes, too. His name is Kee Tso. When he shows up, just put him to work. He'll scrub floors or iron or whatever. He's a good driver, too, if you need him in a pinch." She tossed the Superintendent's letter onto a small stand holding disinfectants, thermometers, a bottle of cotton tufts, and a shock of tongue depressors. "Now about the other things you'll have to do while I'm gone . . ."

As she talked on, we soon realized that the nurse came close to being all things to all people. We were going to be so much excess baggage around Tselani unless we could: run the motion picture projector twice on Thursdays—"at noon while the trading post is closed and again at night because those same people and a lot of others look forward to the movie every week"; conduct a weekday class in Christian education on Thursday afternoons—"because the children will be released from school and they won't know what to do with themselves unless the class goes on as usual"; set up the sewing machines for the ladies on Tuesday—"because Tuesday is 'sign-up day' and everybody comes into the trading post and spends the whole day, and the ladies have nothing to do and no place to go unless they can come here and sew—"

("Lady" is the preferred term, we quickly learned. A lady who does not speak nor understand English still has the uncanny ability to resent being referred to as a "woman.")

The nurse went on and on and on. We, naturally, weren't expected to carry on actual nursing duties. "However," she said, "just

16

remember that whatever you do, using your good common sense, it's bound to be better than nothing, and nothing is what these people have unless you do what you can. Like John Joe's foot, for instance. If he were your boy, you'd dress and disinfect that foot at home. Well, his folks can't do that, and besides, they don't have as much as a plastic bandage in their hogan. He comes nine miles by wagon every day. You can't let a boy like that run the risk of serious infection, and we can't expect him to go all the way to the hospital for mere first aid."

"That's true," we agreed.

"I suppose I can clean and bandage his foot," I said. But my stomach felt a little queasy at the thought of swabbing away the pus.

"Then there's another boy with tubercular glands," the nurse went on. "He must have a shot of streptomycin twice a week. I sterilize syringes in my pressure cooker. I'll show you where it is."

"Me?" I gasped.

The nurse glanced up at me with the same expression I sometimes detect on my pioneer grandmother's photograph when she catches me comfortably running my vacuum cleaner. I always expect her to swat me one with her rug beater. The nurse quickly wiped the look off her face and said, "Of course, you can take him to the R. N. at Black Mountain, if you don't want to bother. But there's really nothing to it. You just give him a shot in the buttock and that's that."

The store and mission that comprise the Black Mountain settlement are only ten miles beyond Tselani, but ten miles of sometimes negotiable road doesn't half tell the story. Between us and the Black Mountain settlement lay The Hill. The choice between giving a shot in a small boy's buttock and driving The Hill is like the choice between turnip and mustard greens.

Squirming for an out, Don volunteered, "We can take patients in to Ganado to the hospital, of course—whenever the road is passable."

"Sure," the nurse agreed, "but accidents happen and emergencies do arise. I'm leaving out my First Aid book just in case you'd like to refresh your memory. And then, there are my ladies. They always wait until the last minute before they think of starting for the hospital." She glanced at our faces and laughed. "Don't worry about it," she added lightly. "I usually get them to Ganado in time."

We had never even seen a baby delivered. "But, what if—" I began.

"You can't tell how much time you'll have by examination or any of the usual methods," she said. "These women are muscular from herding sheep and chopping wood. Their babies arrive easily. The way I tell how soon is, if the lady is sweating on her face, you won't have time to get her to the hospital. Just put her to bed and deliver the baby."

This was a far cry from occasionally handing out a basketball. Before we could ask any more questions, it was time for the nurse to be on her way. She had a plane to catch. We helped load her luggage into her personal car. The Health Center's pickup truck was staying on duty with us.

From nowhere at all five Navahos appeared and silently tucked themselves into the nurse's car among her bags and boxes. With a wave, she went chugging and slithering through the gate, maneuvered herself around the sharp right turn and into the ruts of the road to Ganado and, sixty miles farther on, the Gallup airport.

We were on our own.

As we turned back from the gate, we paid little attention to the gray stone, green-composition-roofed building to our left. Normally it housed the nurse (living-dining room, kitchen, two bedrooms, and bath), and the community-clinic activities. With the nurse gone, we were at least half convinced that no Navahos would show up until she returned, and that all we'd need to do about her house was to "keep the roof on the place."

A Navaho woman and her husband pose
beside a rug she and her sisters have woven

Photo by Arthur Dodd

Canyon del Muerto, where the Navahos holed up
when Kit Carson killed off their flocks and herds

The yellow stucco, green-composition-roofed house set back from the road to our right had been built by a Youth Work Camp for an interpreter. This, for a good Navaho reason—which will be seen later—had proved impracticable, and so it was to be our home for our stay. Didi lived in her own hogan four miles and The Hill away.

We hurried past the red, half-ton pickup truck standing between the two houses. Its nose was poked into a ragged juniper tree that grew from a rounded pillow of yellow sandstone at our back door. We stood on our back porch and somewhat self-consciously glanced over our shoulders, as Don propped the screen door open on his heel and inserted the key in the lock. We saw no sign of life around us, and yet we had a very real sense of being watched.

"Hurry," I whispered, and Don shoved open the kitchen door.

Our house, as we toured it, calling, "Look at this!" and "Come see here," kept slapping us with the familiar until we quickly lost our recent bemusement. Here we were in a five-room cottage, plain as prunes, but clean and comfortable. We had a furnace and a range that burned tanked gas. We had water that spurted, hot or cold, when we turned a spigot. We had electricity (purchased from the trader and supplied by his private manufacturing plant). We had a refrigerator smart enough to defrost itself. The nurse had used a two-way radio until six months before our arrival, when a telephone (four-party and given to days of deadness) had been installed in her living-dining room. We were not cut off from the outside world.

We had hoped, for many years, to get deep into the heart of the Reservation. We had planned that when we could find a stretch of time for a real sojourn, we'd leave the gadgets of civilization behind and just fall into the Navaho pattern and rhythm of life. "We'll slow down and really soak in some of The People's quiet and harmony," we'd said. "We'll relax and learn their way of not-overdoing."

Now we stood in our kitchen, gleaming with porcelain and paint, and felt as if we'd been carried, house and all, by a Kansas tornado into the Land of Oz.

Outside our kitchen window a few juniper trees stood knee-deep in yucca and rabbitbrush. Immediately beyond, rolling folds of yellow sandstone invited us to climb up and renew our acquaintance with strangely eroded figures and pillars standing in sharp relief on the edge of space. Some of these appeared to be giant elephants, lying on their backs, waggling their feet in the air. Still higher, an army of eroded men guarded the top of the mesa.

We went through to our front porch and looked to the east across our rutted, uneven basketball area (recognizable only because of the hoops on posts at its north and south limits), across the road that ran smack into the non-picturesque, purely utilitarian trading post just off to the left, and up to another mesa towering against the bluest sky in the world. In outline, this second mesa might have been a great ocean liner, plowing off to the southwest through the sage-and-juniper desert. An irregular log corral, snuggled at its base, used its perpendicular face to provide the eastern boundary of the enclosure. Beyond the corral and off to the right stood a log schoolhouse (owned by the Navaho Tribal Council, we'd been told) with its two brilliantly red outhouses at the edge of its bumpy playground.

Worming along between the school and the corral, a pair of ruts —now in deep sand, now cut into red or yellow sandstone—worked their way upward to a series of rolling sage- and greasewood-covered grazing lands beyond which jutted a third great, rocky mesa.

A year before, the nurse had taken us up on the petticoat flounces of the mesa at our backs and introduced us to the view from there. Now we could wait no longer to return and claim it for our own. We hurried through the house again and out our back door.

The dry, early evening air carried a fragrance for which we had often been homesick—the roasted, nutlike odor of piñon smoke.

We stopped for long draws on the perfumed air and then hurried through a break in our back fence and along the fence to the right. We followed an ancient trail packed by generations of Navahos carrying water from the spring beyond the brow of the hill.

The path skirted a trampled circle where ponies were often tethered on "sign-up day," and the scent of piñon smoke blended now with the tang of sun-powdered dung and sweat-cured leather and dust. This, plus the fat, sometimes-smell of simmering mutton, made up the privately compounded savor of Tselani. This had been a haunting, half-believed taste in our memories. Now we were enveloped by it. We gulped it down, absorbed it through the pores in our skin, let it seep into our special, all-time reservoir of enticing aromas.

Our feet barely touched the path as it led us to the left between two small log houses, and then we began to climb the slippery rolls of yellow sandstone. After making our way up several ledges with inclined landings between, we came to one ledge higher than the others, that required our full attention. Above us at this point waggled the elephants' feet, and an elongated cone balanced a blob of chocolate-nut icing on its tip.

By means of considerable boosting and pulling, we managed to scale the high step. We were standing then on a kind of tilted counter of sandstone from which our only view was up toward the grotesque wind carvings, or back across our shoulders to the Health Center, the trading post and traders' houses, and beyond to the second mesa. When we climbed the tilted table, we were standing breathlessly on the edge of a whole new world.

A long, narrow shelf of sandstone barely provided room to stand or gingerly sit to take in the spectacle. Below us this flounce of the mesa tumbled down with no more than a ruffle here and there and a few lacy junipers and mountain mahogany shrubs to relieve the drop to the valley, five hundred feet below us.

Our three mesas boxed the valley at the near end. Directly across from us, the wind had discovered a layer of white limestone from which it had carved thousands of human and abstract figures. It had left them displayed, crowded row upon row, in a great stadium-like gallery rising in tiers before us.

On the floor of the valley below and to the right, Old Grand-father Rock looked to our city-trained eyes like a modern sky-scraper, left miraculously erect after its supporting neighbors had somehow been flattened.

One of those rare waves of sensibility swept over us and we turned to each other with the same words on our lips.

"No wonder—" we both began.

"You mean Fort Sumner?" I asked.

Don gazed out again across the cloud-shadowed valley and to the massive mountain beyond. "This is why The People begged to return to their 'beloved Black Mountain.' "

" 'To that land where the sun is always shining,' " I added.

Cutting northward through the valley, the road to Black Moun-tain appeared straight, smooth, and innocent from our vantage point. Before we could travel the ribbon of road through the valley to Black Mountain, however, it would be necessary to descend the five hundred feet to the valley floor. When we climbed around the base of the elephants' feet, we could look down on the series of slender fills, sand pits, and rock ledges that are the so-called road down The Hill.

Tomorrow morning at eight we were to drive down The Hill and four miles beyond to pick up Didibah. Then we should have to retrace the four miles and climb The Hill before the day's work could begin. The idea of actually driving that goat trail was a little too much to stand and bravely contemplate. It looked from here like the sort of thing we'd have to dive into with eyes closed and holding our noses, or else not attempt it at all.

We put The Hill behind us by turning back to look down again on the trading post with its wall-enclosed houses for traders and clerk, on our two out-in-the-open houses, and across the road to the log school. Not an Indian nor a white person was in sight. The only sound we could hear was the rhythmic putt-putt of the trader's electricity-generating plant. Behind Old Grandfather Rock the rays of the setting sun spread a fan of amber light.

Only then were we able to see three round-topped, earth-plastered hogans, betrayed by their shadows, at the base of the Rock. Here and there we spotted other hogans in this light. They stood alone or in groups of three or four together, but always with lonely stretches of sheep-grazing land separating the camps. We still saw no people.

On our first visit here, many years before, we'd fallen in love with this land. Now again, its carved heroic figures challenged our imaginations. Its vast distances and subtle colors calmed our spirits. Its mesas and the tales we had heard of prehistoric pottery and arrowheads to be found on their table-like tops lured us to climb.

We started back toward the house, but not at our usual gait. Already our tempo had slowed and we made numerous stops for breathing in the fragrance of Tselani, now spiced with the sage we bruised in passing. We were deeply regretting that the difference in our color and the traditional Navaho distrust of those with pale skins would keep The People away from the Health Center.

We argued that surely, when we felt so in tune with their land, we could find some common ground for being accepted by the Navahos as their neighbors. We longed to be able to wipe the slate clean, to eliminate from history the Fort Sumner captivity, to blot out all the unpleasant experiences between white people and the Navahos, and disprove the Superintendent's prediction that we should be left strictly to ourselves while we stayed here.

When we reached our house and switched on the porch light, we caught a whisk of movement beyond a large yucca beside the path we'd just jogged down. We heard a high-pitched giggle quickly swallowed. The twilight, then, had not been as uninhabited as it had appeared.

Some time that evening, during the time when we ate and unpacked, our mood took on a new tone. We remembered John Joe's foot with its ragged hoof-shaped wound, and the pus. We called up visions of black-haired, round-cheeked babies who would die of diarrhea unless we did something—the right something. A hollow-hipped boy with tubercular glands was out there in the silent dark somewhere, and we were responsible for his shots. And the ladies —the ladies who were muscular from chopping wood and who waited until the last minute before starting to the hospital! For a full day, we had been feeling a bit rebuffed by the notion that we were outsiders and that the people would hardly deign to recognize our presence here. Now suddenly we were scared to death.

What if they did come, as the nurse had predicted? They could actually rush up to our door with a sick baby, expecting us to save its life. Ladies bulging beneath their fringed blanket-shawls could race to us at the last minute, too late for us to get them to the hospital. What if it rained and the road washed out? What if it didn't rain and the road got axle-deep in sand?

"Listen!" Don said. "There's not a sound." He plopped down in the one big chair in our living room and the crunch of the springs seemed to reverberate through the whole empty house.

I perched gingerly on the arm of the faded sofa, and picked up the First Aid book but I didn't read. "You'd think there'd be somebody passing on the road," I whispered. "When did that generator stop putt-putting? Even that noise was kind of friendly."

We sat listening to the silence and all the horror Indian stories we'd ever read sneaked up on us. We said very little. Somehow we didn't want to be talking and miss some sound that would let us know that all was well.

"I suppose it's time to go to bed," one of us suggested.

24

We neither one moved.

After a while Don mused, "What was it somebody said about the only dangerous Indian being a quiet Indian?"

"Silly!" I scoffed. "These Indians aren't dangerous. Besides, it's not the Indians who are quiet especially. It's the night—everything."

We sat listening again.

I opened the First Aid book to the chapter on Shock. "I wonder how it sounds on Times Square about now," I said. "Seems as if the whole world must have run down and stopped."

Don didn't bother to comment. Finally he asked, "Remember that dark, silent morning before Marcus and Narcissa Whitman were massacred? Remember how they kept feeling Indians lurking around even when they couldn't see or hear them?"

"You read too many books," I murmured, "but I admit I know just how they felt."

Then we heard the wisp of a sound on our front porch. We jumped half out of our hides. I looked up, and there in the frame-size glass set into our front door was the staring face of a man.

CHAPTER THREE

Laughter Is a Language

THE FACE PRESSED AGAINST THE GLASS in our front door gave me a start, but instead of screaming I found myself talking like a ventriloquist, barely moving my lips. "Don't look now," I told Don, "but there's an Indian on our porch."

The face disappeared, but we could hear intermittent scuffing of shoes on the cement.

Don got up to open the door.

"Wait a minute," I objected. "Why doesn't he knock?"

"Bad manners," Don reminded me.

"Oh yes. Well," I said, "there's someone out there. I'm sure of that, so it's not *tchindees*. I saw somebody with my own eyes."

"That takes care of the taboos, then." Don opened the door and I tagged along.

There stood two young Navaho men.

One appeared to be in his late twenties. He was handsome in the tall-dark-handsome tradition. His hair, heavy and black, must have been styled after one of the current high school fads. He had parted it in the middle and slicked it down from the part, then pasted it straight back above his ears, and on back until the ends met in a wake like a rooster's tail feathers. All danger of this tidy arrangement's falling apart into wisps of hair had been insured against by a lavish application of pomade.

Our other visitor appeared to be a few years younger. He scuffed his feet more and stared at them with greater concentration. In fact, he didn't look up at all. While he also had prepared himself for this encounter with much pomade, in his first nervousness at actually confronting us he forgot himself and raked his fingers through his hairdo, leaving it in shreds.

Both young men wore skin-tight Levis with an extra short crotch so that their hand-carved belts circled their hips rather than their waists. Their shirts were of transparent waffle-weave nylon—the first one white, the other yellow—in what we considered two sizes too small. Their shirt sleeves were rolled above their elbows.

We said, "Hello," and waited.

The older young man ventured to lift his eyes long enough for a quick glance at us through the screen door. Then he returned to staring at his own feet.

We waited a proper interval and then one of us asked, "Can we help you?"

The older young man glanced up again and then down.

All four of us watched the bulbous toe of his heavy shoe inscribe a slow circle on the cement floor of our porch. Then, still staring at his shoe, he said, "Hink pan."

"Hink pan?" I asked, trying to repeat it exactly as he had said it, blowing "hink" through my nose and giving "pan" his quite French-sounding final "n."

He glanced up and the beginning of a smile actually tweaked at his mouth. "Hink pan," he repeated. His voice and manner had lost all their tentativeness now. His shoulders squared and the triumphant nudge that he gave his friend managed to convey the idea of patting himself on the back. He had actually broached these foreigners on their own ground, and had conveyed an idea to them in their own language. (His grandfather had undoubtedly won tribal honors for similar feats—stalking up to an enemy camp, sneaking in and actually touching the enemy, and returning alive to tell of his daring.)

Our young man stood back on his heels, waiting for us to bring the "hink pan" to the door.

I searched Don's face for clues. "Hink pan," I muttered. With my index finger marking my page in the First Aid book, our nursing duties were uppermost in my mind. "Hink pan . . . heat pad!" I felt as triumphant as our Navaho friend. "Heat pad?" I asked him a little too loudly.

He really smiled now. "Yiss," he said. "Hink pan."

We opened the screen door and invited our visitors to come inside while we looked for a heat pad. Before I actually reached the first closet, however, little prickles of suspicion took the edge off my triumph. I turned back and asked, "Where do you want to use it?"

"In hogan," the Navaho answered without waiting for his toe to complete a full circle.

Someone was sick at the man's hogan. We had established that much. His hogan, however, could hardly be expected to provide an electric outlet for attaching a heat pad. We made the required mental adjustment and took off on another tack. "I saw a hot water bottle someplace, while we were unpacking," I said. "Now I wonder where that was." As I stood scratching away at my memory, the Navaho spoke again.

"Hink pan on paper," he said.

So, someone had written this thing out for him on paper. That should be easier.

We brightened. "Where's the paper?" we asked in unison. We each held out a hand for it.

His toe took time to make a slow circle on our worn, missionary-barrel rug. "In hogan," he said.

This was discouraging. If he had his request written out, why hadn't he brought it with him?

"I'm afraid you'll have to bring us the paper," I told him. "I'm sorry, but I can't think what a 'hink pan' can be. If I could read it, —"

"Hink pan," he answered. "Paper in hogan."

I never should have separated his request from my preoccupation with our nursing chores, but Don remembered other duties having to do with government forms. "Ink-pen?" he asked. "You have the papers in your hogan. You want to borrow ink and pen?"

Now we needed nothing written out. Our diffident visitors were no longer uncertain and at a disadvantage because of a language barrier. Suddenly all four of us were speaking the same language. We were grinning and then chuckling. We were amused at ourselves and at each other. We were twitting the silly little conventions having to do with placement of the tongue and with tones issuing from the larynx—conventions that kept human beings from finding out what other human beings needed.

The bottle of ink and old-fashioned pen were at the other house. We explained this, between getting-acquainted sorties of giggles, and led the way across the side yard. As we walked along together, the four of us conversed in little bursts of laughter.

When the two young Navahos, armed with the bottle of ink and the old-fashioned yellow pen, started across the washed and rutted basketball court toward the gate, we heard them laughing easily as they went.

Their laughter was far easier to interpret than their English. Their laughter said, "Now look what we did. We went right up to the door of the two *belliganos* who have come among us. We did not sit in our hogans, as everyone else is doing, speculating on what they look like and on what kind of people they are. We went right up to them. They invited us to come inside. We spoke their language, and while at first they seemed too ignorant to understand, the man soon showed some intelligence. We have borrowed these 'hink pan' and tomorrow we can take them back and see these people by daylight. Perhaps we shall all laugh together again. Laughing together makes it clear that we think them a little stupid for not being able to understand their own language, but when they laugh at themselves for not being able to understand, they seem like one of us. We can go tell our people that they need not be concerned, the new *belliganos* laugh the same as we do."

At three-thirty the next afternoon, ten youngsters came directly to the community room from the school across the way.

I had a panicky moment of trying to remember whether this could be Thursday. "This isn't the day for the class," I said accusingly to Didi. "Why are all these children here today?"

Didi barely bothered to glance up from her sewing. "They just coming to play," she said.

Instead of greeting us with a casual, "Hi," or "Hello," as the youngsters we had known would have done, they ducked their heads and grinned at their own feet as they came in. Then, to all appearances ignoring us, they sorted and scattered themselves according to their interests.

Two nine-year-old boys, their hips as thin as a pair of broomsticks in their Levis, their black, flat-topped hats as big as dishpans, started the record player. They kept it going with only as much interruption as is required for manually lifting the arm from the center of a record and replacing it in the groove at the outer edge. The one record they played was "Davy Crockett." They laughed at themselves each time they started it over, and then sat listening and tapping their feet until the last note. Then they laughed and started it once more.

Two boys extracted a checkerboard and checkers from a hiding place behind a bookcase. One boy strode directly to a partly fitted jigsaw puzzle and stood above it, his hands—all but his thumbs—

in his hip pockets and his big hat tipped so low on his forehead that it threatened to wreck one completed corner of the puzzle. One of the older boys (actually a married man with two children) came in and engaged Didi in another checker game.

Five girls ran to the Ping-pong table and wound up in a brief scramble for the four paddles. When the dog pile of hands and paddles had disentangled itself from the table, the small girl with the fat, black pigtails, who had no paddle, spread her empty hands, palms up, and began to giggle. The more she gazed at her empty hands, the more amused she became. The other girls laughed, too, as they took their places at the ends of the table.

The Ping-pong ball was as funny as a clown in a circus to those girls. They had played with the Ping-pong equipment (to say that they had played Ping-pong would be too far-fetched) many times before, but the antics and caprices of the ball sent them into gales of giggles. They always put the ball into play with each girl standing like a proper Priscilla at her half of the serving area. The serve invariably went astray. This set off a bedlam of dashes and wild swipes at the ball which required the record-playing boys to duck and dart out of the way, and resulted in upset checker boards and skewed jigsaw puzzle.

The ball bounced off the ceiling more than off the table. It rolled beneath the piano and behind the gas stove. It landed on "Davy Crockett" and made the player arm skid from where he "killed him a b'ar when he was only three" to the time he "went off to Congress and served a spell," with no interval between for fighting "single-handed through the Indian wars."

Players and spectators all kept batting at the ball, with paddles or palms, as long as they could control their laughter enough to breathe. The ball went out of play only after the last child had succumbed and fallen to the floor or into a chair to give himself over to holding his sides and simmering down.

At first the children sneaked an occasional peek at us to see whether we were laughing with them. When they found us holding our sides and gasping for breath, they took us in and no longer bothered to hood their eyes.

Throughout all the trespassing and buffeting, no one pushed or scowled or even stood up for his rights. The willingness of the girl who missed getting a paddle to laugh about that might be explained by the fact that a paddle was not required equipment for getting into the game. However, the ball went into play and through only one hilarious scamper around the room before one of the other girls passed her paddle on to the fat-pigtailed one called Bah Billy. All were included in the fun. A few words of Navaho occasionally punctuated the laughter, but words of any kind seemed to be quite unnecessary for playing the games.

We were not excluded in any way by our inability to speak the children's language. We were all communicating in a common language, the language of laughter. In that language we all agreed that it was fun to be silly and to enjoy one another's company to the obbligato of toe-tapping music. The conversation at few social gatherings makes more sense than that, and at how many of them do the guests so let themselves go? What a sardonic joke it would be on science and sophistication, if it should turn out that the low incidence of heart diseases among the Navahos is due to their child-like ability to let go and laugh.

Our need of words did not become apparent until after Djdi had caught a ride home. When five-thirty came and went and the children showed no signs of wearing out, we began to wonder how one said politely in Navaho, "It's time for you to leave."

Bah Billy lived with her grandmother in a hogan no more than three city blocks away. All our other guests had to walk a mile, three miles, and as much as four miles to get home. Already the sun had dropped behind the yellow sandstone mesa at the back of the house. We couldn't afford to incur the disapproval of several sets of parents and grandparents by letting the children play so long at our place that they had to walk home in the dark. Still, how could we tell them to leave?

At first we tried to think of courteous ways of suggesting what bored guests we had known (and been) could think of themselves. Our open-door hint and shooing gestures struck the children as more play to add to the fun. We shouted, "Goodbye now," and weren't sure whether we couldn't be heard above "Davy Crockett, the man who knew no fear," or whether we were being purposely ignored.

The record whirled on. The Ping-pong ball hit the ceiling and then sweetly played high C on the piano before wedging itself beneath the treadle of a sewing machine. The players all went into hysterical gales of laughter.

One paddle had been dropped on the table. I retrieved it and then, with no plan in mind, reached for the paddle from the girl nearest me. She handed it over. I stepped to the end of the Ping-pong table and crossed the two paddles on it.

Somehow I had conveyed the idea.

The girl at the far end of the table immediately took the paddle from her partner. She crossed the other two paddles at the exact angle at which I had placed mine. The boys stopped Davy Crockett in the middle of an exploit. The girls snatched at their jackets and took time to shove in only one arm before heading for the door. The checkerboards went back into hiding. The jigsaw puzzle boy spun on his heel, slid his hands—all but his thumbs—into his hip pockets, hunched his shoulders, and joined the exodus. Within two minutes of the time when I had crossed the paddles on the table, the children trooped out the door.

They left quietly, a little sheepishly, with their heads ducked low and their eyes stealing furtive, sidewise glimpses at us. Once they were on the porch, however, they spilled out giggles. They giggled their way across the yard and through the gate, and—for all we knew—all the way home, even though home might have been miles away through the dusk.

We had no thought of trying to converse directly with the elderly couple virtually dumped in our laps one afternoon. Even a glance at their gray hair knots and at their traditional clothing, as they sat on the back seat of the jeep in our yard, told us that they were old-way Navahos who would not know English.

The man and his wife who taught at the trailer school in our area had given the couple a ride from the hospital as far as our place.

"You're to take them on home," one of the teachers said. "Here's a note from the doctor."

"Dear Folks," the doctor had written, "will you please take Grandmother and Grandfather on to their hogan? Grandmother broke her hip a month ago and they've both been at the hospital since then. He slept on the floor in her room most of that time. She's not to be moved except on a chair. We've done our best, but she's well over eighty and brittle as glass. Didi knows where they live. Thanks. D. D."

We looked up from the note. Grandfather, tall and large-boned, sat with his arm around his tiny wife. One fact stuck out all over them—they were in love. It showed in the way her shoulder snuggled into the hollow beneath his arm. It showed in the protective tilt of his gray head above hers.

Don went inside and brought out a Primary chair. The schoolteacher helped him set Grandmother on it and carry her into the community room. Grandfather, lugging a tin suitcase and an armload of bundles, stayed close at their heels.

Didi sat sewing at one of the machines on the far side of the room. She did not turn around.

Don said, "I wonder how far it is to their hogan."

34

Photo by Arthur Dodd

"The roller-coaster topography
kept the crow-straight road from becoming monotonous"
Road from Ganado toward Tselani

Photo by Arthur Dodd

"Strangely eroded figures standing
in sharp relief on the edge of space"
View toward Black Mountain from mesa back of Tselani Health Center

The schoolteacher shrugged. "I wouldn't know, and we've got to beat it. We're late now."

"O. K. and thanks." Don gave him a high sign. "We'll take over from here."

"I can't leave before I dress John Joe's foot," I reminded Don. "He ought to be here any minute."

"I don't suppose anybody's in a hurry," Don said. "I can lay the little lady on the cot to wait, if she'd be more comfortable."

Didi turned on her chair and, without speaking to the couple, said to Don, "Yes, she liked lay down."

We wondered just how she knew this, but Don lifted Grandmother from her chair and onto the cot. Then he swung a full-size chair around for Grandfather.

Grandfather scooted in close to the head of the cot and settled his belongings around him. I could picture him in his youth, quicker and stronger than the wildest horse from the mountains, fought over at every Girls' Dance, and finally allowing himself to be caught and tamed by this little bundle of bones in the blue percale skirt and purple blanket-shawl.

I went on with the job I'd had interrupted—counting out aspirin by twelves into small cardboard boxes—but I couldn't side-track my mind nor keep my eyes from straying to the couple. We had become accustomed to laughter and little bursts of talk whenever two or three Navahos came in. These two seemed to understand each other without words and even without smiles.

Grandmother's birdlike eyes made little undercover excursions around the community room, but they kept darting back to Grandfather's face. Her quick glances were a kind of leaning on him for support and an affirmation of her deep contentment. I could read, in an imperceptible lift to her chin whenever she looked at him, something akin to smugness of the nicest kind. This little lady had been enjoying her triumph since the day she had sat on her heels

35

at the left side of this stalwart young man in her mother's hogan, and eaten the ceremonial mush from the five directions—East, South, West, North, and Up—indicated by a pollen cross on her wedding basket.

Perhaps, I decided, this was the ultimate in communication—this utter quietness, this lack of need to speak or smile. It was as if they had nothing more to prove to each other by means of superfluous words or by the shallow comment that is laughter.

Don edged past me and slipped a clean mattress cover from the bedding closet. "I'll go sweep out the back of the truck and have it ready for Grandmother's ride," he murmured.

An aura of deep calm had spread from the couple in the corner and permeated the room. I could feel it in Don's touch on my shoulder as he passed. I could hear it in the easy sigh that escaped from Didi as she bent to examine a seam. She startled me when she turned back to the sewing machine and set up a clatter of rapid treadling. I counted out another dozen pills.

Didi released the presser foot with a flourish and flicked out her red-print skirt, all finished. She closed the machine and banged the lid. Then she came over to me. Her head wagged toward the cot. "That lady would liked have a cup of tea," she said.

"Of course. I should have thought of that myself," I answered. "I'll go put the water on to heat."

Didi followed me to the kitchen.

"That's a sweet old couple," I commented.

"That lady she's my grandmother," Didi volunteered then.

"She is!" I bit my tongue to keep from asking why she hadn't run out to the car to welcome her the minute they arrived. Instead I said, "Then maybe you and Kee would like to go with us when we take them home."

"Yes, we are going," Didi told me as if it had all been arranged.

I started to measure tea into the teapot. "Would your grandfather like a cup of tea, too?" I asked.

36

"Yes, he would liked it." Didi glanced through the kitchen window toward the gate. "He's been going to the store."

When the water finally boiled, I made the tea and carried two steaming cups and the sugar bowl to the community room. Didi pushed a chair to serve as tea table over beside the cot. Grandfather came in with a large paper bag from the store. He selected one of his purchases and, with stiff fingers, pulled open a crackling nest of cellophane. In it huddled a mound of pink marshmallow cookies, liberally sprinkled with chopped coconut.

Such frivolous cookies would, I felt sure, bring at least a smile to Grandmother's withered lips, but I was wrong. She took one of the pink puffs as her due and tucked her soft high moccasins a bit more modestly beneath the dust ruffle on her blue cotton skirt. Grandfather added another spoonful of sugar to her tea and stirred it for her. In their unspoken language, I felt that this was both "Thank you," and "You're welcome."

Neither Grandmother nor Grandfather had spoken either in words or in smiles by the time I'd finished with John Joe and we were ready to go.

Didi's husband sauntered over from the store. Kee Tso was a typical one of our "boys."

"Boys," in this area may be anywhere from sixteen to thirty-five. They are usually married, but not necessarily so. If they are married, the chances are good that they have from one to six children. Most of these "boys"—in fact all whom we knew—wear their hair cut short. It may have a flat-top styling or one of the swoop-and-swirl effects plastered in place with pomade. The "boys" dress in a uniform. They all wear skin-tight, short-crotched Levis and a wide tan or black belt with the owner's unsacred name carved in the leather and bannered across his back at the base of his spine. Their wide-brimmed, flat-crowned felt hats are shaped every time they're donned, with a high roll at each side.

Kee Tso did not wear a flat-top haircut. His hair was inclined to wave and Kee was not a man to discourage a natural tendency; if it wanted to curl, he gave it its lead and helped it a little. If he saw a pretty girl at a Girls' Dance, he was inclined to give his natural tendencies their lead in that regard, too. If one of the bootleggers— also numbered among our "boys"—found him in funds, his natural tendencies usually separated him from two dollars for a fifth of Tokay. Kee was typical of the other "boys" in that he took spells of working and spells of loafing. The Navahos do not believe in overdoing in anything.

Kee was always willing to help us in any way we needed him. He was always in a good humor. He didn't speak to Grandmother and Grandfather when he came in, but he helped Don lift Grandmother on her Primary chair into the bed of the pickup. He and Grandfather helped her off the chair and onto the freshly-covered mattress. Grandfather sat flat beside the mattress, his long legs straight alongside, and laid his hand on Grandmother's shoulder.

"Do they have a chair at home?" I asked Didi.

She shook her head.

"Then the chair goes, too," we decided.

Didi and Kee and Don and I all climbed into the front seat of the pickup. Don was driving.

The trip to Grandmother's hogan involved, first of all, descending The Hill. The Hill was certainly not the obstacle course we'd have chosen for transporting a brittle old lady in a stiff-jointed pickup. Still, we had no choice.

Before we reached Grandmother's hogan, we had traveled The Hill; ten miles of alternately rutted and wash-boarded road; and another ten miles of wagon trail that led us through a prairie dog settlement, down to the bottom and up the other bank of a steep-sided arroyo, angling into the wilderness toward spectacular monoliths eroded in red sandstone, and finally across an uninhabited arid range. Finally we came to a small camp consisting of two hogans and one rectangular log house. Half a dozen dogs came

barking to meet us. A curl of smoke rose from the pipe in the roof
of the nearest hogan. The scent of simmering mutton and dried
corn surrounded us when we stopped.

We sat for a while with no one making any move to leave the
truck. No one appeared from the hogan. The dogs soon assured
themselves that we weren't really there, and wandered off with a
foolish droop to their tails, admitting that they'd made a mistake.
Finally Kee Tso said, "Well," and opened the cab door.

We got out slowly, taking care to look nonchalant—as if we'd
just happened to stop here with no special purpose in mind. We
didn't, of course, even glance toward the hogan. We certainly
wouldn't walk right up and guide any tagging-along evil spirits
inside. First we must wander around the truck a bit and look off
in the distance and admire the rounded red hills beyond. Then we
might saunter to the back of the truck and find out how Grandmother and Grandfather were doing back there.

Two pregnant young women ducked through the blanket-door
of the hogan and came outside. One sat down on an upended
orange crate. The other leaned against the side of the hogan. They
paid no attention to us.

At last Kee climbed into the bed of the truck and motioned for
Don to follow. Kee and Don lifted Grandmother gently onto the
borrowed chair and eased her down. Pack-saddle fashion they carried her, chair and all, into the hogan.

The two pregnant ladies gazed at their moccasins and said
nothing at all.

Grandfather, still in the truck, pushed his tin suitcase toward the
tail gate where Don could reach it when he came out. Various possessions still seemed to surround him, though, so I held out my
hand, offering to help with whatever was left. He shoved his bag
of store groceries toward me, but awkwardly because he was trying
to hide something behind him. He kept poking a soft, gray bundle
under his thigh, but it insisted on developing appendages that re-

fused to be hidden. Finally, he shrugged and gave up. He tossed the stubborn thing toward me.

I caught the gray wad and discovered, when a leg fell over my arm, that I was holding a suit of long winter underwear. It had quite obviously been worn, night and day, for most of a month. I looked up and surprised a twinkle in Grandfather's eyes. None of the vaudeville jokes based on trap doors ever brought forth a bigger belly laugh than the one that erupted then, simultaneously, from Grandfather and me. He laughed so hard he had difficulty climbing down from the truck.

Grandfather and I stood there, laughing and mopping our eyes, and we were actually talking together in laughter. Without words, I was telling him how sorry I was that Grandmother had broken her hip, and how much we hated to hurt her with the rough ride home. I was telling him how beautiful his country was to my eyes; how delicious the special home-coming meal of mutton and dried corn smelled as it cooked on the piñon fire.

In his laughter, he was telling me of his joy in being home again with little Grandmother still at his side. By laughing with me, he was thanking us for bringing them home. I knew that after we had gone, he and Grandmother would laugh together over his suit of smoke-gray underwear and that he would tell her that I, too, had enjoyed the joke. Their people and my people would never again be quite as far apart now that we had talked together in laughter.

We had another couple, middle-aged, come to clinic one day. They were also in love. Theirs, however, was the teasing, bickering kind of relationship. They were both born clowns. The man pretended that the yellow silk handkerchief around his head had come loose. His bulky wife sat on two chairs, with her arms folded on the shelf of her bosom and refused to tie it for him. He screwed the scarf down until it hung up on his nose in front and on his hair knot at the back of his head.

Other patients in the community room hid their amusement behind their hands as long as they could, but chuckles insisted on escaping.

Finally the man untied the scarf and then he was too tall for his wife to reach him to retie it. He motioned for her to stand up. She refused. He bowed his neck. She tied the scarf around his eyes.

When Didi tried to collect for a bottle of cough syrup from this couple, they began arguing and each pointed to the other.

Didi consulted the doctor. "Which one is taking these cough syrup?"

The doctor stuck in his head from the examination room. "That's for him, Dico," he told Didi.

Dico's wife crossed her arms on her bosom. Dico squirmed his long fingers into every pocket in his Levis. Then he stood and went through his pockets again. At last he came up with the thirty-five cents for his cough medicine.

Didi then turned to his wife and thrust a box of pills toward her. "Twenty cents," she said. The wife tipped her head toward Dico. For answer, Dico crossed his arms on his chest, looked down and saw that they lay too low, and lifted them in the air at the precise angle that his fat wife's arms rested on her bosom.

The other patients were tickled beyond the possibility of containing their laughter. Some laughed behind a fold of their blanket-shawls. Others laughed openly. Children laughed in imitation of their elders. One baby cried because he was receiving no attention, and his mother absent-mindedly explored beneath the flounce of her velvet blouse for her breast, gave him the nipple, and continued wiping laughter tears from her eyes.

Didi patiently stood with one hand out and the other propped on her hip, waiting for the twenty cents. Finally Dico's wife reached down her neck and brought up a flowered cotton handkerchief in the corner of which were tied some coins. She loosened the knot with her teeth, turned her back so her husband couldn't see how

NAVAHOS HAVE FIVE FINGERS

much money she had, and pinched out two dimes for Didi. When she had replaced her knotted handkerchief, clinic was over as far as they were concerned. Dico slid his bottle of cough medicine into his shirt pocket and followed his waddling wife from the room.

If a merry heart doeth good like a medicine, those two were first assistants to the doctor that day. Even after they had gone, the remembrance of their antics kept sporadic giggles alive around the community room.

As the other patients finished their business with the doctor and drifted off, we knew that tales of Dico and his wife would enliven many a family gathering around the stew pot that night. Chuckling remembrances would dissipate many an argument between other men and their wives as to which one owned which sheep, which one would pay to have them run through the sheep dip, which one would spend the credit the new rug on the loom would provide at the store. With the arguments settled, the hogan fire could be banked, and laughter would become the language of love.

People everywhere, primitive or polished, make love in the language of laughter. In later years, given the right conditions, this may become the tacit language of deep joy. What difference then does the sound of a syllable make? In childhood, youth, or old age, as between peoples of disparate cultures, it is understanding that matters. The shape of a word is small reason for clannishness when laughter can so readily serve as a language.

Thus laughter made most of our contacts on the Reservation a happy, two-way experience. But there were times when an unbridged gap yawned between our cultures, and this brought tragedy.

CHAPTER FOUR

Medicine Men

FOR ONCE, Didibah's run-down saddle shoes actually tore across the rutted yard from the community room to our back porch. We heard her coming, but before we could investigate, the screen door banged and Didi stood catching her breath in the doorway between our kitchen and living room.

Barging right in was no breach of etiquette from her point of view. After all, we had left the door open. However, Didi had attended the white man's school for six years and she had become enough accustomed to our ways so that she might have bumped the door a time or two before coming in, except for the fact that she was excited.

I dropped the First Aid book and stood up. "Didi! What is it?"

I'd been in Didibah's country enough to know better than to ask her purpose in such a hurry, but her unprecedented agitation made me forget my manners.

Didibah was a plump young matron of twenty-six. Just how plump she'd become impressed itself on me as I stood watching her fan air into her open mouth after running only the sixty feet or so between the two houses here at the Health Center. Her dark eyes, usually so calm, were wide with a kind of haunted look in them, as if she'd crossed the path of a coyote or discovered that

43

someone had taken her fingernail parings. She ran her arm beneath her heavy mane of black hair, tied with a purple silk handkerchief at the nape of her neck, and gave it a flap as if she were still trying to get more air. She gasped, "You better come, I think."

Didi said "thin" instead of "think," and then stopped the word with a kind of click similar to a snap of the fingers, but done deep in her throat by closing her glottis. Such glottal punctuation ended many of her words and sometimes sliced syllables from each other. On a violin, this sort of thing is done by picking instead of bowing. Most of Didibah's sentences in English came out as a kind of gavotte, easy to understand once we fell in with her syncopated swing, and always intriguing.

Don laid his book aside and stood up too. "Is it a patient, Didibah?" he asked.

"Is a patient," she agreed. "He looked pretty sick. You better come fast, I think." She padded the length of our kitchen, leading the way. On the back porch she turned. Her hand pressed her chest. She shuddered. "He's been coughing—hard, liked hurt."

We hurried past our red pickup truck with its nose in the ragged juniper that served as hitchrack, along the side of the rutted, sandy basketball court that filled most of the yard, and around to the community room.

Our patient stood on the porch. Rather, he leaned against the wall by the community room door. He wore a gray, hard worsted suit that might have been his size at one time. Today it gave the appearance of a medical school joke, hanging on a skeleton. The black wool scarf, crossed at the man's neck, lent his thin, dry face the wrapped-up look of a museum mummy. His eyes stared out from the depths of shriveled sockets with hopeless appeal. His black hair, neatly arranged in a yarn-tied hank, hung askew at the back of his neck. The turquoise nuggets depending from his pierced ears were almost lost in the hollows behind his jawbones.

The red silk handkerchief bound straight around his head and spread to cover his forehead seemed the most alive part of him.

I hoped that, if he saw it at all, my smile looked less forced than it felt. "Have him come inside and we'll take his temperature," I told Didibah.

Don held the screen door back for our patient to follow Didi in as she spoke to him.

The man coughed then—a cough with the sound of tearing burlap—and began slowly to slump down the wall.

Don caught him and helped him inside to a chair.

I shook down a sterile thermometer and placed it under his tongue. His neck might have been a twine string for all the help it gave in holding his head upright. He moaned almost continuously. His breathing sounded like crumpling paper. His body sagged on the chair until his suit jacket rode up around his ears. I had to find his shoulder beneath the folds of worsted and keep my hand pressed against him to prevent his falling forward and ramming the thermometer down his throat.

We waited in silence for the thermometer to register what we already knew—that we'd be lucky if we could get this patient to the hospital in time to save his life.

When the silence had stretched out long enough for Didi to speak, she said, "That medicine man bring him."

With this bit of information added to what I'd read in our patient's eyes and heard in his cough, I needn't have bothered to locate the 104° indicated on the thermometer. "You mean a medicine man has been 'singing' over this poor man and has given up?" I asked.

"I guessed so," Didi answered.

"How long?"

"Two day."

"Sings" are measured by nights. Two days probably meant that

45

our patient had been the central figure in a more or less strenuous healing ceremony for at least forty hours. For a day or two or possibly for a week before that, he had waited, receiving no treatment, while a hand-trembler diagnosed the difficulty and recommended the proper "singer" to set things right.

(The diagnosis had not, of course, suggested anything in the realm of virus infection. It had been in the area of taboos flouted, and the cure would, therefore, involve restoring this man to a right relationship with the spirit world and with his fellows.)

After the "singer" had been decided upon and sent for, and his fee in "hard goods" and "soft goods" determined, the patient had continued to wait, receiving no treatment, while a ceremonial hogan could be built, and prayer sticks properly made and set out to invite—command, really—the attendance of the gods. Desperately in need of modern drugs and protection from exposure, this man had been sitting for a large part of a day and a half at least, on a sand painting in a hastily constructed hogan, drinking emetics and receiving an occasional ritualistic massage.

We'd heard about this sort of thing, but had heard it and then automatically disassociated it from the present and the personal. This is the kind of protective disassociation that we all practice at times, I'm sure. We hear about ten thousand children starving in some Asian province, and we keep ourselves from caring too much by pushing the situation back in time and off in space. By letting a mass of ten thousand faces drift beyond us somewhere, out there and back then, we can keep ourselves from looking into one hungry child's eyes, here and now.

But here was a man of fifty or fifty-five who should have years of living before him, and he was dying for what seemed to me like no good reason. After all, this was the age of penicillin. My hand trembled as I replaced the thermometer in its sterile solution.

"Didi, tell him he must go to the hospital at once."

He nodded weakly when she transposed my words into his language.

"And please tell him," I added, "that he should have come here first. This is not the kind of sickness a 'singer' can cure."

As she spoke, he nodded again. When she finished, he answered in murmurs and paid for the effort in racking coughs.

"He says," Didibah reported, " 'Yes, that is what I should done. Should coming here first.' "

We helped the exhausted man to the cot where he collapsed in a heap of gray worsted.

"I'd better bring the pickup over here," Don suggested. "I'll put a clean cover on the mattress and he can lie in the back. Give me five minutes."

"I'm not sure we have five minutes to spare," I answered.

Didi looked up. "Here is coming that medicine man," she said. "I guessed he must laughed a lot when he's a young boy."

Didi sometimes forgot that we couldn't immediately perceive the humorous innuendos that she found in her native language. We learned later that the "singer's" name means "laughter."

He came inside and spoke to Didibah after the proper time lapse. They were both mannerly enough not to look at each other.

Didi found a small snag in the white cotton bedspread we'd hung on a wire to partition off the cot from the rest of the community room. She picked at the loose threads as she talked. The "singer" had removed his wide-brimmed hat, and he gave his full attention to turning it round and round in his hands as he and Didi conversed.

The "singer" was a pleasant-looking, well-fed man of sixty or so. He wore a wrinkled brown flannel suit with a blue and gray plaid gingham shirt. His broad chest and rounded belly provided ample display space for his heavy necklace of turquoise nuggets and wampum.

Finally Didi turned to me. "He says he pay you one dollar for take that sick man to hospital. He says he go 'long. He want that sick man ride up front seat."

"Just a minute. I have something to say to this medicine man," I told her.

She spoke to him and murmured my name.

He extended a plump, clean hand.

I remembered not to shake his hand in the white man's way, but merely to press my palm against his.

He looked me in the face as he would not have done had I been one of his own people. His eyes weighed me, dared me to criticize him.

I could feel the respect of his people upon him. Here was a man accustomed to being right and, even now, secure in his personal consciousness that in sending his patient to the hospital he was performing meritorious service far beyond the call of duty.

His dignity and self-righteousness, I admit, kept me from speaking as sharply as my inner disturbance prompted. However, I knew that his motives were mixed. He might be sending his patient to the white man's hospital in a last ditch effort to save his life. More likely, he was willing to take him and even to pay us for our trouble, in order that the man might live long enough to die on the white doctors' hands. In that way, he himself would be relieved of responsibility for the death. Even more desirable, the disposal of the patient's body would be up to the white men.

I said, "Didi, tell him that this man is very sick. Next time, when a man is sick in this way—with fever and coughing—he should not wait to have a 'sing' for him. Next time, he should send him to the hospital at once."

Didi stood picking at the snag in the curtain and her interpretation of my words droned on and on.

The "singer" gazed at his hat endlessly turning in his hands.

I resisted the urge to stamp my foot and insist that Didi tell him, straight to his face, what I'd said. I felt sure she was softening the tone of my rather high-handed advice. I could read nothing on the "singer's" face as he listened, if he were listening.

When at last Didi finished, the "singer" said nothing. For an instant, however, he glanced up and his eyes met mine. In that instant, I knew that I'd wasted my breath. This man had no intention of letting a foreign upstart come in here and tell him how to pursue his profession.

Don hurried in. "The pickup's all set," he said. "I brought it around."

I reached into the closet and pulled out a rough, gray blanket. I shook it open and draped it around our patient's shoulders. Don helped him off the cot and all but carried him to the pickup.

The "singer" spoke to Didi.

"He says he want that man ride up front seat," she relayed.

I tried to keep the impatience from my voice. "You tell him that we can keep this man warmer in the back on the mattress." I wagged my head toward the "singer." "He can ride up front, if he likes. I'll ride in the back with the patient."

Don dropped the tail gate and we lifted our frail patient into the bed of the pickup. We managed to prop him up with his back against the cab and his bony legs prone on the mattress. Then I scrambled out and went for more blankets.

During the few moments I was gone, two women in full satin skirts and fringed Pendleton shawls, a grown young girl in a purple cotton flounced skirt and silk print head scarf, a small boy of three or four in Levis so stiff they almost refused to bend with his legs, and two babies on cradle boards appeared from nowhere and established themselves in the back of the truck.

I took one astonished look and called Didibah. "Who are all these people?"

Didi ducked her head and giggled. Then she started fiddling with the zipper pull on the canvas cover over the truck bed, and spoke to our surprise passengers. When the round-faced lady answered, Didi explained to me, "They liked go to the hospital with that man."

"But who are they?" I asked. "Do you know them?"

Didi giggled again. "Yes. I know them."

I didn't know them, of course, nor understand why so many people should pile into our pickup uninvited. I did know enough to keep still and wait, on the chance that Didibah might get around to volunteering more information.

Instead, she asked, "You want this flap it zip down?"

"Yes," I told her. "We must keep this man warm or he won't live for thirty-five miles. I just hope we don't get stuck in the sand."

Didibah unrolled the canvas back flap. "These ladies been at that store," she happened to mention then. "That store close now for noon," she added.

"Oh," I said. This wasn't the information I wanted, but I might be getting nearer, provided I could contain my curiosity a little longer. I glanced beyond our gate and off to the left where eight or ten men lounged against the front of the trading post. A cluster of women and children (pardon me, ladies and children) sat on the ground in the ragged shade directly beneath a twisted juniper across the road from our gate. Another cluster huddled in the lee of a rubber-tired wagon parked outside our fence.

Two young men had climbed the sandstone base of the mesa behind our house. They pretended to be admiring the view across the valley while they surreptitiously drank wine and kept one eye peeled for the Navaho Police who patrolled in a blue- and cream-colored carryall. From farther beyond the road and a bit to the right, came the squeals and yells of two dozen school children at play on the slides and teeter-totters set between the long school building and its two fire-red outhouses.

These were the signs of noon and I thought, "At least, it's the warmest part of the day. We may be able to get our patient to the hospital in time." I scrambled into the small corner left for me in the bed of the pickup, and gave Don a high sign through the cab's rear window.

He backed the truck onto the basketball court, turned, and gunned through the sand trap on our side of the gate. He'd barely managed to spin the front wheels to the right and into the furrows leading to Ganado and the hospital when he slammed on the brakes.

I got to my knees to peer through the cab window. Don was talking to someone I couldn't see beside the road. Then he swung out and came around to the back.

"Another patient," he said. "A girl has broken her arm at school."

The excited schoolteacher came around then. She was the kind of flustery little dried-up woman who is sometimes highly successful in handling children. "Bah Billy's best friend pushed her off the top of the high slide," she burst out. "Her arm's broken at the wrist. I've sent for her grandmother. Somebody ought to go to the hospital with her." She whirled and shaded her eyes to squint down the road. "Here comes Sadie now. I guess you'd better drive over to school and pick up Bah Billy. I tied her arm to a board and gave her an aspirin. She didn't cry, but maybe we'd better not make her walk over here."

"You're sure it's her grandmother coming?" I asked. "We don't dare lose any time. We're taking a very sick man."

"That's Sadie, all right," the teacher said. "She lives in the second hogan down there—down that path from your place."

Didi came sauntering through the Health Center gate.

"Bah Billy has broken her arm," I told her. "We're going to take her with us to the hospital."

Didi poked her head under the canvas flap and grinned. "You think you having enough room with all that man's family?" she asked.

So, at last I knew! These ladies and children were members of our sick man's family. "That depends on how many of Bah Billy's family want to come along," I said.

Didi made some shoving-back gestures to accompany a few staccato words to our passengers. The ladies, sitting on their doubled-up legs, scooted off the side of the mattress and packed themselves against the tool box.

Our patient coughed and toppled sideways.

"Which is this man's wife?" I asked Didi.

She poked out her chin and lower lip toward the plumper of the two women, but before I could make my suggestion, she also pointed out the long-faced one in the same way.

"Both?" I asked.

"Yes," she answered with a shrug.

I gulped and said, "That's good. Have them arrange themselves on each side of their husband to keep him sitting up so he can breathe. Tell them to leave room on the mattress for Bah Billy."

As soon as Didibah began to speak, the ladies started moving around to brace their backs against our patient. The young woman wedged herself into the niche beside the tool box, and the small boy did his best to squeeze himself behind her. We had ample room for Bah Billy on the mattress. Her grandmother, Sadie, could fit herself into the corner opposite me.

Sadie, however, when she hurried up, appeared to be ninety. I worried about where we'd put her without breaking her. Her face was the color and texture of a wadded paper bag from the grocer's. Her grin had only three teeth in it. Still, she came scrambling over the tail gate with the nimbleness of a ten-year-old. She grasped her bony shanks and tucked them beneath her turquoise satin skirt, folded her arms across the rows of dimes running down her velvet blouse, and sat back to enjoy this unexpected journey.

Don invited the schoolteacher to get in front with him and the medicine man, and we drove across to the school.

Bah Billy, a pretty seven-year-old with an inverted pear-shaped face and her two fat, black pigtails, walked out to the truck with her left hand under the board to which the schoolteacher had tied her broken arm. Not one tear stain streaked her face, and she gave no sign of being in pain even though above her wrist she appeared to have developed an extra elbow. The broken end of the bone had not come through the skin, but it was so nearly through that I could almost count the splinters.

Don and I lifted the child into the truck. She and her grandmother did not speak.

Our sick man moaned. His chest heaved.

Don backed the truck toward a red outhouse to turn and swing onto the road again. I looked around me and wondered how our first innocent curiosity about Indians could have deposited us at the heart of the Navaho Reservation on a brisk April day, and thrust on us the responsibility for a man's life and for a child's uncrippled future.

As Don built up speed, our man was seized by a fit of dry, searing coughs. He was still coughing when we hit the stretch of road that humps over bare, water-scarred sandstone. Don barely inched along, but I still suffered for Bah Billy. Each jolt must have been agony for her. When we hit a wooden culvert that bounced her half off the mattress, I reached over and lifted her broken arm for her, and she squirmed back to her place without one wince of pain. Five grains of aspirin had never before produced such fortitude.

The miles to the hospital had never stretched so long. I sat with every muscle tense against the jolts and tilts as if I could in that way avert some of the buffeting from our patients. I cringed against every draft that whipped under the flapping canvas.

This coughing, fever-baked man, I thought, was in the same kind of misery and danger that any man with pneumonia would be. His family had gathered around to be near him at this time. He would, no doubt, like to see his babies grow to manhood. This young lady —who would put the pollen around the edge of her wedding bas-

NAVAHOS HAVE FIVE FINGERS

ket when the time came for her to bring him a son-in-law, if he should fail to recover from his illness? This boy would need his father through the growing years to instruct him beside the hogan fire at night, in the ways of the old ones.

Then I felt the truck shudder and roar. The tires clutched at footing and gave up. The engine gasped.

A spasm of coughing that I felt sure must be our patient's last kept me from hearing what, exactly, was happening. The motor roared, the tires ground into shifting sand, jarring my teeth but failing to move the truck, until finally we began to chug, inch by inch, backward.

Don maneuvered into a packed rut. I knew that next he'd try to explore a new trail beside the road, out through the sagebrush and Mormon tea. The truck bucked once and came down with a clatter, we went rearing and snorting over shrubs and hummocks, but we were at least moving forward toward the hospital.

I laid my hand on Bah Billy's broken arm to steady it and reached back to help his wives keep our other patient upright. When Don was able to take to the road again, it felt like a paved highway in spite of its broken culverts, miles of washboard, and whip-cracking stretches of loose sand.

Somehow we made it to the hospital.

The hospital at Ganado was at that time of native stone. It would have been an impressive building in any Midwestern town. Set in its own oasis, sixty miles from the railroad and completely surrounded by sagebrush and medicine men, it looked to me that day like a safe harbor miraculously appearing in the center of a stormy sea. Don drove to the end of the ramp where outpatients were admitted. A few steps more, and skilled hands took over for us.

The "singer" made it clear at the hospital office that he was the one who was entering the cough-racked man. He had arranged to have him brought here, the interpreter explained, and he wanted his man to have the best room in the place and shots of the white man's medicine—the same shots he himself had had in the winter when he had come to the hospital with that bad cold. He followed along to the private room as nurses wheeled his patient away.

We entered Bah Billy and bragged on what a brave girl she'd been. Nurses hurried her off to X-ray.

We were free now to head back to Tselani, but we stuck around. Sadie sat outside on the hospital porch railing. We couldn't talk with her directly, but her hands lay loose in her lap on her green and brown striped blanket-shawl. Her eyes did not question us as we wandered past, waiting until the X-rays were processed, hoping to learn the doctor's verdict on our other patient before we must leave.

Our man's two wives and their babies, his daughter, and his small son had disappeared. We couldn't find them in either of the hospital waiting rooms. Across the road at the community house, the matron hadn't seen them. We killed time by walking around the grounds, searching for them.

They had vanished.

We wandered back inside the hospital and upstairs. The doctor was examining Bah Billy's X-rays. He shook his head in our direction and murmured, "Poor kid," as he hurried away.

"Two breaks," the technician told us. "One in the wrist and one just above."

We waited around until the arm was set. Still, Bah Billy hadn't whimpered.

"What would you think of staying overnight?" I asked Don.

"I hate to leave without knowing about our man," he answered, "but what would his family do . . . and Sadie?"

"They can sleep at the community house," I reminded him.

"They'll probably want to go right back," Don said, still thinking like a white man, "but we can ask them."

"If we can find them," I added. "Let's go back to our man's room. Surely the doctor can tell us something about him by now."

We found the "singer" on the room's one chair, and the ladies of our patient's family perfectly at home on the floor, each in a circle of colorful skirt. The small boy tried to hide behind the young lady when I stepped to the open door.

"How is he?" I asked the nurse with the empty syringe.

She came into the hall and shook her head.

The "singer" disappeared before midnight, the night nurse told us the next morning. At four o'clock our patient died. By dawn, no member of his family could be found.

The "singer," by disappearing well before death came, had saved the necessity of a long, expensive ceremonial to cleanse himself. Those members of the family who had been in the room at the end would have to be ceremonially decontaminated. They had vanished, however, for another reason.

We returned to Tselani with instructions from the hospital to go to the dead man's home and find out what his family wanted done with his body. This was a squeamish kind of mission so we dropped off Sadie at her hogan, and stopped at our place barely long enough to pick up Didibah before driving on to carry out our mission.

Three hogans set in a windswept col at the base of Old Grandfather Rock comprised the family camp. After the proper interval following our arrival, the blanket-door of the center hogan fluttered and our man's plump wife appeared. Didibah climbed down from the truck and strolled over to speak with her. She soon came back alone. "They liked him get it Christian burial," she reported.

Don said, "Oh-oh!"

"Did you explain that they must pay the expenses?" I asked. "And that they should attend the funeral?"

"I explain it," Didi said and sighed.

I waited as long as I could contain myself. "Well," I pressed then, "do they want us to take them back to Ganado? Or what?... And what about paying?"

"They all herding sheep out." Didibah shrugged. "Nobody is home but just that lady. . . . She must taking care those babies."

We looked again, and "that lady" was hurrying toward us from the corral beyond the farthest hogan. Before her, as one might dangle a dead rat by the tail, she carried something that looked like an old-fashioned salt sack containing a lumpy handful of heaven-knew what. Her quick steps rippled her blue satin skirt, making it wink in the morning sun. Suddenly, instead of coming on to our truck, she stopped. She dropped the salt sack on an up-ended stump beside the woodpile. In a twinkling, she turned and disappeared behind the blanket-door of the center hogan.

Didibah had seen all this, I was sure, and yet she'd taken pains not to be caught looking. Now she continued to sit. She said nothing and made no move to pick up what we assumed to be the lady's payment for her husband's funeral.

Finally I asked, "Is that for the hospital, for the funeral expenses?"

"Yes," Didi answered, but she continued to sit, staring straight ahead.

Don and I exchanged puzzled glances.

Don asked, "Are we supposed to take it?"

"Yes," Didi answered and sighed.

Don opened the door and stepped down from the truck.

Didi's hands fell open in her lap and I watched the color slowly return to her knuckles.

Don walked over and casually picked up the contribution from the stump. As he came toward us, lightly tossing the sack on his palm, I felt Didibah tighten up again beside me. She actually shuddered before she spoke. Then her voice erupted as if she'd held back as long as possible.

"Tell him that sack it ride in back."

Don started to slide the salt sack into his jacket pocket as he stepped up on the running board.

Didi cowered and drew away.

"She says you should put that in the back of the truck," I told Don. I hoped he could read the urgency in my tone.

He shaped the word "Why" but looked across at Didibah before the sound came. He went around at once and dropped the sack with a careless clatter into the bed of the truck.

I happened to turn as Don started the motor and the truck began to growl its way through the sand. Beginning at the woodpile and coming toward the place where we'd stopped, the plump lady in the blue satin skirt was wielding a handful of brush, carefully sweeping away Don's footprints.

Christianity personifies evil and calls it the Devil. The Christian opposes him with various practical and theological weapons.

The Navahos personify evil influences and call them *tchindees*. Their way of overcoming these devils is to propitiate and outwit them. If it is possible to dispose of a dead body by leaving it in the hands of white men, one can avoid much of the personal risk of contact with the *tchindees* pertaining to death. If the white men wish to be paid for handling the dangerous body, that is fair enough. One can pay with jewelry belonging to the dead man—jewelry that is now *tchindee*-infested and must be disposed of anyway. Finally, one can brush out the footprints by which *tchindees* might be guided back to the camp made vulnerable by death. If one takes all these precautions, all may be well again for a time.

The following day we delivered the expense payment of necklace and bracelets to the hospital, and made the lady's excuses for not attending the funeral.

The Superintendent shrugged. "Any excuse is better than none," he said. "We like them at least to see that the service is nice instead of frightening, but many of them still don't understand." He brightened. "By the way, you're to take Bah Billy home when you go."

We felt cheered. We had one patient on the mend—one who was responding to medical treatment, one who would surely grow up believing in anesthetics and X-rays and plaster casts. Perhaps Bah Billy's hospital experience would help her to think about and decide for herself what she believed regarding medicines and death and *tchindees*.

Bah Billy said nothing all the way home. She neither frowned nor smiled. From all appearances, she came close to fitting the wooden-Indian myth.

When we approached her grandmother's hogan, four pickups stood at the camp and another was humping toward it along the back sheep path that served as road. Half a dozen men scurried here and there with fresh-peeled logs. Women hustled between the hogan and a green brush shelter, half-finished, beyond it. Laughter drifted over and cut off short as Don stopped the motor and went around to help Bah Billy down from the truck.

No one came over to say, "Thank you for bringing Bah Billy home." The buzz of activity slowed, but no one openly looked in our direction. Bah Billy, without a backward glance, trudged off toward her grandmother's hogan.

We learned two days later of the "sing" at Sadie's camp. "Blessingway Chant" had been sung over Bah Billy to neutralize the evil effects of her contact with white people at the hospital.

Human beings—all human beings—are instinctively afraid until they make a satisfactory adjustment to the universe. The nature of our fears and the terms of our adjustments are shaped by fascinating little accidents.

Perhaps you were born thirty years too late for your mother to teach you to run and hide beneath the feather bed during a thunderstorm. My mother learned that trick from her mother, but when I grew up, we had no feather bed. I was taught never, during danger of lightning, to use the telephone. Navaho mothers teach their children not to laugh aloud in the face of a storm.

A whistling girl
And a crowing hen
Are sure to come
To some bad end.

Who is to say that this jingle makes more sense than the Navaho taboo against whistling in the dark?

Whether we are living on the twenty-fifth floor of a New York apartment building or at the Health Center deep on the Navaho Reservation, we ourselves and those around us are always searching for the most satisfying adjustment to life. Wherever we happen to be, we find ourselves among human beings searching.

Parents handing down beliefs and children testing them out, wagons giving way to pickups, atoms submitting to smashing, "singers" consulting doctors, outer space revealing its secrets, uranium mines displacing sheep, electron microscopes revealing the coded secrets of life—our adaptations to our environment are always changing in the direction of what works best in the light of new facts.

We had no more than unpacked at Tselani when we knew that we had moved onto a two-way sheep trail. Two diverse backgrounds were to meet in the "little." Inevitably we would exchange notes on the search.

The nurse had left us with the airy prediction, "But the people will come for help. You can't avoid doing something for them."

Almost at once we knew that we, too, had come for help and that The People could not avoid doing something for us. We were all human beings, held back by various prejudices and misconceptions, but in search of the same answers. We could not avoid helping each other, and what fun we were to have, discovering each other's human foibles!

But when warmer weather and contaminated water combined to attack the black-haired babies in our area, we found that life or death rode on our success or failure to make ourselves understood; and we added to our spiritual vocabulary of understanding, two words of Navaho.

CHAPTER FIVE

Déh, Not Txó

A STOCKY YOUNG NAVAHO with a crew haircut appeared at our back door when we had barely started our six o'clock breakfast one morning.

"Oh-oh," I said. "No interpreter."

Don went to the door.

"Good morning," our caller said in perfect English. "I've brought our baby. He's sick. Is the nurse here?"

Explaining the absence of the nurse and our own inadequacy seemed almost too easy. We had become accustomed to speaking single-syllable words and three-word sentences to Navahos who strained hard to understand and then stood, head hanging, in utter bafflement. This young man looked us in the eye when he spoke and looked us in the eye when he listened. We felt no need even to choose the simpler of two words in talking with him.

"What are your baby's symptoms?" I asked.

"He's got diarrhea," the father answered.

I remembered the nurse's agitation when she'd thought we were going to do nothing here except hand out the basketball and put it to bed at night. "But these babies get diarrhea and there's no time to shunt them around from place to place," she said. "First thing you know, they die."

"How long has he had diarrhea?" I asked, and belatedly reminded myself that this is a foolish thing to ask a Navaho. Navaho time, the same as a Navaho mile, is elastic.

When the father answered, "Three days," however, his manner made me believe that he actually meant seventy-two hours.

"We can take his temperature and we'll call the nearest nurse," Don said. "How are you traveling?"

"Car," the father answered.

"Good," Don said. "Maybe you can drive on up and see the nurse at Black Mountain, but we'll call her first to be sure she's there."

We left our breakfast and followed the young man across to the other house. He had parked his pickup near the community room door. We went inside and started the fires while our visitor helped his wife and baby from his car.

The contrasts between the young man and his wife could hardly have been greater. He wore Levis, a blue work shirt, and a brown leather jacket. With his crew haircut and his easy manner, he might have been any young, healthy American with a friendly, well-tanned face. As he came into the room, he proudly displayed his son on the cradle board across the crook of his right elbow.

The baby on the board had the square-shaped face of his father, but he did not look healthy. His head fell limp and listless against the gray blanket laced around him. He was softly whimpering.

The baby's mother hesitated in the doorway, and even while her husband held the screen door open for her to enter, she turned toward the pickup as if she might run to its familiar protection. She was as slight as a breath of air. Timidity hovered over and around her. One small hand covered her mouth. The other smoothed loosened strands of hair back from her face and nervously tucked them into the neat hank that hugged the back of her head. Her eyes remained on the tips of her moccasins. In her cerise satin skirt and green velveteen blouse, she made me think of a hummingbird, and I expected her to dart away at any second.

"Come in," I urged, but not until her husband had spoken to her in Navaho could she be persuaded to take the frightening step over the threshold. Then she stood with her chin among the silver and turquoise necklaces around her neck and her eyes on the tips of the moccasins peeping from beneath her full, ankle-length skirt.

"Your wife doesn't speak English?" I asked the young man.

"No," he said, "but you just tell her what you want done and I'll interpret for you."

I indicated the cot in the corner. "If she'll sit here with the baby, we'll take his temperature," I said. "Then we'll call the nurse."

He spoke to his wife in Navaho and she sat down on the cot. He placed the cradle board across her knees. He turned to me. "You'll want him off the cradle board to take a rectal, won't you?"

"You must have been in the armed services," I said.

He grinned. "I sure was."

I busied myself with selecting a rectal thermometer and preparing it for insertion.

The baby kept on whimpering.

When I turned around, the little mother had unlaced him from the board, removed his diaper, and properly turned him on his side across her lap. Her eyes were still fixed on the toes of her moccasins. I inserted the thermometer and stood back to wait.

The baby's father said, "We took him to Keams Canyon yesterday and they gave him a shot, but he's still sick. I wanted to bring him here."

"I'm sorry the nurse isn't here," I told him, "but we'll do what we can."

He wandered across the room to the Ping-pong table. He picked up a ball and began to bounce it on the table. Then he picked up a paddle and bounced the ball on the paddle.

"Where did you serve in the war?" Don asked him.

"All over. South Pacific mostly," he answered.

"You got English down pat," Don complimented him.

He grinned. "Had to."

When I looked at the thermometer, it registered 101°. "This isn't too bad," I said to the young man. "You tell your wife so she won't worry."

"What is it?" he wanted to know.

I told him.

"No, that's not too bad," he agreed, and came over to tell his wife about it in soft-spoken Navaho.

I went into the living room to telephone the nurse. The line was busy at first, as it always was when I needed it, but I finally got through and heard the nurse's, "Hello." By the breathless quality in her voice, though, I knew that I had interrupted something. I described my listless, heavy-headed little patient and asked whether I should send him on up to her.

"What's his temp?" she wanted to know. When I told her, she said, "We're just ready to start for the hospital with a hip fracture. But you can handle your case yourself. You'll find Kaopectate among your medicines. It's a white, chalky-looking liquid, and—"

"I know Kaopectate," I told her. "The doctor left us a fresh supply last Wednesday."

"Good. Prescribe one teaspoonful every two hours. And tell them not to give the baby any water, just tea. That way the water will get boiled. Suppose she knows how to sterilize a bottle?"

"I'm sure the father must know," I said. "He was in the South Pacific, and I'd be willing to bet he had his eyes open all the time."

"Better take a look at the baby's bottle anyway," the nurse advised. "Good luck. If he isn't better tomorrow— Tomorrow's Wednesday, your clinic day. Tell them to bring him back tomorrow, if he isn't better, but I think he'll improve before then."

I went back to the community room and took a bottle of Kaopectate from the medicine cabinet. The doctor had left it so far forward and so conspicuously labeled that I almost missed finding it.

The baby's mother had him neatly diapered and upright now, but he still whimpered and he still acted as if his head were too heavy to support. I shook the bottle of medicine and poured out a teaspoonful. When I squatted and attempted to give it to him, he stopped whimpering and began to cry. I could see that the mother's thin arm around him was tense. I realized that she was actually frightened. I turned to the father.

"I wonder whether you'll try giving him this," I suggested. "He must have a spoonful every two hours and the sooner we get him started, the better. And tea," I added. "He's to have tea instead of water. Do you have any tea at home?"

The father didn't think so, but he put the question into Navaho to his wife. As he did so, he squatted on his heels and gave the baby the medicine.

"We don't have any tea, but we can get some at the store," the father said when the spoon had been licked clean.

"What's the Navaho word for tea?" I asked him.

"*Déh,*" he said, ("e" as in met, and said on a high tone.)

"And the word for water?"

"*Txó,*" he told me. (The "x" is a kind of blowing sound.)

"I'll go boil *txó* and make *déh,*" I said.

For an instant the baby's mother glanced up at the familiar sound of the two words, but she did not relax her guard.

I had all but forgotten the other part of the nurse's instructions. Actual medicines are apt to take precedence in our minds, although conditions may be even more conductive to health than anything in the way of drugs. I had the water boiled and the tea made, and then I finally remembered about sterilizing the baby's bottle. Before I went back to the community room, I filled the tea kettle again and turned the fire high.

66

I found Don and the baby's father batting a Ping-pong ball back and forth across the net.

"Does the baby have a bottle?" I asked.

The father turned to his wife. She answered his question and he hurried through the door and out to his pickup. When he came back, he handed me a nursing bottle and returned to his game. "How do you keep score?" I heard him ask Don as I started to the kitchen. (He was the only Navaho who ever asked us how to score a game.)

I saw at once that the nursing bottle looked cloudy and well covered with fingerprints. I thought little of it until I got to the sink and removed the nipple. When I started to pour out the water remaining in the bottle, I discovered a quarter-inch layer of silt and sand.

I scoured and scrubbed and then sterilized both bottle and nipple. The incongruities to be found within this small family group would, I knew, hound them through the years. The father and mother, while of the same generation, were of two distinctly different cultures. Still, the father had not moved from the Navaho way to the white man's way in the orderly process of weighing and choosing one set of understood beliefs and practices in preference to the other. He had been thrust from one world into another, and he had missed many of the intervening steps.

He had learned from Uncle Sam that clothes should be kept clean. Uncle Sam, on the other hand, had come across no normal occasion either in boot camp or the South Pacific for teaching him that a baby's nursing bottle should be kept clean. This young man had undoubtedly been taught in the South Pacific to add certain ingredients to water to purify it before drinking. He had not been taught that water drawn from an open spring should be boiled before it is given to a baby.

Fifty years ago diarrhea-enteritis was one of the three leading causes of death among people generally in the United States. Today most of us need hardly think about it at all. Even today, however, gastro-enteric diseases rank first in causing deaths among the Navahos. They are twenty-eight times as deadly among Navaho babies as among our babies generally.

When I returned to the community room with the clean bottle, I had it filled with strong tea. I said to the baby's father, "You know, this kind of sickness causes more deaths among your people than any other disease. You boys who served in the armed forces should get together and stop it."

"It's the drinking water," the father said. "The Tribal Council and the Bureau are working on it. They dig a few new wells every year, but they don't ever catch up with what we need."

Don said, "Most of the people living around here dip their drinking water from the open spring. We see their buckets setting around in manure or any old place. Their dogs and sheep drink from them whenever they feel like it."

"I know," the father agreed. "I guess the flies don't help things much either."

"You be sure to boil your drinking water," I warned. "This boy of yours is too valuable to lose."

The baby's father left his Ping-pong game and seemed eager to understand everything connected with getting his son well again. I showed him the sparkling clean bottle filled with tea. I insisted that it must be washed and boiled each day. He explained the process to his wife. She did not look up.

The method of making tea came next. "The water must be boiling," I insisted. "Build the fire up and let the water boil awhile before you pour it on the tea."

He explained it to his wife. She did not look up and did not speak.

"And the medicine," I added, "every two hours." I checked the price list on our medicine cabinet door. "This size Kaopectate is twenty-five cents," I told him. "You'll need to buy a little package

68

of tea at the store. Remember now, no water!" I recalled my two words of Navaho. "No *txó*," I said, "just *déh*."

The baby's mother was caught off guard by the familiar sound of the words. She looked up quickly and smiled. Then, following the lead of her husband, she laughed aloud. For the first time, I felt that she might really make an effort to carry out the unintelligible instructions from the white man's way. Two words of Navaho had opened a chink in the wall between us.

We are all subject to brilliant flashes of hindsight. These frequently provide us with knowledge which, had it come earlier, would have been labeled profound intuition. I wondered how many more Navahos might now speak English, if the white people going on the Reservation with helpful purposes had learned, first of all, to speak even a little Navaho. As for us, I felt that we had been far too slow in realizing that a person who wants to help another must find some point of personal contact first, before help can be accepted without a loss of dignity.

Thinking about it after the little family had gone on their way, we could visualize them, as they had begun that day in their hogan. The baby had fretted all night. The diarrhea had grown worse instead of better. The mother was scared—both by the baby's symptoms, and by her consciousness of having flouted the ways of her people. She had given in the day before and allowed her son to be taken to the white man's hospital. There they had jabbed him with a needle and made him cry. Now he was still sick. How did she know what kind of poison they had stuck into him? After all, the white man did not care what happened to the Navahos. If only she had not listened to the pleadings of her husband! Perhaps it was true, as her father had often said, that her husband had been made half white man in his mind. If only she had sent for the "singer" when the baby's sickness first started!

And then, even with the baby's bowels still running, her husband continued to hold out against going for the "singer"! "The nurse at Tselani—we will take the baby to her," he had insisted. When they had learned that the nurse was away, he had still argued that they should let just any white person say what was to be done about her sick baby. He had taken the child from her arms, in spite of her pleadings. He had carried it inside to those strange *belliganos*.

We soon became amateurs with a reputation for successfully treating babies with diarrhea. Fortunately it came in a mild form this particular spring. When we worried aloud to the doctor about our lack of training, he said, "You're not administering prescription drugs. Anybody off the Reservation can and does go to a drug store, ask for it by name, and buy the same medicine you're providing. If you don't do this here, there's no one else to do it. Besides, nobody is going to accuse you of malpractice when the most important thing you're doing is giving lessons in how to boil water."

So word passed from mouth to mouth, "The white people at the nurse's house at Tselani know what to do for it."

No day was quite complete until we had treated at least one baby for diarrhea. On some days, they came by threes and fours. We often watched, fascinated, as a mother unlaced her baby from his cradle board and began to lay back his wrappings. Sometimes only a sprinkling of sand fell out upon the clean sheet on our cot. Sometimes we found as much as a cupful collected in the cot's center sag after our patient had been rewrapped and taken away.

We treated clean babies and dirty babies. Most of them were completely clothed, down to a shirt and a diaper. One little girl was different. Her grandmother brought her in. The old lady refused to tell us her name or the name of the baby.

(The old-way Navahos consider a name a power-invested personal possession. A name is not for everyday use. It is saved for momentous occasions. If a person inadvertently mentions a friend's name, he apologizes with assurances that he meant no harm. Nicknames and circumlocutions—"my sister-in-law's brother's wife's mother"—help The People to avoid wearing out by casual use the potency of their names.)

This grandmother thought the baby might be about a year old. She appeared to me to be nearer six months of age, but malnutrition could easily account for her shriveled, undeveloped appearance. The grandmother thought the baby had been having loose bowels for "a short time." Didi tried various means of getting "a short time" defined in days or weeks, but she had to give up.

I asked to have the baby taken from the cradle board. The grandmother laid the board beside her on the cot and untied the laces. Then, with a shrug, she leaned back and left the rest to me. I pulled the dirty muslin strings from the loops along the sides of the cradle board and unwound the child's outer wrapping—a blanket that had once been white but was now grease-spotted and gray. With the blanket laid back, the child looked like an authentic Navaho doll— a very dirty doll.

She wore a blouse made exactly like her grandmother's, with seams down front and back as well as under the arms and along the shoulders, a V neck with a small collar, and three-quarter-length sleeves. Small yellow daisies grew helter-skelter on the once-white background of her calico blouse. Her skirt, made like her grandmother's with three tiers of ruffles, was of turquoise rayon satin. It covered her feet as she lay on the cradle board. I had a moment of alarm when I thought of a child attempting to walk in a skirt so long, and then I reminded myself that this was a dress-up skirt, no more intended for everyday use than her name. It had been taken from one of the tin suitcases stacked in the grandmother's hogan, and put on especially for this visit to the nurse. I almost decided that the grandmother was right in her calculation of time. Surely the child's dress-up clothes couldn't have got so dirty in only six months.

My two weeks of specializing had not prepared me for what I found next. I turned back the baby's skirt and three grimy petticoats in order to remove her diaper and take a rectal temperature reading. Beneath the skirts I found shredded cedar bark—the sort of nest one might expect for a bird or wild animal. In fairness to the grandmother, this was the cleanest part of the child's attire.

As I picked off shreds of bark in order that I might safely insert a thermometer, I wondered whether I dared offer the grandmother a dozen diapers. Then I decided that diapers could be made a part of my prescription. Don went to the storeroom and brought back the necessary addition to the medicines in our cabinet. I found my ever-present bottle of Kaopectate.

"Give her this—one teaspoon morning, noon, afternoon, and night."

I had learned to accompany these times for medicine with a gesture. Facing south, the index finger indicates the east which is the place of the sunrise and, therefore, morning. The finger points straightup for noon. It comes down part way toward the west to indicate the middle of the afternoon, and drops low to mark the time of sunset and night. Using this gesture, the bottle of medicine, and a teaspoon, I could now give accurate directions even when we had no interpreter. With Didi beside me, I still used the gesture because it made our patients smile and I knew they would remember my marks in the air because they had smiled.

It was not until I had read two related articles in *The American Journal of Nursing* that I burst out to Don, "And I'm the dodo who thought those cedar bark panties were old-fashioned!"

Don laid aside the First Aid book. "Don't tell me they're advertised in the *New York Times* this week."

"They're using sawdust beds in hospitals now!" I exclaimed. "For patients requiring long-term bed rest. Sawdust is more absorbent than cotton. The resins and turpentine in the wood are astringent and antiseptic, and they even act as a deodorant. Can you beat that!"

"And we think we're so smart!" Don commented.

"I get so mad at myself," I fumed. "Sometimes I decide that I must have quit thinking about three days after I was born. From then on, I think I've had a closed mind. I felt a nudge to think the other day, when I peeled that child down and came to that clean, sweet-smelling cedar bark. But did I think? No, not me! I didn't have to. I've always known that babies are supposed to wear cloth diapers." I wagged the *Journal of Nursing* at Don. "Now here this comes along. Every white person who ever had a bedsore could have had relief, if we hadn't been too pig-headed to learn about cedar bark and sawdust from the Navahos."

"I guess the Navahos, who have a reputation for it, aren't quite as pig-headed as we are, are they?" Don said. "At least most of them around here have seemed willing enough to let you teach them how to boil water."

I knew when I was being razzed. "All right, I admit that's not a very complicated medical procedure, but to those babies, it could make the difference between life and death."

"I'm serious," Don said. "Most of the profound answers to life's problems are as simple as Déh, not txó, or 'Love thy neighbor as thyself.' What a lot of us aren't smart enough to see is that even the simplest people have as much chance as the most sophisticated to stumble upon these answers and test them out against life."

"Like that first father who started this whole diarrhea business for us," I said. "The trouble was, he got shoved so abruptly into off-Reservation life that his answers were hit-and-miss—wash the baby's clothes but never mind his bottle."

"That's one big reason for the slow process of education," Don, the ex-schoolteacher, reminded me. "Those beginners of all ages,

73

sitting down there at the trailer school now are learning the uses of soap and water along with how to pronounce our 'th' sound and that beans are forty cents a can at the trader's."

" Let's hope they learn how to get soap and water along with learning what to do with them," I answered.

"Education should help with that, too. It's the best answer we've found so far," Don persisted. "Even the Tribal Council agrees. You remember the Chairman's inaugural address. He went all-out for education."

"The Chairman and the Tribal Council, yes, but I wonder sometimes about the people—these people up here who have so few outside contacts."

"Well, the trailer school is running at capacity," Don reminded me. "Why don't we go see for ourselves how the people—these people, as you say—are taking to it?"

74

CHAPTER SIX

Town Meeting, Reservation Style

AMERICANS ARE GOING EVERYWHERE in trailers these days—to the mountains, to the shore, to glamor trailer parks, and to the poor house. Almost a thousand Navaho children are even attending trailer schools.

The trailer school a few miles from Tselani was one of the largest of the twenty-eight then operating on the Reservation. Three teachers—a man and his wife, and a single woman—taught a hundred boys and girls at this school. When the teaching couple stopped by our place one day and said, "We're having Parents' Day tomorrow. Why don't you come?" we quickly accepted their invitation.

"Be sure you're there by noon," the man said. "We're going to feed everybody mutton stew. In the afternoon, we'll have a get-together and listen to them air their grievances." He said this in a somewhat weary tone of voice. He might have been a father who had tried repeatedly to explain to his small son the reasons why he should wash his hands before dinner.

Even before Didi arrived the next morning, we had taught two mothers how to boil water and sterilize their babies' bottles. After Didi came, we thought we might leave her in charge, and spend most of the day at the trailer school. But then we had to paint the sores in a lady's mouth. Next, we spent half an hour persuading a man with inflamed eyes to go see the doctor at Ganado. We had to search to the bottom of a dozen cartons of used clothing before we could find a warm coat that almost fit a thin-blooded grandmother. No, she couldn't wait until tomorrow, she said. Her lambs were beginning to come, and she got too cold in the corral. We then helped Didi match the plaid and cut out a gingham dress that she wanted to make while we attended the school meeting. Just when we thought we might possibly get away in time for the mutton stew, John Joe arrived to have his foot dressed.

By the time we approached the trailer school in our pickup, the two women teachers had the children all circled up in a group game beyond the windmill. Two men in large hats were the only grown-ups in evidence, and they were sauntering toward the nearest of the two Quonsets.

Dinner was obviously over and the afternoon meeting in session. Four pickups were parked beside the second Quonset—the one that served as kitchen and dining room. Two more pickups and a jeep sat beside the two trailers in which the teachers lived. A dozen or more wagons, tongues lax, were bunched beyond the schoolroom Quonset near the shower-and-toilet trailer. Hobbled horses grazed around the edges of the tramped-down area that was the playground.

We left our pickup just off the road (hoping we'd be able to start for home, when the time came, without shoveling sand) and followed the two Navaho men into the near Quonset. We found ourselves at the rear of a modern schoolroom in which sat forty or fifty adult Navahos at undersized school desks.

The schoolteacher who had invited us to attend the meeting lounged in a chair at the right-hand end of a table at the front of the room. At the middle of the table sat a short, round-cheeked

76

Navaho man. His elbows rested on the table and his fat, interlocked fingers formed a cushioned support for his double chin. His eyes were fixed on a spot in the center aisle between the school desks. At the left-hand end of the table sat a Navaho whom we had met. He was Hastiin Chee, a "singer," and a man who carried great weight in this area.

Hastiin Chee, a man of sixty or so, wore a fresh, professional haircut. This haircut had, we knew, required a round trip of two hundred miles; this occasion was obviously one of considerable significance to Chee. His gray worsted business suit was shiny at the elbows—it had probably been purchased at the Health Center for a dollar or two—but it fit his tall, lean body as well as if it had been custom tailored. With the suit, he wore a scarlet, rayon velvet shirt that had been made two weeks before on one of our Health Center sewing machines by his daughter. The shirt was open at the neck, and a string of turquoise nugget beads lay warm against the velvet and ended in a heavy *nacall* just above the silver and turquoise buckle on his belt. His red velvet cuffs extended an inch beyond the sleeves of his suit jacket. Against the red, turquoise-set silver bracelets adorned his wrists.

The schoolteacher delayed starting the meeting until we had slid into school desks at the far side of the room. Then he was delayed again by the arrival of three plump Navaho women in Pendleton blanket-shawls. Two of these carried babies on cradle boards, and their efforts to maneuver their bulk into the narrow space between the back of a school seat and its attached desk, while holding a shawl in place and balancing a cradle board, caused a ripple of giggles the length of the row.

The display of velvet blouses with rows of silver buttons and silver collar-corners, the squash-blossom necklaces, the strings of turquoise nuggets and wampum, the massive sand-cast belts all marked this as a special occasion.

Any normal gathering of forty or fifty Navahos automatically includes a large number of children. Today, with the school-age children on the playground, those attending the meeting were babies—babies on cradle boards, babies in arms, babies learning to stand alone by clutching at their mothers' knees, babies experimenting with walking by toddling from one desk to another up and down the aisle.

The schoolteacher frowned at his wrist watch and stood behind the table. "Ladies and Gentlemen," he said with a smile, "we have invited you here today so you can see just what we are doing in this school. You visited the classes this morning. You ate dinner here the way your children do every day. Now this afternoon, we want to know what you think about the school. I know some of you have been talking among yourselves, saying, 'This is wrong,' 'That is not the way we think it should be,' and 'We don't like the school for this reason.' Now we want you to tell us all these things that you think are wrong. If anybody happens to like something about the school, it is all right to tell that, too."

He sat down and the well-fed Navaho man next to him let his interlocked hands swing forward to rest on the table before him. He did not shift the point of his gaze away from the center aisle. He spoke in the staccatos and gutturals of Navaho, but in such a muted tone that it seemed impossible for those at the back of the room to hear him. Still, no one asked him to speak up. His interpretation of the teacher's words went on and on and on, and then ended on a rising inflection. Once more the interpreter propped his chin on his plump, intertwined fingers.

The teacher stood up and turned toward Hastiin Chee. "You all know Hastiin Chee," he said. "You have picked him to speak for you on the matter of our school here. So we will hear from him first, and then everybody who has anything to say will have a chance to say it." He turned the meeting over to Hastiin Chee with a wave of his hand, and sat down again to listen.

Babies, born only a few years too late to escape all schooling, blithely tugged at their mothers' breasts. Their sucking and cooing sounds were soft with contentment. They never once raised their voices to protest either against compulsory school attendance or against the white man's methods of education.

Hastiin Chee, as far as his facial expression indicated, was neither pleased with nor annoyed by the school. He stood tall beside his chair. The tip of his long index finger barely touched the table top as he reached out to flick away an imaginary speck. He began to speak very quietly. His finger continued to make little sweeps in a six-inch arc on the table. His eyes fixed themselves on his finger and stayed there.

This was oration in low key. Without raising his voice or his eyes, Hastiin Chee held his audience at the tip of his finger. A mother reached down beside her to hoist a fallen toddler by one arm without taking her eyes from the speaker's moving finger. A young father unlaced a baby from its cradle board and changed its diaper without a break in his attention to Chee. An elderly man wearing nugget earrings and a thinning hair knot sat running his hand over the high-domed crown of his hat on his knees, but his eyes were on Hastiin Chee's finger.

Occasionally a shy little laugh caromed through the audience. Usually a bit of weight-shifting and the whisper of moccasin soles moving on the floor seemed to communicate his hearers' assent. After each of these little flurries, Hastiin Chee shifted his own weight and the tiniest twitch at the left side of his mouth betrayed his knowledge of the power he was wielding.

At long intervals he stopped and waited for the interpreter to lay his clasped hands on the table and report in telegram-style English what Chee had spent five minutes saying in Navaho.

"Say, 'Children not like food at school. . . .' "

"Say, 'Children get too tired at school. Not work much when get home. . . .' "

"Say, 'School too far. Long walk. Children not like get up early. Too dark. . . .' "

"Say, 'Children stay too long at school. Time they get home, sheep already in corral. . . .' "

"Say, 'What good is to figure? Trader always figure different answer. . . .' "

"Say, 'Mighty hard get good clothes for school. Government ought to give children clothes for wearing to school.' "

Hastiin Chee had everyone's complaints corralled in his mind. He needed no notes. He marched them out, one by one, like calling out the black sheep from a flock. He admitted that there were a few white sheep lurking around somewhere—even though the children did not like the hot school lunches, they did gain weight and grow taller—but the black sheep made up the bulk of the flock.

When Hastiin Chee finally finished, his words ran out before his finger had completed its arc on the table top. He finished the gesture and ended it with a visible period. Instead of sitting down then to wait for the teacher to answer his complaints, he merely stepped back, folded his arms across his velvet chest, and leaned against the blackboard behind him.

The teacher nudged the interpreter. "Ask whether anybody else has anything to say."

One by one, with easy, leisurely waits between, half a dozen members of the audience got to their feet and spoke. According to the interpretation given each speech, no one added any new complaints but rather stressed the one that he felt about most strongly. No one spoke with any apparent heat, however, the whole tone of the meeting was quiet, peaceful, and good-natured.

Something intriguing and recognizable about the whole business kept teasing me to remember where I'd attended similar sessions before. The unfamiliarities of language, dress, jewelry, and setting kept getting in the way of my memory.

When all who wished to speak had been given a chance, the teacher's turn came. He stood up.

He is not a placid man. We half expected him to give these parents a lambasting. We felt sure that the least he'd do would be to deliver a pointed lecture on gratitude. After all, he and his wife and the other teacher had left their comfortable homes in the East and come to this barren wilderness to devote their lives to teaching boys and girls who otherwise might never have the opportunity of any schooling. When he turned to Hastiin Chee, leaning against the blackboard, we expected that the least he'd say would be, "Now you sit down and listen to me!"

Instead he smiled at Chee and then smiled at the audience. "Well," he said with a shrug, "we've said it all again, haven't we? It's good to see you here. We're glad you came to tell us what you think is wrong with the school. We'll have another meeting next year and I hope you'll all come. So, that's all for today."

At last, my memory clicked. This was like dormitory bull sessions I had known. Nobody here was actually against the school. What a furor the schoolteacher would have blown up, if he'd stood up on his two hind legs and said, "Well then, since you don't like the school, we'll slip the wheels under these trailers and Quonsets again and haul them away." The complaints had all been in the nature of college students rapping their food, the grade system, a housemother's restrictions. Tell a griping Junior to pack up his belongings and go home, if he thinks his college is so derelict, and he can quickly think of a thousand desirables about his campus life.

These Navahos on this Parents' Day were typical Americans, given a chance to shoot off their mouths. They didn't really want anything changed very much. They were glad for their children to have a chance to begin their English education this close to their homes. They were grateful for the well that had to be drilled here before the school could be set up. But the white teacher had asked them to complain, and what real American can resist such an invitation?

The interpreter lowered his hands and spoke briefly in Navaho. As his voice trailed off, ladies pushed their breasts up under their velveteen blouses and made little "Chi . . . chi . . . chi," sounds through their teeth to quiet the interrupted babies. Men stood and settled their wide-brimmed hats on their heads: the young men rolled their brims high on the sides and plunked their creased crowns flat; the older men wore their hats as they came from the store, with high-rounded crowns and straight-out brims. No hubbub of behind-the-hand comments marked the end of an unsatisfactory meeting. No pent-up feelings were released in pushing for the door.

A small boy, hampered more by plumpness than by age in learning to walk, clung to his mother's purple skirt and stared up openmouthed at me. His mother corrected his impudence by slapping his broad-brimmed hat upon his head and pushing it down over his eyes. When I laughed, she laughed, too, but she did not openly look at me.

Slowly, as if reluctantly, families separated themselves and trailed toward their wagons or pickups.

The schoolteacher stood on the steps of the classroom Quonset, shaking his head. "It's always the same," he told us. "Same old complaints every year."

"They seemed to enjoy the meeting."

"Sure they enjoy it," the teacher said. "We give them a good mutton stew and all the coffee they can drink. Besides, they like to get together for any reason."

A father, standing beside his pickup with a colorful load of women in its bed, called to a boy who just couldn't stop playing basketball. Two girls in long, full skirts ran squealing past us. A larger girl in blue jeans started into the schoolroom, stopped when she saw us, said, "Hi," and went on about her business. Hastiin

Chee walked by with no more than a slight settling of his tall hat on his head to indicate that he knew we had come to the meeting to hear him speak. We watched as a rubber-tired wagon squeaked around the far Quonset. The young man on the seat hauled up at the well and climbed down to fill his water barrel.

Gradually the rutted roads in all directions from the school became populated with pickups and wagons and people afoot. By the time the sun had spread its amber fan behind Old Grandfather Rock, parents and children would be snug in their hogans. Few if any families would have mutton stew bubbling on the stove this night. They had eaten well at the school and could save their own meat until tomorrow. The coffee pot or gallon tin can would simmer on the stove, no doubt, sending out little whiffs of rich brown fragrance. Coffee mixed with talk of the school meeting would fill the people's bellies.

In the hogans the talk would not be of children disliking the food served them at the trailer school; it would not touch on the difficulty involved in securing school clothes. The elder J. P. Morgan once said that for every action there are two reasons—a good reason and the real reason. He may or may not have realized that his rule was universal enough to apply to Navahos living in isolation as well as to Wall Street financiers. This night, family groups would gather around the stoves in two dozen scattered hogans, and consider their real objections to the school. Their "good" (meaning "acceptable to white people") reasons for objecting had been voiced at the meeting. Suppose we make ourselves invisible and visit Hastiin Chee's own camp.

His two married daughters are busy in their rectangular log houses—Dezba's twenty-five feet to the south, and Ebah's to the north of the large, central hogan where Hastiin Chee, his first wife, his brother, Kee Chee, and Kee Chee's wife have gathered. With the younger people of the camp occupied at their evening chores and child-tending, the older people are free to hold a heart-to-heart post-mortem on the school meeting. Kee Chee and his wife have driven ten miles through sand and sagebrush in order to relieve their pent-up feelings in talk not shaped to fit the white man's ears.

The packed dirt floor of the hogan has been freshly swept. Around the stove and running back to the slightly inward-sloping walls, have been spread fluffy goat- and sheepskins. Since Hastiin Chee is a man of some wealth, the skins are spread three and four deep on the floor. A graduated series of tin suitcases is stacked at the rear of the hogan. This is the Navaho equivalent of a clothes closet—a practical way to store clothes in the space available, and an effective means of keeping out the dust.

A loom with a gray and red saddle blanket, finished except for two or three rows, makes a small partition out from the north wall. Hastiin Chee's wife could have finished the blanket off yesterday, but she knows that to overdo is to tempt the gods to take away her ability. So she left the blanket not quite finished, and today of course she has been at the school since early morning. But the loom doesn't really interfere. The women sit on their heels on either side of it, and the edge of the blanket has pulled away from the frame enough for them to speak, if they wish, through the slit.

The men sit cross-legged opposite the fire. The stove door has been left open to provide light. The nut-like scent of burning piñon mingles with the rich pungence of coffee boiling in a gallon tin can to give the hogan an aura of well-being. No one speaks as yet. All sit enjoying one another's company in silence, and thinking through the opinions they will express when the proper time for speaking has come.

Hastiin Chee, as we have said, is a man of some wealth, but we should point out that he has been careful not to acquire too much. Too much wealth, especially if acquired suddenly, subjects a man to suspicion. It is a well-known fact and constant worry among the Navahos that life is hard. A man does not make a living easily. If one appears to do so, it is immediately suspected that he is in cahoots with a witch or has become a witch himself, and so is unduly able to influence the forces of nature in his behalf. Hastiin Chee would not have been selected to speak at the school meeting for his people, had any talk of witchcraft ever cast a shadow on his reputation.

So we can enjoy the lush scents and cozy warmth of the hogan, rich as it seems, without fear of having entered the domain of evil forces. Hastiin Chee and his wives have worked to achieve this comfort, and his standing among his people is of the highest. His opinion is worth seeking. It will be passed from hogan to hogan and will, eventually, bring some weight to bear upon the district's representatives on the Tribal Council.

When Hastiin Chee, called then Bahe Chee, was five years old, he started herding sheep. He was one of six thousand Navaho children on the Reservation at that time. This was thirty-five years after the United States government had agreed by treaty to provide a schoolhouse and a teacher for every thirty children between the ages of six and sixteen. During these thirty-five years, the government had got around to providing two schools with a capacity of three hundred. Five thousand seven hundred children, including Bahe Chee, had no possible opportunity to attend school. From the time of the treaty until 1946, thirty-nine thousand Navaho children grew up without the chance of going to school to learn to speak English, to learn to add up the prices of beans and coffee when they went to the store, to learn to read for themselves the printed forms to which the government required them to affix their names or X's.

As young Bahe Chee grew and learned from his fathers and grandfathers the Navaho ways to appease the malevolent spirits surrounding him in this world, he also learned to think for himself. Always careful to observe the proper taboos and to hold the required ceremonies for counteracting the inevitable disorders in his life, Bahe Chee added to all this a large measure of common sense.

While he was still a young man, his relatives began coming to

85

Chee for advice when their corn failed. They came to him when a new son-in-law demanded his marriage gifts returned on the ground that his bride was not the innocent girl for which he had contracted. When Bahe Chee himself became prosperous enough to bring his wife's sister to his camp and build her a hogan of her own, his relatives and friends began to refer to him as Hastiin Chee. He had become a man of distinction.

Thinking for himself, Hastiin Chee decided that white men surrounded the Reservation on every side, and that a man must deal with white men at the stores and in Washington. So, he decided, it would be wise to have a member of the family learn to speak the white man's language, to read the white man's papers, and to figure with the white man's markings. It was, of course, too late for him to go to school himself. If a school had been provided when he was growing up, now he would know these things and be able to meet white men on their own ground. The best he could do at this late date would be to send a child or two to school, he reasoned.

At the time, he could spare girls more easily than boys. So Dezba and Ebah were sent to Chinle to the government boarding school. Their expenses were not great and their chores at home could be taken over by other members of the family. At first, Hastiin Chee felt well satisfied with the course he had taken even though some of his people no longer respected him as highly as they had, and they were inclined to forget the "Hastiin" when speaking his name.

"That Bahe Chee," it was reported to him that they were saying at the store, "he is deserting the ways of our fathers. Soon Dezba and Ebah will be turned into white girls and will forget the language of our people."

Hastiin Chee walked with his shoulders a little straighter. He knew what he was doing. When, through the months, the people saw that Chee himself did not neglect to observe the proper taboos, they remembered to say "Hastiin" when referring to him.

The first trouble came when the girls returned home from school for the Christmas holidays. It was, of course, necessary to hold a Blessing Way Ceremony to counteract their long contact with white teachers. Otherwise none of their friends would have felt free to come to the Chee camp. Otherwise who could tell what disasters might befall the Chee family?

So Hastiin Chee called in a respected "singer" of Blessing Way, settled the financial arrangements, butchered a large portion of his first wife's flock to provide meat for all the friends and relatives who would come for the "sing," and pawned his two best bracelets to the trader in order to secure the necessary cornmeal and coffee.

It would take the Chee family the rest of the year to recover from the financial drain of this ceremony. Still, this was not the worst of having two daughters at the white man's school. Dezba and Ebah had come home with some mighty highfalutin notions. "We should have chairs for sitting on in the hogan," they said. "We should have windows in the hogan for letting in the light." They once were caught using water to wash their bodies. This was too much!

Hastiin Chee had put his foot down at that. The girls had not been so long away from home that they had forgotten that every drop of water was required for the squashes and corn. They promised not to act so foolish again with the water. They also spoke to each other in English and walked away from their father with a kind of superior air about them.

It was their changed manner that disturbed the girls' father more than any of the things they did or said. They questioned with a raised eyebrow the real necessity of carefully gathering up and burning their nail parings. When Ebah started to comb her hair at night and Hastiin Chee reminded her that bad luck would result, she shrugged and said offhandedly, "I forgot." Before going away to school, she would not have forgotten.

All of these things made Hastiin Chee squat on his heels for long hours at a time, watching the sheep but thinking only of his daughters. He had sent them to school for learning to speak English and to read. They were learning much more than he had intended. They were learning disrespect for the Navaho way.

A father living in the middlewestern section of the United States may sacrifice personal luxuries in order to send his daughter to an Eastern school. He sends her, expecting her to come home with a speaking knowledge of the French language and a practicing knowledge of polite social usage. This father may be astonished, in the same way that Hastiin Chee was astonished, to discover that the girl who returns from her sojourn at school is not the same girl plus refinements, but is instead a different girl. She has learned new skills at school, but she has learned also to look down her nose at her father's table manners, to criticize her mother's clothes, to question the minister's theology, and to refer to her home town as "the village."

"If it were only the trailer school," Kee Chee begins, now that the time for speaking has come, "things would not be so bad in my opinion. But after trailer school, comes riding the bus to the big, new day school. Then there is nothing for it but to send our children on to high school at Ganado or Brigham City. After high school, even the Tribal Council is now insisting they should be going to college. It would appear that the longer our children go to school, the more ignorant they become since they must always go longer and longer to school and can never stay at home to help with the work."

"The ways of the old ones are being forgotten," Kee's wife adds. "Look at the tight skirts the girls wear home from boarding school. They have no room beneath them for even one petticoat, which is not decent."

"And some even come home wearing blue jeans the same as their brothers'," her sister-in-law points out.

A car rattles to a stop at the edge of the camp. A half dozen dogs go barking to meet it. No one in the hogan gives any evidence of having heard the commotion, except that talk is cut off short. Soon footsteps, purposefully loud, can be heard beyond the hanging-blanket door of the hogan. Still no one inside the hogan moves.

The sounds at the blanket door die down and then increase again. Someone seems to be slapping his leather boot with a strap. Men's voices can be heard in an exchange of murmurs. Now sure that visitors have really arrived and that these sounds are not being made by the Wind People, Hastiin Chee gets lightly to his feet and goes to thrust the blanket aside.

Without a spoken greeting the visitors come in. They are three "boys" in their late thirties. They have come from up Waterless Mesa way. They walk around the fire clockwise and squat on their heels beyond Kee Chee. Two of these boys served as marines during World War II. The other one worked in a defense plant in Los Angeles.

Hastiin Chee adds two sticks of yellow piñon wood to the fire before taking his place again, cross-legged beside his brother.

These young men do not observe the proper time of orienting silence. The one known as Ned Todacheenee picks at a tiny burr caught in the goatskin on which he squats and says, "We think it is a mistake to speak so many complaints against the trailer school. The young ones must learn English. They must learn how to get along with the white man. This is a thing we found out when we went to war. We knew nothing at first. We had to be taught to speak and taught to read before we could help fight the war."

Roger Tso Benally, just home for a visit from Los Angeles, has spoken English for so long now that his Navaho words come in jerks and starts, as if he can barely remember them. He does remember, though, to draw circles with his index finger on the floor of the hogan as he speaks. "What good is it to make trouble about the trailer school?" he asks. "It is here to stay. Even the Tribal

Council is doing everything it can to get all Navahos to go to school near their hogans at first, then later to day school or boarding school to learn more, and finally to high school and on to college. It is the only way our people can live with white people and get along all right."

Tsiko Tsosie had become a sergeant in the Marines. He hangs his broad-brimmed hat on his knee and turns it round and round, giving it his full attention while he speaks. "You people stay on the Reservation so much," he says, "that you do not see how many white people live every-place else in this country. You think there are a lot of white people when you go to Gallup. Let me tell you something. I have been in towns where people were walking up and down the streets so thick they could hardly pass each other and I could not find even one Navaho in all those people. I tell you, it is no use fighting them. Once we have learned their language, we can get along with them without much trouble. You are only making it hard for your children when you complain against the school."

Hastiin Chee sighs and even the young men allow him to hold the floor in silence long enough to arrange his thoughts. At last he speaks. "If you young ones are thinking in these ways, you should have told it to the teacher when he asked that you speak. As for me, the ways of our people have always served me well. The ways of the white man have often been bitter on my tongue."

Here, at last, is the real reason!

Hastiin Chee has spoken himself dry of "good" reasons—neat black sheep, curried and driven in, one by one, for all to see. Now, he speaks from the depths of the resentment sucked in at his mother's breast, and kept fanned into flame by big and little mistreatments and slights. Now he speaks in thrown-out wads—like a man cleaning his corral with his bare hands. "Don't forget Fort Sumner! Four years in captivity! And then no schools—year after year, no schools! Then it was 'Cut down your flocks. Kill off your horses. They eat too much.' Remember how they made us get rid of our sheep! It is 'Jump now. Turn this way. Do as we say.' "

"But that is all past," Roger Tso Benally interrupts. "Times have changed."

"Times have changed," Hastiin Chee scoffs. "How often have I heard this!" A broken thong in the toe of his moccasin occupies his hands. He thinks, "I suppose these young men would say, 'Feet have changed,' and have me discard my moccasins in favor of those stiff leather boxes sold as shoes," He says aloud, "You may be right. Maybe times have changed, but I have not. I am still the descendant of Sun and Changing Woman. I am still one of The People. I do not blow with every shifting wind, first to the south and then to the north just because a white man comes from Wah-sheen-don with papers in his hand."

"It is time for coffee," Hastiin Chee's wife proposes, and goes to the orange-crate cupboard at the back of the hogan to get the white graniteware cups. . . .

Long after the visitors have gone, Hastiin Chee sits cross-legged beside the dying fire. He knows that his generation will soon pass on to the next world, and that those who will follow are less concerned than he has been with keeping the old ways pure and undefiled. After those will come the ones who went to war along with the white man and can see little wrong with his ways. After those will come the children who now sit at desks in trailer schools, and boarding schools, and the big, new day schools, and mission schools, and off-reservation schools, learning that the Navaho ways are to pass into darkness, the white man's ways are to be taken up.

Slowly he shakes his head. He knows that he cannot hold back the wind that blows his people toward the changing ways. Neither can he stop remembering the white man's broken promises, his high-handed orders, his know-it-all bearing, and his uncouth man-

NAVAHOS HAVE FIVE FINGERS

ners with his prying eyes and clicking cameras. He cannot help wishing that, as his children and his grandchildren sit in the white way schools, they might be sure of learning to live in freedom without overdoing, to make a living without also learning greed, to get along with all men in the Navaho way of harmony.

Perhaps, if he himself had not allowed his hair to be cut . . .

CHAPTER SEVEN

Ladies Do Sweat

THE ROOM THAT HAD BEEN A CHURCH on Sunday and a play room on Tuesday would be a schoolroom and a movie theater on Thursday, but on Wednesday it became a clinic.

Didibah and Kee Tso arrived early on Wednesdays. We didn't know this on our first Wednesday. As soon as we'd finished breakfast and gone across the yard, we were surprised to find the cotton braided rugs in a wad on the porch of the community house. Inside, Didi was bent double, slapping a long-handled, chlorine-scented wet mop at the yellow linoleum, poking it under sewing machines and stacked chairs. Kee Tso flung the mattress from the back of the pickup onto the porch with the rugs. He swept the floor of the truck as if he were killing rattlesnakes.

Don and I fitted ourselves in around the edges of this house-cleaning frenzy. We dusted, watered the potted caladium, and—when the floor had dried—set the chairs down the east wall, across the room along the Ping-pong table, and up the west wall in front of the sewing machines.

Didi took her mop to the kitchen and rushed back to turn on the record player. Davy Crockett pursued his exploits at ear-splitting volume while she hurried into the living room to come back

93

lugging the big 1920 typewriter. She centered the machine on the small table near the supply closet that doubled for an examination room. Next, she found the green steel file in which patients' records were kept on six-by-nine-inch cards. She placed the file on the table beside the typewriter and let her arms fall to her sides.

"So that's finish," she said. "Think I going out where Kee is play basketball."

She and Kee Tso practiced shooting baskets for an hour. We still had two hours to wait before the doctor would arrive.

When the store closed at noon, patients and visitors wandered into our clean clinic room and settled themselves on the lined-up chairs. Some of the ladies carried babies on cradle boards. Others held babies astride their hips. Many had young children clinging to their skirts. Little girls in long dresses like their mothers' and little boys in stiff Levis ducked their heads behind the most convenient shawl or skirt if we happened to glance in their direction.

Our "boys" all gravitated over, but they didn't hang around inside on clinic day the way they did on days when the community room wasn't scented with chlorine and scouring powder. They'd come in and stand with their backs to the door, apparently seeing nothing except the hangnail at which they were picking. Then they'd quickly decide to sidle out.

Soon we'd hear them on the basketball court. Their characteristic "Ya-a-a," a deep-throated gargle let loose when they wanted another player to intercept the ball or try for a basket, gave clinic day a special sound all its own. Their laughter over silly plays called more "time outs" on clinic day than at any other time. You see, on clinic day, they had spectators. They played ready to laugh, ready to show off, and with a ripping "ya-a-a-a" always ready to spill from their throats.

Inside, on clinic day, we got the older men, the *hastiins*—men of distinction in the realms of horse sense and prestige.

The difference between men and "boys" was not necessarily marked by age. Not all of the *hastiins* wore their hair in a hank, either, but most of those living in our area did. Even more distinctive was their manner. They had none of the "boys' " restlessness in their eyes or in their movements. They might or might not wear Pendleton blankets clutched around their shoulders. From their ear lobes might or might not dangle turquoise nuggets. A man's whole-hearted adherence to his tribal beliefs and practices can be detected in the way he sets his feet when he walks, in the expression barely lighting his eyes when he comes face-to-face with a white man, and in an at-peace-with-destiny air that touches his whole bearing.

I watched one of these *hastiins* at noon on our second Wednesday at Tselani. From behind our living room curtains I peered, fascinated, as he crossed the dusty road from the store and came through our gate. The English word for the way he walked has not yet evolved. "Stride" isn't it, although he took long steps with power in them. "Stroll" isn't it. Purpose is missing from that word. "March" is too restricted—it leaves out the freedom of his movements, but its suggestion of rhythm is certainly apropos.

I wanted to see him better, so I hurried into the community room, then stopped and leaned nonchalantly against the door frame. My man opened the door as the President of the United States might open the door of the White House—with the air of one owning the place for the period of his term of office. His manner was not offensive. Here was a man wearing his rights and privileges like a shawl.

He came in and bumped the door shut. His eyes swept all of the room except the spot where I was standing. There is a knack to this—a knack most Navahos seem to acquire at birth. White people are avoided in any remote trading post, in this same manner, and then later described in minute detail to the members of the family who weren't at the store that day.

Unsmiling but with a wholly pleasant expression on his face, my man moved across the room and seated himself on a chair at the far end of the Ping-pong table.

"Is he a patient?" I asked Didi.

She shrugged. "I don't know." After the proper interval had elapsed, she wandered over and spoke to him in Navaho. He must have murmured an answer, but he seemed to be giving his undivided attention to the leather thong that tied the large, cone-shaped silver button to his moccasin-boot.

Didi came back to the table. "His granddaughter, she having baby soon. He just visiting. See what doctor saying 'bout his granddaughter."

"Have you found all the patients' cards?" I asked Didibah. "What about those ladies in the corner?"

"They just visiting," Didi told me.

I was accustomed to a certain amount of conversation between visiting ladies. One of these coaxed, nudged, and finally insisted that a dimpled, black-haired infant stop staring at the ceiling and finish nursing. The other lady held her friend's empty cradle board across her lap and straightened the blankets and laces while she waited. This is the way these ladies visited. I remembered having been involved in a good many visits that featured far less communication.

We heard no complaints about being made to wait for the doctor. No one mentioned having another engagement, and needing to see the doctor ahead of the others. No one consulted a watch.

One small boy whimpered. His mother grasped his upper arm, and when he let his knees give way and threatened to slide to the floor and start kicking, she hoisted him to the chair beside her. She said only one pleasant-sounding word of Navaho. He stopped whimpering and sat, legs straight out before him, his eyes fixed on the scuffed toes of his bulbous-nosed shoes.

We had no candy wrappers, nothing but a few trails of dusty

footprints across our floor when the doctor's carryall spun through the gate, across the basketball court, and up to the community room door.

The doctors at the hospital took turns coming from Ganado to conduct our clinic. Today we had the young, six-foot-four-inch one.

We still weren't skilled in the art of being properly indifferent to new arrivals. We hurried out to greet him.

He was wearing a sport jacket and well-pressed brown slacks. He swung down from the carryall and pulled out from behind the seat his medicines and instruments.

"How are you folks getting along?" he asked.

We assured him that, so far, we hadn't lost a patient.

"Delivered any babies?" he teased.

"We haven't even had any close calls," I bragged. "The West isn't half as wild as advertised."

We went inside and the doctor visited with Didibah for a bit. He turned then to his waiting patients, lined up on chairs around the room. He gave them a smile reassuring enough to heal any minor ailments. Then he took off his sport jacket and slid into a starched, white tunic.

Didibah sat at the little table, ready to handle the card file and the typewriter.

"Well, Didibah, who's first?" the doctor asked.

Didi grinned up at him and handed him a card. She wagged her head toward an unkempt girl of four or five who kept swiping her long sleeve beneath her nose.

The doctor reached for the child's hand and led her toward the tiny examination room. "Well, Juanita, let's see what we can do for you."

He turned to Didibah. "Temperature?" he asked.

Didi waved toward the card in his hand. "I write it down."

The business of clinic was under way.

Didi found patients' cards in the file and slid them out. I helped her read and record temperatures. We passed thermometers around and patients sat sucking on them as if they were lollypops.

Pregnant ladies each had a turn with the doctor in the examination room. They came out tugging their velveteen blouses into place, and covered their embarrassment by turning at once to Didibah with questions about the bottle of capsules the doctor had given them. Didi explained dosages and routines and accepted twenty-five cents, the clinic's charge for a dollar's worth of vitamins.

The doctor squatted on his heels to swab small throats. He asked Don to set up the infrared light and train it on a thin-faced *hastiin's* back. Pains in his back had kept him awake nights for a week, he told Didibah. Still, he'd sat on a Primary chair for two hours, waiting without complaint for the doctor and whatever meager relief might be had from the light.

The doctor scolded one lady. "Do you mean to tell me your husband still hasn't gone to Fort Defiance to the sanatorium? You promised me a month ago that you'd get him there."

When Didi put his outburst into indignant-sounding Navaho, the lady lifted her hands and let them fall in a helpless heap to her lap.

The doctor would not be put off. "Tell her to bring the whole family to Ganado or else take them to Fort Defiance Hospital for tests. Tell her next she'll have to move everybody from her camp into the sanatorium, if she doesn't quit this fooling around."

The trader's wife from a store twenty miles away drove in for a checkup. She'd been having headaches.

The doctor dispensed pills, ointments, and sympathetic, concerned advice which Didibah put into low-toned Navaho.

John Joe came late. I saw him limping across the basketball area, dragging his crutches behind him. When he stepped upon the porch, he wedged the crutches into his armpits and hobbled on in.

I put his foot to soak while the doctor finished with the trader's wife.

98

"This foot looks all right," the doctor told me when he got to John Joe. "You've done a good job."

"Can I not walking on crutch?" John Joe pleaded without taking his gaze from the now spongy-looking wound.

John Joe had never spoken to me in English, so this was obviously a case of being desperate.

The doctor examined the foot, turning it from side to side. "Use the crutches awhile longer," he suggested. "Be sure you come back every day, and I'll see you next Wednesday. Then we'll decide." He looked up at Don. "Bring him to the hospital for another X-ray the first chance you get."

Two tears splashed into the washpan. Those crutches were a humiliation to John Joe, and I felt quite sure that he used them now only in the presence of us *belliganos*.

The doctor treated the foot and dressed it. He stood up then and laid his hand on John Joe's touseled, black hair. "I promise I won't keep you on crutches one minute longer than I have to," he vowed.

John Joe grinned at the pan of soapy water as he reached for them.

Within two hours, the doctor had seen everyone who wanted to be seen. Our proud-walking *hastiin* still sat on his child's chair at the end of the Ping-pong table. I reminded Didi of his presence and insisted that he must want to see the doctor.

"He's just waiting," she said.

The doctor traded our syringes for the sterile ones he'd brought. He left a roll of gauze and replenished our medicine shelves with Kaopectate and baby aspirin.

He loaded his belongings into the carryall and got out his camera.

Don and I climbed with him up the sandstone mesa at the back of our house. We soon reached our favorite lookout. Billows of sandstone fell away from both sides of the ridge on which we stood. Above us towered the abstractions suggesting elephants' legs. Beyond the gently undulated sandstone stood the white wall of carved figures like a mile-long reredos in a fifty-acre cathedral. The doctor did as we had done so often—examined various pinpoints of this vast display through his lens, sighed, and snapped the case shut on his camera. He stood for a long minute, drinking in space and beauty, taking pictures in his memory.

"Well, here we go again," he said.

When we got back to his carryall, six Navahos were waiting to ride with him. Some would ask to be dropped off along the way to the hospital. Others would ride as far as Ganado, and then hitch another ride for the sixty miles on to Gallup.

The doctor shifted his load and fitted his passengers in around medicine bag, water jugs, and shovels. "Have you heard anything about Grandma Greymule?" he asked us then.

We hadn't and Didi hadn't.

The doctor glanced at his wrist watch. "I may swing in by her hogan," he said. "It won't take more than ten minutes, and I was worried about her eyes the last time I saw her." He slipped behind the wheel then, and was off in a cloud of dust.

It had been a full day and we were ready to relax.

"Let's have a cup of coffee," I suggested.

We went across to our house and Don filled the percolator. I sat down at the table and kicked off my loafers. "Well, one more clinic day down!" I said.

But it wasn't—not by a Navaho jugful!

Didi rushed up our back steps. "You better come," she said. "It's another lady."

I shoved one foot into a shoe. "What's the matter with her?"

"Nothing," Didi answered.

I flopped the shoe off again.

"She might having her baby soon, I think," Didi added.

"Oh no!" I wailed. "Not when the doctor has just left. Why didn't she come sooner?" I fumbled under the table for my shoes.

Didi giggled.

I left her to come tagging along and ran across the yard to the community room.

There sat the lady, all right, on a Primary chair, her shawl clutched around her. Her free hand was what worried me. With it she kept mopping her perspiring face.

I heard the nurse's voice as clearly as if she'd been standing beside me, and just then I'd have given a good deal to have her there. "If she's perspiring on her face," the nurse's voice said evenly, "you won't have time to get her to the hospital. Just put her to bed and deliver the baby."

I had no intention of being maneuvered into a medical education without a struggle. "Ask her when her baby is due," I begged Didi, who came sauntering in. I hid my shaking hands behind my back and waited for my reprieve to come out of their mumbled exchange.

Didi giggled. "She say, 'Sometime 'bout now.' " I half suspected that Didi was enjoying this.

"How often do the pains come? Ask her that." I was fighting for my life.

Didi and the lady carried on quite a lengthy conversation.

"She say, 'Twenty minute . . . 'bout that.' " The shrug that Didi used to help interpret her words told me plainly that the lady had no idea of time. A Navaho twenty minutes could be two or forty.

The lady swiped her hand across her upper lip. I reached for a box of facial tissues and held it toward her. She took two tissues and gave her whole face a good mopping.

"Where's Kee?" I asked Didi.

" 'Round somewhere."

"Hurry. See if you can find him," I told her. "Tell him to get in the truck and try to catch the doctor."

This was pure cowardice on my part, but I'd been haunted at night by dreams of stopping in a dust hole halfway to the hospital to deliver a baby in the back of our pickup. I grabbed a handful of tissues and started mopping my face.

Didi found Kee Tso in record time. I ran out and thrust the keys to the pickup at him. "Hurry," I pleaded, "but don't drive too fast. Look around when you get to the windmill. The doctor thought he might go to Grandma Greymule's hogan." When I saw Kee roar through the gate, I remembered to breathe again. Next I remembered our lady and hurried inside.

Not until then did I notice our round-faced *hastiin* still sitting on his Primary chair at the end of the Ping-pong table. When Didi came in, I inquired about him again. "Are you sure he didn't want to see the doctor?"

"Yes," she answered.

I needed another interpreter for that, but I turned back to our perspiring lady. If only by some miracle Kee Tso could overtake the doctor! "Would you like to lie down?" I asked the lady.

Didi put my question to her. For answer, she mopped her face. I offered her the tissue box again, and she helped herself. She thanked me with an apologetic, split-second smile.

"Ask whether she has the pain now," I prompted Didi.

She had no pain at that moment.

"Tell her to let us know when it comes again," I said. "We'll time her." It was something to do. I went to the door to peer down the road.

Don came over from the other house. "Coffee's ready," he said. "Have you delivered that baby yet?"

"If you think you're joking, you're not."

"You're trembling," he said.

"You'd better be, too," I told him. "You're the doctor. I'm just the amateur nurse around here."

He followed me inside and we took up our questioning again. The answers we received did nothing to put us at ease. We learned that the lady lived about a mile (or five miles) beyond The Hill. She had come on foot. No, she didn't have the pain again, not yet.

Yes, the pains had started during the night. No, this was not her first child. This would be her fourth.

Fourth! The one obstetrical fact I knew what that the first one might come reluctantly, not the fourth one.

And why hadn't the lady come earlier?

Well, she had tried. Actually she had run most of the way in order to get here before the doctor left.

She had run! She had run up The Hill! In three petticoats, a velveteen blouse, and a folded Pendleton blanket, she had run! What lady wouldn't sweat?

My trembling stopped.

Then we heard a motor. Don, at the door, said, "Here they come —two cars, raising an awful dust. . . . Yes, it's Kee and the doctor."

The doctor came in with a grin on his face.

"Darn her, she ran!" I told him. "That's not fair."

"I'll take her off your hands," he said.

We handled her as if she were rare china, getting her into the carryall. I'm sure I don't know why. If I hadn't been so relieved, I'd have given her a lecture on promptness that would have blighted her baby's whole life. As it was, we were delighted to see the doctor gun his carryall through our sand trap and disappear in a billow of beige dust.

Didi and Don and I stood on the porch, giggling from relief.

"Want a cup of coffee, Didibah?" Don asked.

"Where's Kee?" I added. "If anybody gets coffee, he does. He saved my life."

We turned when the screen door slammed. Again we had forgotten our *hastiin*. He came toward us now and, without a glance in our direction, angled across the basketball court toward the gate.

"I wonder who he is," I said, more to myself than to anyone else. His dignity intrigued me.

"That man?" Didi asked. "He's that lady's grandfather. He coming to see that doctor taking care of her all right. Now he's in big hurry for getting home."

"In a hurry!" I scoffed. "He's been sitting in there since noon, and not a peep out of him. If he was in such a hurry, why on earth did he let the doctor leave before his granddaughter got here?"

Didi shrugged. "I don't know."

We watched the man's slow, lord-of-the-earth tread.

"What's he in such a hurry about?" Don asked.

"Say lambs starting," Didi explained. "He need being home."

"Lambs? Starting where?" I asked.

Didibah's glance was incredulous at first, and then, when she read the abysmal ignorance on my face, she became indulgent. "Lambs starting to get borned," she explained. "This getting 'bout lambing time 'round here."

I still had no inkling of the work, the odors, the excitement, the joy, and the frustration that were "lambing time 'round here," but we were soon to stand ankle-deep in corral droppings and find out.

CHAPTER EIGHT

Lambing Time

BEN LEE BEGAY had attended Intermountain School at Brigham City, Utah, at the expense of the Bureau of Indian Affairs. He was a tall, serious young man. He had returned to the Reservation, after four or five years of schooling, wearing a pair of horn-rimmed spectacles that added to his serious appearance, but with an almost easy manner and a comfortable command of English. We didn't need to hold back and wait for Ben Lee to accept us. He was openly our friend from the day of our arrival. He stepped forward at once and offered his palm to be pressed in turn by each of ours.

Ben Lee's quick, toothy smile gave us a warm, wanted feeling at times when we might have been inclined to interpret as uncordiality the normal Navaho reserve. (Most of us live amid so much social effusion that we forget the possibility of honest neutrality in relationships. If a new acquaintance doesn't throw his arms around us, we're likely to assume that he doesn't like us.)

Ben Lee, however, appeared only infrequently at the community room with time to kill in playing Ping-pong or listening to records. He conscientiously gave his full time to making a living for his wife, his mother-in-law, and his wife's unmarried sisters.

We hadn't seen Ben Lee for two or three weeks. Then, just at noon when the store closed, he came across the road and through our gate. He wore clean Levis and a maroon, rayon gabardine shirt in the fitted-body, scroll-tabbed pocket, cowboy style, and a navy blue, long-billed cap.

Seeking Don out, he offered his hand and his nice smile.

"How've you been?" Don asked him. "We've missed you."

"Been to Phoenix," Ben Lee said. "Stay one week. Could you taking me home now?"

Don was surprised. Ben Lee was one of the few Navahos who hadn't asked favors with the air of divine right. Because he hadn't made a practice of pre-empting our pickup and our adhesive bandages, Don decided to go along with his request.

"How far do you live?"

Ben Lee waved toward the southwest. "Not far."

Three or four ladies in their best satin skirts and full savings account of jewelry were sitting on the Primary chairs in the community room. They were saying nothing, and covering their mouths with their hands whenever we went in and out about our business. "Do they want anything?" I asked Didi.

"Just visiting," she told me. Then, with a mere hint of strained patience, she added the explanation, "Store close now."

Don suggested that I bring my camera and come along with him and Ben Lee. "Didi can take care of things here, and you might get a picture."

This turned out to be the short-sighted prediction of the century.

I grabbed up both the movie and the still cameras and we headed for the pickup. Instead of joining us, Ben Lee ambled toward the gate. Don watched him for a moment and then shrugged. "I guess we're supposed to follow him," he said, and stepped on the starter. When we'd turned around on the basketball court and whipped through our sand hole, we could see Ben Lee's back still retreating up the middle of the road toward the store. We ground along in low after him until he stopped by the gasoline pump. There we saw why he needed a ride home.

Don got out and helped him load his purchases into the bed of the pickup. He had bought cornmeal, flour, sugar, coffee, canned peaches, canned tomatoes, canned milk, Pepsi-cola—enough to fill two large cardboard cartons. In addition, he had bought an iron stove in a wooden crate, four lengths of pipe for the stove, and a white graniteware coffeepot.

With his purchases loaded, Ben Lee motioned us down the road toward Ganado. Then, in about a mile, he waved off to the right. "Turn on next road," he said. After awhile he very quietly murmured, "You pass road." Don stepped on the brake. We backed for a long quarter-mile before Ben Lee grinned and pointed out the double sheep path that he had intended for us to take.

Experience had taught us implicit faith in our pickup by now. Don cut the front wheels around, let the right one fall into the angling ditch before us, and hoped the rest would follow on through. We were soon rolling along at a dizzy ten-mile-per-hour rate over sagebrush and saltbush that had been somewhat flattened by the occasional passage of an iron-wheeled wagon. At intervals we dropped with a jolt into an eroded ditch across our highway, but we were soon accustomed to the truck's being equal to these small hazards, and we could give our attention to the scenery.

We were headed almost straight west, along the back of our third mesa. We hadn't seen this mesa from the lower side until now. From here it appeared to be six times as large around and three times as high as it did from our back porch. We promised ourselves that we'd come down here at the first opportunity and explore on foot its sinuous sandstone base and its jutting, burnt sienna terraces. Beyond the mesa, the sky opened up above a straight horizon as if we were riding along the lower edge of a tilted table top.

"Over that way is pretty lookout," Ben Lee said.

"It's pretty ahead of us, too," Don commented.

Ben Lee smiled. His eyes were fixed on the gentle mesa that rose before us. Silver streamers of sunlight marked its perpendicular

107

ridges. Its gun metal cap absorbed the noonday sun as if it were a great round saddle blanket, woven from the wool of black sheep. Ben Lee's head turned to the right where a sinewy, cream-colored hill sprawled beyond the sky-tilted tableland. Slowly he turned back to the left where the dark-capped mesa was attached by a high fill to a chalk-white, block-walled mountain that might have been built by Egyptians. On the near face of this mountain, a boldly eroded sphinx watched us from the corner of its eye, ready to pose us the riddle of man if we should dare to pass beneath it.

With just a whisper of pride in his voice, Ben Lee finally said, "This is my place," and then added, "for wintertime."

Not more than five hundred feet ahead of us, then, we were able to distinguish, from the sheltered high valley on which they stood, two mud-plastered hogans. Their brown-and-white-striped blanket doors, facing us as we approached from the east, gave them away.

Soon Ben Lee scooted forward until he was barely hanging on the edge of the seat. Then he lifted himself, and pressed his nose almost against the windshield as he shaded his spectacles with his hand. "Lambs!" he breathed.

The corral was even harder to separate from its surrounding landscape than the hogans. It was built against the side of the sprawling hill and into an extending ridge that curved around like an arm. By building two additional sides, Ben Lee or his father-in-law or grandfather-in-law had been able to enclose a snug corral. Those two sides had been woven rather than laid. Many wagon trips to the mountains, many gleanings from flash floods, many seasons' accumulations of scrap had gone into those two man-made sides of this corral.

A flood-carried dead tree had probably been laid down for a start. Piñon branches, heavy trunks of sagebrush, and pieces of scrap metal had been woven in and out among the dead branches and among the roots. Railroad ties, here and there a few mountain-cut posts, and an old car spring had been driven into the ground and buttressed with rocks. Old shoes, old jackets, old Levis had been used along with coffee cans and flattened cardboard cartons and boards from packing crates to make this fence secure against lambs sneaking out, against preying animals sneaking in. It was, I'm sure, a good, utilitarian corral.

Today, under a spotlight of late April sun, the corral was touched by the more-than-real magic of a good stage set. The drama being enacted there, with its accompanying sounds and odors and dialogue, made it hard for Ben Lee to remain in the truck until we had jolted through the last and deepest ditch and cut over to the right to stop between the near hogan and the corral.

"Lambs not starting when I was going to Phoenix," Ben Lee exclaimed.

Now lambs were everywhere.

Before we stopped, an elderly lady in a man's suit jacket and a long blue-and-white percale skirt herded a dozen ewes, each with a spindle-legged lamb, around our truck and off to pasture. On any other day, this lady would have ducked her head and covered her mouth with her hand in an effort to pass without being seen. Today she tossed her head and grinned from ear to ear. Then, just for good measure, she lifted her arm and waved.

Her mood and Ben Lee's bursting excitement proved to be the tone pattern of the day.

We flung the doors open and hurried into the thick of things. I slung a camera over each shoulder, hoping that pictures of newborn lambs and kids would be permissible.

Ben Lee had not been at home for a week. Even so, he now appeared not to notice that his pretty young wife stood in the center of the corral. She recognized his arrival (or ours) by turning her face away and nervously tucking imaginary wisps of gleaming black hair into the heavy chignon, rolled white-lady fashion, at the back of her head. She appeared to be giving full attention to her guard duty—seeing that ewes and nannies didn't interfere with each other during their deliveries. However, she kept running her spread fingers down the wrinkle-pleats of her long blue-and-pink print skirt, and tugging the collar of her worn denim jacket higher and higher around her throat. Probably our cameras frightened her. She was dressed for work, not for having her picture taken, and she had no way of knowing that we would respect the difference.

Ben Lee approached the corral very quietly and slowly lifted one leg and then the other over the gate—two removable boards laid horizontally into crotches of tree skeletons. He took up his corral duties at once, helping a macaroni-legged lamb to a spraddled, propped-up stance from which it dared not lift one foot. When Ben Lee's tasks naturally took him to the area where his wife was working, the two appeared to pick up an on-going conversation where it had been interrupted a week before. Anything by way of a greeting must have been deferred by mutual consent and tribal custom, until they could be alone in the privacy of their hogan.

Ben Lee worked with his wife and with her two older sisters, who were also busy in the corral, with the same kind of impersonality. His mother-in-law hurried from the near hogan, clutching a cascade of inch-wide torn strips of calico and percale. She smiled and waved the gay string mop at us as she trotted to the corral.

We don't know whether she and Ben Lee observe the mother-in-law taboo. Their observance of it that day couldn't have been very strict. While they probably didn't look into each others' faces, they worked together around the corral in too close quarters for complete avoidance. Maybe all rules are modified at lambing time. Certainly a special rule of happiness and excitement had gone into effect for the occasion. I had felt the same kind of exuberance in the air, years before in Oklahoma, when a "gusher" came in and spewed oil over everything and everybody within ear shot of its whooshing roar.

Like an uncontrolled gusher, lambs and kids were being born all over the corral. A din of discordant baa-a-as and stuttered bleats accompanied the drama. Ben Lee's wife and her mother and sisters stepped over laboring animals to get to those delivering so they could tag mothers and their off-spring with matching strips of calico.

Usually the lambs came one by one, limber-legged and bare-looking in their plastered-down wool. Kids came more often than not in pairs, their fleece expertly brushed and curled on delivery. They arrived, also, with a fully matured instinct for butting heads together.

The seven-year-old sister of Ben Lee's wife scampered to and from the corral, grabbing up a damp, doddering lamb and lugging it draped over her arm until a cuddlier one appeared. She wore a blue-and-yellow print skirt that came to her high-topped tennis shoes. Her blouse of black velveteen was soon spotted and slobbered on by her pets, but no one marred her joy by delivering a lecture. Her lovely, deep-set eyes glowed with greater and greater delight as her fickle arms released a squirming lamb for one that couldn't stand alone, and then relinquished that one in a pile of droppings for love of a curly-haired kid.

I asked Ben Lee whether I might take some pictures of the baby lambs and kids from outside the corral.

"I guess that be all right," he said.

At the time, I attributed the tone of reluctance in his permission to the Navaho's usual restraint and to a kind of rigidity in his use of English. Since then, we've wondered whether the fear of enemy possession and the possibility of witchcraft's being worked against the animals might have been lurking in Ben Lee's mind.

If so, all adversities affecting the family's flocks may now be charged against us, for I did take pictures. I exposed yards of motion picture film to the pitiable-comic antics of ten-minute-old lambs, struggling to learn the uses of legs with every-which-away joints in them. At birth, these lambs would lie as they fell, in a heap with loose ends protruding until their mothers started licking them. The licking always began as a toweling-off process and always ended with a few purposeful swipes around the head that seemed to say, "Now get up. You're on your own."

The lambs could usually manage to lock their hind legs into some kind of linear continuity and hoist their hollow-hipped posteriors into the air. From there on, the going got tough. If the hind legs pushed too hard, the lamb nosed over into the brown, ripe droppings that carpeted the corral and came around with a wet face full of odorous polka dots. If one hind leg pushed harder than the other, one front leg got crimped underneath, and walking at a list on three legs and one bent knee presented problems of a different sort. When all went well and the hind legs pushed just enough to assist with a forward boost as the front knees unbent, a lamb was still likely to find itself elevated high in the air on four unmanageable stilts with ball bearings where one-way hinges should have been.

Any lamb in Ben Lee's corral could have taught a comic dancer a lifetime of routines.

The kids seemed to find their legs somewhat less astonishing. Of course, the kids arrived done up in yellow celophane bags, which their mothers peeled off, and there they were, all neat and finished. I am inclined toward the view that feeling better dressed and perfectly groomed, they had the self-assurance required for immediate walking. I used but little film on the kids until they started butting their heads together. They began this as soon as they discovered that mere walking was difficult for no one except those awkward lambs.

One kid would find another walking around minding his own business, give him a playful tag, and at once they'd be squared away, neatly curled white or gray heads down, and wham! The report of their cracking foreheads would sound above the continuous din of bleats and baas, and they'd back off to try it all over again. Another pair would get a loping start and frolic up onto a foot-wide ledge of rock, where they'd turn and start whacking their heads together from there, upstaging all the others.

I took many nature-written, perfect continuity films of the birth process. Ben Lee's smallest sister-in-law ran around the outside of the corral and squatted down to point out to me, through the hodge-podge fence, a large nanny beginning her labor. The child stayed beside me, clutching a skin-and-bone lamb around the middle, until I had the event complete on film. The happenings around us seemed so natural and everyone was so elated by them that it didn't once occur to me to wonder about the methods and materials of a seven-year-old's education.

Don came up behind us. "I don't know just why you're taking all these pictures. If you showed them to any of your friends, they'd faint."

I looked down on the blue-black top of my small companion's head and couldn't resist brushing a strand of hair back from her eyes. "My friends faint too easy," I said. "It's time they grew up."

As ewes and nannies were delivered and their babies learned to stand, Ben Lee's mother-in-law drove them from the corral by swinging a tomato can rattle on a string. The ewes came nodding wearily along, paying no attention to their staggering offspring until they happened on a tuft of something green that lured them to stop and nibble. Then, with awkward lunges and bobbles, the concave-sided, knotty-jointed lambs would finally find the proper milk dispensary and hang on in spite of being buffeted along to the next tuft of green for mother's nibbling. The tufts were widely scattered.

The mother nannies came with their heads high and the mere hint of a superior attitude in the way they swung their silky tippets as they strolled along. After all, they had for the most part given birth to twins. In addition, their children, instead of looking like toys made of worn-out plush and only half stuffed, were groomed and fluffed and tinted pink at the tips of their noses. What mother wouldn't be a trifle proud?

"How many are there?" I asked Ben Lee when he seemed to have a minute.

" 'Bout two hundred," he answered. "Maybe fifty more coming."

"That many sheep and goats will be worth a lot of money," I commented. Then I asked the question that we were frequently asked about our possessions. "How much are they worth?"

Ben Lee shrugged. "I don't know."

"But why don't you figure it out?" I persisted. "Wouldn't you like to know how rich you'll be when these lambs and kids grow up and you can sell them?"

"'They won't growing up," Ben Lee said. "They soon be starving."

"Oh no!" I wailed. "I thought you took them to the mountains in the summer. Surely there's grass up there."

"They will starving before." Ben Lee's tone was resigned. "We don't get permit for keeping many sheep. Not enough people in family. Not good enough land. Tribal Council give out just 'bout two hundred permits for raising two-hundred-fifty sheep. Those men having big family, good land. My family getting small permit."

Don had come up while we were talking. "Does your permit give you enough sheep and goats to make a living for your family?"

Ben Lee shrugged. "Can't making living since Wah-sheen-don tell us cut down. 'Too many sheep causing erosion,' Wah-sheen-don say. 'Horse eating much as five sheep. Get rid horses. Get rid goats.' " Ben Lee pushed his long-billed cap back on his head and swiped his sleeve across his damp forehead. "The People don't like Wah-sheen-don saying how many." He waved his hand toward the corral. "Mother nature better say how many."

"But you've just told us they'll die off," Don reminded him.

Ben Lee shrugged. "Ought to be raising many as can. Tribal Council is not knowing how many we needing here."

"The Tribal Council? I thought you said Washington made you cut down."

"First Wah-sheen-don then Tribal Council," Ben Lee said in a tone that lumped the two together.

So, it was authority—white or Navaho—that rankled him. I remembered the disgruntled talk I'd so frequently heard in the 'thirties—just when the big stock reduction program was being fought by the Navahos—against plowing under crops, against the government's interfering with a man's freedom to plant whatever he wished and as much of it as he could, against Washington setting itself up to play God.

"But, Ben Lee, your land is eroded," I pointed out in my most reasonable tone of voice. "We drove through all those ditches to get here. Don't you think it's better to do something about it now? Otherwise it will just get worse and worse and soon there won't be any grass at all."

Ben Lee stood silently gazing across his corral for a long minute. "I think same like my grandfather," he said at last. Then his shoulders squared. His head lifted. "My grandfather go from this district, being on Tribal Council, you know, till he die."

"And you agreed with him?" Don prodded.

"He was not scare tell that Wah-sheen-don man what he's thinking," Ben Lee said with pride. "That Wah-sheen-don man coming to Tribal Council with little bunch papers saying, 'Do this for stopping erosion.' Next year, same man come with more papers, saying, 'Maybe do this for stopping erosion.' Next year, same man come from Wah-sheen-don again. This time bringing big thick bunch papers, saying, 'Here more way for stopping erosion.' "

Don and I exchanged an indulgent glance. We were used to shrugging off the endless sheaves of papers coming out of Washington.

Ben Lee wasn't amused. His livelihood was at stake the same as his grandfather's had been. "My grandfather standing up in Tribal Council, telling that Wah-sheen-don man: 'Three year past, you coming here, papers in hand, we thinking, This is honest man. He mean well. Next year, you coming, more papers in hand, we thinking, This man mean well, but he is fool. Now you coming, papers stack high, we thinking, This man is liar and fake. I advising,' my grandfather said,"—Ben Lee hesitated as if he were trying to decide whether to repeat his grandfather's words, and then plunged ahead on one long breath—" 'I advising you take these papers. Wipe yourself with them. Then throw papers in arroyo. That stopping erosion.' "

The necessity for most wide-scale planning programs isn't usually observable in one season in one corral. However, when we went back a week later, to visit Ben Lee's place, his lambs and kids had died off in alarming numbers. Starvation carried out that season, and has carried out for decades, a stock reduction program of a size to make the government's planned purchases and slaughter look picayune.

With such close-at-home lessons in their own corrals, the Navahos might have been expected to limit their flocks on their own initiative long before the government stepped in. Still, for generations they had swung along in the rhythm set by nature, allowing themselves and their animals to do what came naturally. In the same spirit, white men have allowed oil to flow as freely as it would, have refused to limit the horsepower of their cars, have glutted markets with beef or wheat or butter.

It was evening and the sun had slipped behind the dark-capped mesa beyond Ben Lee's hogan. The shadow of the mesa fell across the corral where nannies and ewes stood baa-a-a-aing and bleating while those that were left of their offspring tugged away at their suppers.

"Are these all that are left?" we asked Ben Lee when the proper interval had elapsed and he came outside.

For answer, he waved helplessly toward the corral.

"But what will you do?" I asked. "How will you and your family get along?"

"I think I working on the pipeline for 'while," Ben Lee answered. "Out of Needles."

"Do you like that kind of work?" Don asked.

Ben Lee made a half-turn, gazing off toward the dark-capped mesa and on to the great white sphinx eroded in the mountain face beyond. "I liked staying home," he answered softly, "but—" He finished with a shrug.

At least the desperate necessity for lambs will be relieved by Ben Lee's wages. Perhaps, though, his love of the Reservation and his longing to make his living there with his sheep and goats may be only intensified.

The answer? We don't know it. We don't expect, and neither do the Navahos, that the answer will come full-blown out of Washington. Many of the men and women living in their scattered camps across the Reservation don't expect the answer to spring ready-made from Window Rock and the Tribal Council.

The People now are in the stage of "rugged individualism," with each man bucking controls of all kinds and looking for a job off the Reservation whenever the trader will no longer extend him credit at the store. This, of course, is not the final answer and he knows it. This is merely the way he gets along while he searches for the ultimate solution to the problem.

It may still be that the Navahos will learn to conserve their resources before the white men do. They are all working on the problem because they are up to their necks in it. Our record hardly confers on us the role of all-wise teacher, and the Navahos are not people to be easily fooled by sheaves of paper plans that grow faster than the grass to feed their flocks. Mother Nature may teach them in time. Or they may discover the answer, as they have so remarkably at various stages in their history, in a whole new way of life.

Sometimes we wonder about teaching. Our own human nature seems to insist on sending most of us to the school of hard knocks.

I, for instance, "taught" until I was hoarse on my first Thursday afternoon at Tselani. I half-decided that all teaching was for the birds. Then I discovered how Mother Nature does it—by setting up conditions that open a small door. I certainly hadn't expected that the question, "How would you like to be in the movies?" would open a door to the camera-shy Navaho children.

CHAPTER NINE

The Good Samaritan—Navaho Version

"TELL ME A STORY," and "Once upon a time," are phrases as familiar to Navaho children as to any children of any period in any land. Aesop may have had nothing on some nameless Navaho except a better press agent.

Coyote tales are The People's fables, told and retold around the hogan fire at night for purposes of entertainment and instruction. We'd read the recorded English versions of some of these tales and of some of the legends from the ceremonial Chants before going to the Reservation. Some struck us as having a great deal in common with shaggy dog stories. Others, however, pointed a real moral (meaning, of course, one understandable to us). The very fact that parents used such stories to instruct small Navahos gave us and them one culture pattern in common, and so the stories interested us.

We would have given a great deal to be able to sit down with eight-year-old Haskie Chee and listen to him repeat the tales he'd been taught at home. We were curious, not so much about the stories themselves, as about The People; and legends are windows. Through them we felt that we might see clearly The People's fears, their humor, their aspirations, and their recommended behavior patterns, and so understand them better.

We'd been immersed in "sign-up day" and "clinic day" and in learning the foibles of the movie projector in preparation for our Thursday noon and night showing of whatever Western the nurse had ordered for this week. We'd almost forgotten that the nurse had said, "You'll have a class in religious education on Thursday afternoons. The kids get dismissed from school, and a priest comes from St. Michael's. Unless you take the Protestants, they'll just be turned loose with nothing to do."

We felt certain that the small Protestants who attended the school across the road were as much in need of religious instruction as were the small Catholics there. Still, I felt squeamish about attempting anything as basic and so abstract as teaching religion in a language which the children were only beginning to learn. (This, I felt, would be like trying to convert me to Hinduism after I'd attended Primary classes in India for a year or two.)

"What can we teach them?" I'd moaned.

"Bible stories," the nurse had answered. "I have a study book I follow. Since Sunday is Easter, the Easter story comes next in the book."

Wednesday night I was still keyed up over clinic and hesitant about attempting to teach the class, when Don suggested, "This might be just the chance we've wanted. Maybe we can work out a kind of exchange of stories that will help all of us to understand one another's religious beliefs and practices a little better. Children are usually more talkative about such things than adults."

Don is an optimist. He was also away on Thursday afternoon— driving a patient to the hospital.

I'd spent most of Thursday morning getting ready for the class. I'd rehearsed the Easter story, putting it into as simple and solid terms as possible. Then I wrote the words, "Getting attention," at the top of my notes and jotted down three sure-fire, opening-wedge questions. I didn't really anticipate any major trouble.

The children who would come that afternoon, plus those who

would meet with the priest, had been well-behaved in spite of their high spirits when playing in our community room on other days of the week. I expected them to pop in for class and run at once to the record player and Ping-pong table, so I was all set to calm them down into a teachable mood. I felt sure that I could quickly interest them in exchanging one of their stories for one of ours, and that we'd get along "just find," as Didi so often said.

Don had threaded the movie projector and arranged the chairs with a center aisle down the community room. By the time the store closed at noon, my mind was at ease about the class. I pulled the green shades, collected ten cents from each of our customers, and switched on the "Our Gang" comedy that had come along with the inevitable Western.

After the show, I had barely time to push the table with the projector on it to one side, and arrange a dozen Primary chairs in a semicircle down by the movie screen. Then my class arrived.

Eight children, boys and girls, slipped into the room in a well-behaved mood, all right. They came in, eyes downcast, silent. They didn't look up or speak when I greeted them. They squirmed out of their jackets and sweaters, and waited for me to point out the Primary chairs where they were to sit. There was none of the easy, making-themselves-at-home that had sent them scampering for checkerboards and Ping-pong paddles on those other days. This was formal. Today they had come for their class in religion.

I was a bit taken aback, but I began the session with my most sure-fire question anyway. I got not one peep out of even one child, let alone getting the interest and attention of the class. I kept re-wording my questions and finally committed the cardinal teaching sin of setting up my queries for simple, "Yes" or "No" answers.

When nothing continued to happen, I hurried into the kitchen. Didi was mixing dough for fried bread. "You'll have to interpret for me," I told her. "I thought these children knew me well enough by now that they'd admit they can understand English."

"I always interpreting for the class," Didi said and sighed. "They don't liked understanding English too much." She washed the flour-and-water dough off her hands at the sink.

Back in the community room, I placed a chair for Didi in the teacher's space, facing my semicircle of mute pupils. We began again, but I fared only slightly better this time. Didi bullied the children into grunting and nodding once or twice. Still, we were getting nowhere.

I knew that I'd have to establish some sort of interest contact before even hoping to make any headway with questions about Navaho coyote tales or religious legends. "Once upon a time, a long time ago," I said, "a young man called Jesus lived in a land across the ocean."

When Didi came to the word "Jesus" in her interpretation, I found my place and was ready to go on.

"He was a good man," I continued, "but some people didn't like the things he did, and some didn't like the stories he told to teach the people how to act. So one day some of these enemies of his killed him."

I felt the slight tremor that went through Didi, and looked to see whether I'd also made some impression on the children. I could read nothing from the tops of their heads.

"But Jesus had friends as well as enemies," I went on. "One of his friends went and got his body, and he dressed it nicely, and buried it in his garden."

Before I'd gone much further into the Easter story, I realized that Didi was horrified. Belatedly I recalled the Navaho taboo against contact with bodies of the dead. Then it dawned on me that regardless of Easter's coming the following Sunday on the calendar used by most of the United States and by a good part of the world, the isolated Navahos were not ready for that story.

I floundered for a moment during which I heard the words of a friend of ours: "We ought to leave the Navahos alone. They'd be better off. They've got their own religion. As long as it suits them, why should we try to make them over into something they're not and don't want to be?"

I was tempted to give up. I remembered that Christian missionaries had worked on the Reservation for almost a hundred years now; and still, the Navahos have not adopted Christianity in numbers anything like commensurate with the efforts that have been expended. The missionaries themselves are the first to admit this.

But just before I conceded that I had no chance of getting across where so many others had labored with such meager results, I recalled a talk we'd had with a high official in the Navaho Agency of the Bureau of Indian Affairs. This man is not a missionary, not a minister, not a religious educator. He had talked to us of the future, and of the practical, down-to-earth necessity for the Navahos to understand Christianity.

"The People are emerging into our culture," he had said. "They're learning English and they have to get off the Reservation in order to make a living. Our civilization is set up on Christian concepts and morals. The Navahos will stub their toes on everything from our laws to our conduct at parties until they learn to understand Christian ethics and underlying principles. Missionaries have simply got to get across to the Navahos now, or else we're all in trouble."

Every newscast concerning our relations with Russia pointed up his opinion. Whether two basically conflicting cultures can co-exist in the world is a moot question. For two fundamentally dissimilar cultures to co-exist within the United States is obviously impossible, now that the Navaho culture is no longer isolated on the Reservation.

I decided to make another stab at doing something, although I'd obviously started at the wrong end for a story exchange. I said, "I'd like to hear one of your stories. Who can tell me a story about Coyote or Rabbit or Crow?"

All eight heads dropped lower even before Didi interpreted my request. I caught only one girl glancing up from beneath her lashes, and I felt a little flick of resentment in her look.

I waited, though, prodding a bit, until Didi said gently, "They don't liked tell you these stories."

So, that was that—at least until we loosened up more with each other. In desperation, I looked around for some point of contact that might help me open the way for teaching. I found myself gazing into the lens of the motion picture projector.

Very softly, without making anything of it at all, I asked, "How would you like to be in the movies?"

Not one child waited for Didi's interpretation. They all looked up. Then each smiled, and shot a wagging hand into the air.

Didi started to interpret and stopped herself with a grin. "They understanded," she said.

I'd been using the nurse's motion picture camera occasionally. The people around Tselani were accustomed to that camera, and paid it little or no attention. I still don't know whether motion pictures are, in The People's minds, different from "still" pictures, and not subject to the same taboos. In any case, the boys and girls in the class before me had no qualms about appearing in them.

"Next week, I'm going to tell you a story," I said. "We'll act it out here in the community room. Then the next Thursday, we'll go outside and take a moving picture of it. Later on, you can all see yourselves in the movies."

Once more, Didi started to interpret and then dwindled off with a giggle. "They understanded."

The story that came to me for this project proved to be a natural, or at least it practically adapted itself into a natural. Of course any teacher shapes a story in the telling, taking it up here and letting it out there, adding a ruffle or a bit of embroidery for decoration—making it fit the listeners in the same way that a good seamstress finishes a dress.

On my second Thursday, I began something like this:

"You have stories about Coyote that teach you certain lessons. They show you how to get along with each other, and how you ought to act. Well, we have stories, too, that teach us how to act." I stopped and waited for Didi to interpret.

She was as interested as any of the children. In a tone edged with impatience she said, "You all understanded, don't you?"

The children's grins were sheepish as they nodded. Now that they wanted to, they could understand my English.

"While Jesus lived on the earth," I went on, "everybody kept talking about him and the things he was teaching. Some people said, 'We ought to live in Jesus' way.' Others said, 'No, we ought to live in the old way, the same as our fathers and grandfathers did.'

"One day a well-educated man stood up in a crowd and asked Jesus a question. This man thought the old way of living was right, and he wanted to make Jesus look silly before all the other people. He asked, 'Teacher, what shall I do to be sure I have the kind of life you are talking about?'

"Jesus didn't answer his question. Instead, he asked the man one. He asked, 'What did your father and grandfather tell you about it?'

"Well naturally, when this man was a boy, he had to listen to his father and to his grandfather, instructing him beside the fire at night. He knew the teachings of his people. He said, 'We believe that a person should love God and that he should love his neighbor as much as he loves himself.'

"Jesus said, 'That's a good answer. You do this, and you will live.'

"But the man still hoped he could trap Jesus into saying something that would make the people stop listening to his teachings. He asked, 'Just who is my neighbor?'

"Instead of answering that question by saying, 'Your neighbors are the people who live in the camp nearest you,' Jesus told a story.

"Jesus, as you know, lived a long way from here, across the ocean. He also lived a long time ago. When he made up a story to answer the man's question, he made the story about the people and places in his country. It was the same with the old ones among your people. When they wanted to teach boys and girls not to take things away from weak people, they made up the story about Coyote and Horned Toad because you have those animals right here on the Reservation.

"So today I'm going to make Jesus' story about the Reservation and the people you know today. That way we can understand better about who our neighbors are, in the way that Jesus taught. This is the story:

"A man was going from Tselani down to Phoenix. Naturally he dressed in his red velvet shirt and his cleanest Levis. He put on all of his turquoise beads—except the ones that the trader was holding —and all of his silver bracelets and rings. He put all his cash and his padlock key in his pocket. He took the sheepskins off the fence and off the sagebrush where they were airing, and carried them inside his hogan. Then he shut the door and snapped on the padlock. He herded his sheep as far as his brother's camp, and left them there. His brother promised to take care of them until he got back. Next he went by the trader's and gave him money to redeem his best string of turquoise beads. Then, he was ready to start on his trip.

"He walked down the road as fast as he could because it had taken him a long time to get started, and he was afraid it would get dark before he got to the community house at Ganado where he planned to stay overnight. He caught a short ride in a pickup, but the people's hogan was over toward Beautiful Valley, so they had to turn off a little way past the windmill. The man walked on and on then, and nobody came along to give him a ride.

"Sure enough, the sun went down over toward Keams Canyon, and by the time the man got as far as the cut this side of Hubbel's Trading Post, it was quite dark. He felt a little skittish about walking through those black shadows made by the cliffs there, but he hurried on anyway.

"Just as he got where the road was the blackest, somebody jumped out and grabbed him around the neck. Somebody else jerked his bracelets off his arms, and wriggled and worked the rings off his fingers. Somebody else pulled off his belt with the big turquoise and silver buckle. Last and worst of all, they jerked off his turquoise beads.

"These robbers had been drinking Tokay wine. He could smell it on their breath. He felt sure they didn't know what they were doing, or else they wouldn't have taken everything from one of their own people. So he begged them to let him keep just one of his strings of beads, at least. His beads were the most valuable of all his possessions. If they'd only leave him the beads that he had just redeemed from the trader, they could have everything else.

"Instead of giving him back the beads, the robbers jerked off his velvet shirt. Then they kicked him and beat him with their fists, and, by the time they left him, he was half dead. He couldn't even get up on his feet. All night long he lay there beside the road, all beaten up and bloody. His head was cut and his arm was broken and he was bruised and cut from head to foot.

"When it began to get light, the man ached and hurt all over. Still, he thought, 'My people who pass this way can see me now. Surely someone will come along and help me.'

"And sure enough, he heard footsteps coming toward him. But then he saw that the man he had heard had crossed over to the other side of the road. He wasn't sure, but he thought from the way he was dressed and from his stoop-shouldered walk that this was the old 'singer' from up on the mountain. Perhaps the 'singer' had seen the blood on his head and decided that it was too late to conduct a healing ceremony.

"The sun was getting high now, and flies were coming around.

The man tried to straighten out his leg, but it was too stiff and sore to move. Just then he heard someone else coming and he thought, 'If he will only give me a drink of water, that will help.'

"This person did walk up close and take a good look, but he must have got the notion that the man was dead. He ran back across the road as fast as his moccasins would carry him.

"The poor, wounded man gave up hope then. If his people wouldn't help, he would soon be dead. He tried once more to lift himself. He raised up just enough to see a man on a horse riding toward him. For one minute, he began to hope again that someone would help. Then he blinked, and he could see more clearly. His head dropped back with a thud. The man riding toward him was a Hopi.

"The Navaho man gave up all hope now. If his own people wouldn't help, he certainly couldn't expect a Hopi to take pity on him.

"The Hopi rode up and almost past.

"The Navaho man didn't even bother to lift his head. He knew it was no use.

"Then the Hopi reined in his horse.

"The Navaho thought, 'He's trying to see whether the robbers left any of my jewelry for him to snatch.'

"The Hopi swung down and came scuffing across the road, leading his horse. He snubbed the horse to a little juniper at the edge of the wash, beyond the cut in the road. Next, he untied a canteen that was hanging on his saddle. Then he knelt beside the Navaho and lifted his head so he could take a sip of water.

"The Navaho saw that the Hopi's eyes were kind. He asked the Hopi to help him straighten out his leg.

"The Hopi's hands were gentle. He tied his head scarf around the Navaho's broken arm. He brought his horse over close and helped the Navaho into the saddle. He slung the reins across his shoulder then, and walked the rest of the way to Ganado hospital, leading his horse.

"At the hospital, he helped the Navaho get off the horse, and let him lean on him to go up the steps and into the admissions office. He found the wounded man a place to sit in the waiting room. Then he stayed nearby, while the doctor examined the Navaho and treated his wounds.

"That night, the Hopi stayed in the community house. The next morning when he went back across the road to the hospital, he reached into the pocket of his Levis and got out all the money he had with him. 'Here, you take this money,' he said to the doctor. 'I have to go on to Gallup on business, but when I come back in a few days, I'll have more money. I want you to take good care of this Navaho and make him well. Whatever more it costs, I will pay it when I get back.' "

"When Jesus finished his story," I said, "he asked the educated man who'd been questioning him, 'Which one of these persons who passed turned out to be a neighbor to the man who was robbed?' "

My pupils had forgotten that other time and place. "The Hopi!" they answered. "The Hopi! The Hopi!"

"Jesus said," I added, no doubt needlessly, " 'Now you go and do that way, too.' "

The children were eager to set the Primary chairs in rows, marking off a road. We collected jewelry from everybody and loaded it all on the boy chosen to play the role of the Navaho man. Our only rehearsal bog-down came when the robbers, two of whom were of necessity girls, refused to hit The Man.

Didi let me urge them for a while before she gave a little self-conscious laugh. "Girls like that age don't supposed to bother the boys," she explained. (The word "bother" means to a Navaho something different and considerably more than it means to us.)

We had to cut our robbers down to one (male) and find nurses' roles at the hospital for our extra girls. Our priest and Levite were already female, so we had no need there for adjustments in line with scruples. I couldn't help wondering how many seven-, eight-, and nine-year-old white girls I'd have needed to coax in order to persuade them to beat up a boy.

We had some turnover in our cast the following Thursday. Our robber had stayed home from school to herd sheep that day. So we put the girls back in as robbers and commandeered Didi as leader of the gang to do the actual robbing and hitting.

We found a wagon trail up behind the school that looked, I'm sure, a good deal more like the road from Jerusalem to Jericho than from Tselani to Phoenix, but it made a picturesque set. We made-believe the hospital stood between two juniper trees near the foot of the road.

Our movie of "The Good Samaritan" has won no Oscars, but it is even more popular than Westerns or "Our Gang" comedies around Tselani.

The role each pupil begged to play was that of the Hopi. This, for a class of Navahos, was more to be desired than an Oscar.

We have no illusions about the significance of this one experience with this one class. It certainly proves nothing more than that small Navahos are normal children. They like movies. They enjoy role-playing. It is possible to condition their reactions.

I had stumbled on a point of contact.

Various students and friends of the Navahos have made detailed and excellent suggestions for the guidance of Bureau of Indian Affairs personnel, teachers, public health nurses, and others in the matter of employing accepted customs, beliefs, and thought patterns as a point of contact for helping Navahos to understand our health practices, our social usages, our animal husbandry methods, and the like. Our limited experience with this Thursday afternoon class led us to conclude that someone might do well to write a version for Navahos of selected Bible stories.

The Navahos are meeting us more than halfway by learning our language. The least we can do is to find points of contact through which we can help them to make the adjustment they are being forced to make to our way of life.

Some of our theology cuts so sharply across their ingrained taboos, and is so removed from their beliefs and experiences that it must wait. But we see no harm in beginning at the points where our two ways of life meet, and building understanding. Navahos who have been steeped for generations in taboos against contact with the dead are not ready for the Easter story. These same Navahos, who govern all their activities by their code of not overdoing, can understand the Christian ethic of moderation.

The Christian concept of God will in time relieve the Navahos of the worrisome unpredictability of their supreme beings. In the Navaho religion, no one being is more important all the time than any other. Neither good nor evil is characteristic all the time of any one being. "Sun" has great religious significance, but he isn't always represented as good, and while he aims to be of help to man, he does some things that can only be considered evil and detrimental. It would be pretty difficult for a Christian or a Jew or a Moslem to find in a Navaho's concept of "Sun" a prototype of the idea of One God, infinite and unchangeable, a being wholly good; but even that can wait.

When the house we occupied was built at Tselani, an interpreter and her husband moved in. Within a week, their relatives began moving in with them. Soon the Health Center's budget was being drained by utility and food bills. No amount of explanation or pleading changed the situation. Navaho families stick together. When one has mutton fat, they all have mutton fat, no matter how thin it must be spread.

It takes a white man to succeed as a trader on the Reservation. A Navaho must, both because of his own conscience and because of social pressure, extend credit to all his family and friends without regard to their credit rating. The Navaho can readily understand Paul's, "Let each of you look not only to his own interests, but also to the interests of others."[1]

We have many other ready-made points of contact. The Navahos are prepared now to agree with us, or to allow us to agree with them, that life is predestined toward Good. Perhaps, if our Prince of Peace were so presented, they would welcome the discovery of a prophet who embodies their own ideal of harmony. It would take very little uncovering to show the Navahos that the central purpose of their religion is the same as ours, namely, to maintain a right and helpful relationship with the supernatural. Their prayers, like ours, culminate in the plea, "Restore everything to harmony again."

The Golden Rule serves them and us, as a practical, workable means of getting along with one another. So far, they haven't generally extended its application to white men, and we haven't extended it to the Navahos. They have looked out across the borders of the Reservation, and remembered Fort Sumner. We have looked in across the borders of the Reservation, and seen wooden Indians instead of human beings. Now that the borders of the Reservation are being trampled out, we are all up against the inescapable question, "Who is my neighbor?"

Missionaries have for almost a century demonstrated Christianity on the Reservation. The Navahos have taken them for granted, and often presumed upon their helpfulness. They have said, in effect, "Helping us is your business." Off the Reservation, the rest of us now have an opportunity to prove that our Christian culture pro-

[1] *Revised Standard Version of the Bible*, Philippians 2:4. Used by permission, Thomas Nelson & Sons.

vides the moral and philosophical basis for a workable way of life.

"After all," as Don said, "the Navahos are undoubtedly as susceptible to a practical, everyday presentation of Christianity as they were to wearing Levis."

But transitions are seldom as painless as changing pants. With our many points of contact, we were tempted to conclude that the step from the Navaho way to the white man's way might be taken on airy feet. Then we were quickly reminded, when Sarah came with her vague aches and pains, that the steps to be taken from one way to the other should move in both directions.

CHAPTER TEN

Psychosomatics and "Sings"

WHITE PEOPLE have been considerably behind the Navahos in the field of psychosomatics. Many Navahos, reading that statement, would say, "See, just as we have known all along! White men are trying to get possession of our songs and rituals. They know that our old ones found out the right ways of approaching the spirits to gain their favor. They want to learn our tribal secrets and work their benefits for themselves."

Here is one area, actually, in which learning could profitably be a two-way street. We are all aware that our doctors frequently give salt or sugar pills and unmedicated injections in a legitimate effort to convince patients that their physical symptoms are being treated by physical means. Their real treatment is taking place on a different level and against strong resistance.

These same doctors would be instantly relieved of all necessity for subterfuge, if a patient were to come in saying, "Doctor, I feel terrible. I ache all over and I can't sleep nights. The diagnostician I called in says that the trouble is, I've been pocketing a little of the company's money from time to time, and my conscience is about to get me down." Or, "Doctor, I just can't seem to get rid of this rash on my hands. I think the cause of it all is that I know my life is completely useless. I'm not contributing anything worth-while to anybody or anything, and I'm dying of boredom."

How simple it would be to relieve, at least temporarily, the symptoms of the bored woman who is suffering from lack of attention and the fear that life is passing her by! The doctor could get her family to give a huge family reunion at which she would be the center of attention.

They would spare no expense in securing and preparing succulent food to feed the visitors. For days in advance, everyone would be roasting turkeys and baking hams and preparing molded salads and frozen desserts, and all the gaiety would whirl around the patient, making her feel spoiled and petted and important. They might go so far as to build or buy her a special house for this occasion, or they might have the side yard covered with red-and-white striped canvas.

As each member of the family arrived, from far and near, he would go to the patient. He would tell her how important her health is to his happiness. He would express his hope that everything will be just wonderful for her from this day on.

The doctor would be the master of ceremonies for this one- to nine-day party. He wouldn't claim that he could make the patient well. He'd simply affirm that he knew how to call in the gods who could do whatever was necessary. During the party, he would spend the entire time telling stories of great heroes of the past who had overcome the vicissitudes of this life, and thus set an example for the patient and her family to follow.

The efficacy of such treatment for a Navaho patient is multiplied many times by something that few white people will ever know. We are never so completely dependent on family approval and acceptance as almost all Navahos are. We can't possibly know the depths of loneliness suffered by the Navaho who is separated, either physically or spiritually, from his family. For certain illnesses and for certain patients, a "sing" can provide the social restoration that either amounts to or effects a cure.

A teenage girl was brought to us in tears one evening after Didi had left for the day. Her mother herded her into the community room.

The girl seemed to understand some English, but she either couldn't, or refused to, speak it at first. She sat with her eyes politely downcast (to look directly into the eyes of the person with whom you are conversing, may indicate that you don't believe a word he's saying), and the only sound out of her was an occasional sniffle.

She was tall and slender, quite a pretty young lady of sixteen or seventeen. She wore turquoise ear pendants, telling me that she was unmarried. Her black hair gleamed from a recent shampoo with yucca root suds. It was combed straight back from her small-featured face, tied with a green scarf at the nape of her neck, and then left loose to fall in a heavy, soap-fragrant cascade. She wore a pink percale skirt, fashioned with the usual three tiers. It had been freshly starched and pleated on a broomstick. With the skirt, she wore a white cotton blouse, commercially made, in the style of a boy's shirt. The shirttail hem in her skirt came just above her ankles. She wore white cotton socks and brown-and-white saddle oxfords with rubber soles.

Except that her skin had a richer color than most, and her skirt was a trifle too long, she could have passed for a high school girl in New Milford, Connecticut. Her face was mottled and her eyes puffed. She had been crying her heart out.

After making three or four bad-mannered attempts to get her name for our records, I finally learned that she was called Sarah.

(When a stranger enters a Navaho family gathering, no one would think of asking his name. He will be asked the name of his mother's clan and where his parents live. He will tell in terms as definitive as a Philadelphia street address that his parents' home is near the edge of the red canyon beyond White Rocks Standing where the water runs through the blue shadows beneath the five-forked pine tree. To tell his name, however, is too personal, and no well-mannered host would be nosy enough to ask such a thing.)

My questions about Sarah's symptoms brought a helpless shrug from her mother and nothing but additional sniffles from the girl. Then Sarah hiccoughed. I remembered something from my reading. "Aren't you supposed to make a wish?" I asked.

The girl glanced up at me for the first time. A disparaging little grin tweaked at her swollen face—the kind of grin we don for going around instead of under a ladder.

Now that we both understood how it is about superstitions that we observe but don't quite credit, I was able to ferret out the information, imparted through single-word sentences and gestures, that Sarah had pains in her chest region. These had started three days before, in the late afternoon. She had been out herding sheep, and had fallen off her horse.

I knew one injury caused by a fall that would result in chest pains, and I knew a test for it. "Take a deep breath," I said, and demonstrated the procedure in case she needed the words made clearer. She breathed deeply. Instead of causing her to cry out, this seemed to be interesting enough to slow her tears for the moment. I asked her to breathe again and again, until we had done it four times. So, I concluded, she did not have a broken rib.

I asked about cold symptoms—headache? . . . cough? . . . runny nose? She had none of these, and I had exhausted my meager store of questions.

"I'll telephone the nurse at Black Mountain," I said.

For answer, Sarah's tears welled up again.

I left her on the cot sitting beside her mother, while I went into the next room to the telephone. The nurse, when I got her, completed the name for my record. "Oh, that's Sarah Benally. She was up here yesterday. I couldn't find anything wrong with her physically."

"I can't just send her home without doing anything," I demurred. "Something's wrong, or she wouldn't be crying the way she is."

(I wonder how many doctors, confronted by a weeping woman, have also felt the necessity for doing something—anything—that might look to the patient as if he were at least trying.)

"Do you have any wide adhesive tape?" the nurse asked me.

"I've seen some around here someplace."

"Well, you might tape her," she suggested. "You know how to do it?"

I told her that I'd once been taped myself. I thought I could do it. (I wondered whether I'd been taped, at that time, because the doctor couldn't think of anything else to do for my vague pains.)

The nurse went on, "Taping might make her feel better. At least, it won't hurt her."

"Not until she goes to take it off," I said, remembering my own experience.

"Well, it's something to do—all I can think of," the nurse concluded.

I found the wide adhesive tape and led Sarah into the small examination room. She continued to dab at her eyes as she fumbled with the buttons on her blouse. When she got her blouse off, she allowed me to help her with the hooks on her cotton lace brassiere.

She submitted docilely to my request that she lie on the leather-covered, old-fashioned examination table, turn toward me so I could stick the end of a strip of tape on her back, and then roll, pulling hard against my grip on the tape. I continued the process, as it had been done to me, trussing up her firm young body, knowing that I was doing nothing at all for her aching heart.

I did take the ceremonial precaution of leaving an open space down her back. If I had completely encircled her body with tape, naturally I should have enclosed all the evil, leaving it no path of escape, and Sarah would never have recovered.

I wish I could say that I probed and found the cause of Sarah's sadness. It could have been a mood. Most Navahos are given to moods, and what adolescent girl is not given to weeping at times for no more definite reason than that she feels like weeping? But since Sarah had fixed a time and the circumstances marking the start of her distress, I suspected that this was more than a mood.

Young, attractive girls alone on the great, empty desert with a herd of sheep are not always left alone. Perhaps an older man had found her and jerked her from her horse. If so, her turmoil now might be caused by a bitter, corroding memory. Or, it might be caused by fear that after her marriage, her husband would step over the hogan fire from west to east and leave, demanding the return of his marriage gifts on the ground that he had contracted for a virgin. If she had been found and drawn from her horse by a young man of a different clan from her mother's, her distress might now be due to the fact that in three days he had not returned.

Whatever the cause of her state, I had no pills or ointment that would help her. The proper "sing," however, would have done her good. Clearly she needed fresh assurance that her family really loved her, no matter what. She needed to feel them gathering round her, sparing no expense to restore her to a state of happiness. She needed to hear again the myths of her people, with their repeated reminders that certain heroes have in the past been able to overcome the very problem that she faced. She needed to have her faith renewed that the gods would come to assist her.

"Be sure you come back on Wednesday to see the doctor," I told her. I wondered whether I should have added, "And come on Sunday to see the minister." Then I wondered whether I might not better have said, "Call in a 'singer.' "

The situation on the Navaho Reservation has been historically and is today such that neither the whites nor the Navahos are quite free to work out the creative cultural interchange that might have been most valuable to both groups. The uneducated Navahos have been and still are under the fear-motivated domination of their "singers." Many acts of their daily lives are regulated by superstitions. Superstitions and taboos are the stock in trade of medicine men the world over. On the Reservation, taboos either flouted or neglected provide the occasions for conducting the profitable chants of healing and restoration.

Taboos and traditions along with the chants have been synthetized into a religion, and so they have come to be considered sacred. Religion and precedent authorize or prohibit almost every act that a Navaho contemplates. One authority says that the average Navaho spends 40 per cent of his time in religious activities.

In general, the white people who have gone into the Reservation have gone for profit or for propaganda. Cultural exchanges between white traders and Navahos have been precluded by high fences and aloof traders' wives. This, of course, is a generalization and is for that reason partially false. By and large, however, the traders and their families have had nothing to do with their customers on a common level of cultural exchange. The two or three exceptions have been widely publicized in print, in vegetable dye rugs, and in dolls and jewelry.

The word "propaganda" has fallen in with bad company at times and, for that reason, may be a little surprising as the motivation for missionaries. In its strict and original sense, however, propaganda is the right word. Both Catholics and Protestants have gone into the Reservation to propagate Christianity. The very nature of this aim has caused them to lock horns with the Navaho "singers," keepers of the tribal religion.

If the Navaho religious system seems to be all-inclusive, touching on everything from killing snakes to ceremonial cleansing after contact with the dead, propagating Christianity has not been a mere matter of preaching and building churches either. The Reservation situation has required that missionaries dig for water, teach both children and adults to read, care for the sick, build power plants to supply their schools and hospitals and churches, and carry on a thousand tasks in support of their preaching.

Christian doctors found tuberculosis rampant on the Reservation. They also found that the cause of tuberculosis was often given as ghost infection brought about by the patient's having been in contact with Pueblo ruins or burial places. The cure prescribed was apt to be an Evil Way Chant if Navaho ghosts had caused the trouble, or an Enemy Way Chant if the ghosts were those of some other people. During the ceremonial, an herb infusion was passed from mouth to mouth in a gourd dipper or pottery bowl. Naturally doctors pleaded with the people to come to the hospital instead of sending for a "singer."

Some of these doctors automatically ruled against all healing ceremonies. This seemed legitimate to them on both religious and hygienic grounds. Few had the time or the grasp of the Navaho language necessary for studying and distinguishing between the troubles for which Navahos employ a "singer." Some of these doctors might—had they been entirely unprejudiced and had they understood fully—have agreed that for cases of bad dreams during pregnancy, a Blessing Way Chant would do more good than logical explanations or pink pills.

On the other hand, it has not been easy to explain germs and viruses and contagion and organic degeneration to people who, with religious zeal and sanction, consider all disease to be brought about by failure to observe certain taboos. The natural reaction was, "I don't care if the medicine man did say that you had slept in a hogan where someone had died. I say that you have eaten too much fat mutton and that you must come to the hospital and have your gall bladder removed. No other ceremonial will make you well."

Evangelists and schoolteachers and carpenters and nurses all went to the Reservation under religious compulsion. They came up against a complicated system of religion, but found that its morality did not match that of Christianity in many particulars. They had neither the time nor the language facility to separate the worthy from the unworthy. They were unable to make the distinctions clear to the Navahos with whom they talked, usually through meagerly-educated interpreters. So they said, in effect, "Your way just won't do. You must give it up and accept our way."

The old ones, especially the "singers," whose profession was that of preacher-doctor, got their backs up. They were ready to fight everything that the missionaries touched—from water to paper-learning to medicines to Jesus-talk. They no doubt fostered the generally-held opinion that "white" medicine works all right on white people; but it won't work on a Navaho except, possibly, if his disease is one that The People have acquired from the white man.

The situation has been dramatically changed in recent years. It will change even more as the thousands of Navaho children now in school complete their education.

The old-time "singers" are dying off and fewer and fewer young ones are undergoing the exhaustive training required for carrying on the profession. In time, no doubt, as Navahos are dispersed from the Reservation, their special family solidarity will disintegrate. Then the need for "sings" and their peculiar efficacy will gradually disappear.

As Navahos work and live among white families more generally, they will discover that their new neighbors don't despair of their lives because they have inadvertently harmed a snake. They will not be expected to go out of their minds as the result of killing a coyote. Soon the Navahos themselves will begin to pooh-pooh the danger in such things. By then, they may be knocking on wood to ward off evil, and avoiding black cats instead of coyotes.

How long will it be after that, we can't help wondering, before these same Navahos will become so completely integrated into our Christian culture that they will develop guilt feelings as a result of promiscuity or lying? Some may become so imbued with our spirit of competition that they will be gripped by frustrations for which their doctors can only prescribe getting away from it all.

"You're being driven by the clock," a doctor may declare to his "assimilated" Navaho patient. "You'd better slow down, or you're headed for trouble. Relax. Stop being so intense. You need to get into a different rhythm. Why don't you go to northern Arizona for a few weeks? Just soak up the peace and quiet for a while."

When this happens, and hardly until then, that intense Navaho will be able to appreciate what we went through one Sunday night, while a prospective father took his good old Navaho time, and left it for us to race the stork.

CHAPTER ELEVEN

Navahos in Labor

SUNDAY AFTERNOONS at Tselani were inclined toward dullness in the Kaopectate and adhesive bandage business. The store was closed. The school was closed, of course. Undoubtedly it seemed like poor planning to a Navaho to make the trip in from his hogan in order to get a box of aspirin for a Sunday headache or to have a cut finger bandaged, on a day when he couldn't also buy a can of tomatoes and visit over a bottle of warm pop with his distant neighbors. So, having only stray customers, we were free to walk and climb mesas, searching, as we always did, for pieces of ancient pottery.

We came down from the third mesa just before dusk one Sunday afternoon. We had hurried the end of our walk on account of rain-threatening clouds, squalling northward toward us from down the valley. On this particular Sunday, we had weighted our pockets with brown rock beads. We had happened on nature's bead factory, and had come away with a load of free samples.

We rounded the nurse's house and started for ours, anticipating hot baths and a feet-up evening. Just beyond the porch of the community house, we met a man of twenty-eight or thirty. He was tall and slender. His skin was light. His features had no distinctively Indian accents. My first assumption was that he was a white man.

But when he saw us, he turned away. He pulled his roll-brimmed black hat low over his eyes, and hung his thumbs over his silver belt buckle. He gave the impression that he'd been trespassing and was embarrassed for us to have found him here. We knew then that he was a Navaho.

Since he said nothing in answer to our "Hello," we decided that he didn't speak English, and that we'd relieve his embarrassment if we hurried on to those hot baths. We started to pass him by, but he stopped us by side-stepping into our path.

"Can we help you?" Don asked.

This was too abrupt, of course, but we were tired. Besides, we hadn't quite learned—never quite learned, as a matter of fact—the fine art of just standing until the proper time for speaking had come. This was especially hard to do with a Navaho who looked like any white person.

Our man now conveniently discovered a sliver of petrified wood in the dust at his feet. He nudged it forward with the blunt toe of his shoe, and then hooked his heavy sole around it to pull it toward him again.

Don and I exchanged nonplused glances. "We'll have to find an interpreter," I said.

"Wife," the Navaho man said then distinctly. He gave his full attention to pushing and retrieving the piece of petrified wood on the ground. "Ready for going hospital," he added, finally. Then he looked up and grinned before tacking on the one word that we had already surmised, "Baby."

We asked several fast questions, white man fashion. Of all his slow answers, the one that gave us the most concern was, "Ride horseback. Long time."

When he said that he lived ten miles away, we knew that he could mean two miles or thirty. His wave toward the northeast told us all too clearly that he lived in the opposite direction from the hospital. He had left his horse at the foot of The Hill. He would like to pick up his saddle and ride with us. The horse could find his own way home. Yes, he had been waiting for some time for us to return from our walk. He didn't know how long. "Maybe hour." This would be his wife's fifth child. Yes, he thought her time was close.

We saw step-by-step visions of his wife giving birth to her baby during the fifteen minutes required for tapping his well and siphoning out these dribbles of information.

All right, we told him, he could go get his saddle. We'd collect some things we'd need and be right along to pick him up on The Hill.

He gave the piece of petrified wood a final shove with his toe and buried it in the dust. With the heel of his hand, he shoved his hat far back on his head. Then he turned slowly toward The Hill.

We hurried into the house, and emptied our pockets on the kitchen work counter.

"Her fifth child!" I wailed. "It could come any minute; may have come long before now."

"Just so it doesn't come on the way," Don said.

"I'd better take some sheets and a blanket," I decided. "If you mention hot water," I threatened Don, "I'm going to drive, and you can ride in the back with the patient."

Don said, "I hope that rain holds off. Chances are good that man came on horseback because there isn't a road in to his hogan. Let's take our toothbrushes. We can stay overnight in Ganado, if we're late getting in there."

We were ready in less time than it had taken us to question our expectant father. Don slammed the pickup through our sand trap and hurtled, with a sharp left crimp, into the sand ruts that guided us toward the store and then around to the left, and onto the roller-coaster locally known as The Hill.

For once our prospective father had got a move on. There he stood, beside the road, his saddle over his arm. Off to the right and

146

"The vast distances and subtle colors calmed our spirits"
Distant view of Tselani mesas

"Her face was the color and texture
of a wadded paper bag from the grocer's"

on down the drop-off from the second mesa, his dappled gray horse had begun to graze his way home.

We told the man to heave his saddle into the back of the pickup and climb in front with us. The sky, with an assist from the rain clouds, which had caught us now and spread themselves over our heads, had grown prematurely gray. Following a rutted road by the headlights of a pickup is tricky. Following a sheep trail at night, especially a strange sheep trail, requires a mixture of luck and daring for which traveling Highway 66 had never prepared us. However, the knowledge that the stork had a good chance of beating us to the end of that sheep trail served as an effective spur.

Don gave the pickup its head, and we covered ten miles of our so-called road in record time. Then our guide waved us off into the sagebrush to the left. We kept to a pair of wagon tracks across a high plateau for a mile or so before we came to a perpendicular-banked arroyo that definitely needed a bridge.

Don's foot on the accelerator didn't like the looks of that black gash across our way. By the last smudge of light in the sky, we saw our guide's hand swoop down below his knees and up fast. "Go down-up fast," he said. "Sand down bottom. Go fast or else getting stuck."

We took a nose dive into the sand at the bottom of the arroyo. The pickup, however, objected to the climb up the other side with no footing. The wheels, spinning in the sand, felt as if we had suddenly acquired tractor lugs. Then, having loosened our molars, they caught something and up we went, into the air and over the top where the faithful grooves of our wagon track were waiting to lead us on.

I felt relieved enough about the road to shift my worrying into high gear and concentrate it on delivering babies in transit. I tried to recall exactly what the nurse had said when I'd insisted that I was a babe in the woods when it came to babies. "If you start to the hospital and don't make it," she had tossed off lightly, "just stop long enough to deliver the baby. Don't cut any cords. Lay the baby on the mother's belly, and keep on down the road to the hospital."

Night had really caught us now, and because of that the trip to the man's hogan was beginning to seem endless. When the wagon tracks deserted us after four or five miles, Don managed to align either our right or left wheels—depending on the lay of the land at any moment—along the sheep trail that continued to lead us through the night.

I spent the time alternating between hope that we'd beat the stork to the hogan and fear that we should. I knew from our reading what might be happening while we chugged and bumped along this endless sheep trail.

If the lady's pains had become frequent during the afternoon or evening, someone had long since gone for a "singer." Someone else had brought in a long pole and wedged it, slanting toward the west, into the roof at the south side of her hogan. Some member of the family had taken a shovel or a knife and loosened up a small space in the packed floor of the hogan, beneath the pole; and sheepskins had been placed over the softened ground. A sturdy belt had been looped around the middle of the pole and left hanging down for the lady to grasp for support.

The "singer" had started to sing as soon as he'd arrived probably, but he was also occupied with other preparations. He had the lady untie her hair. Then he took corn pollen in his hand, and letting it run out in a fine line beneath his thumb, he trickled pollen down the belt hanging from the pole. Then, starting at the lady's head, he ran a line of pollen down her body to her feet. If necessary, he'd make patterned downward gestures over the lady, using sacred feathers and stones from his "medicine bundle."

Each time her pains recurred, the lady would clutch the belt above her head and raise herself upright. Between pains, she'd sit back on her heels and wait.

The lady's mother and sisters and aunts were busy around the hogan, I knew. I could all but see them. One brought in cedar boughs and layered them into a bed for the lady to lie on after the baby came. One collected cedar buds and mashed them with a rock. One tended the fire to keep the hogan warm.

The lady was never left without one or two members of her family nearby to help at any moment. Sometimes a lady fainted from the pain, and then she might fall on the baby. Sometimes a baby came so easily, with the mother lifting herself high by the belt on the pole, that it fell on its head or was crippled in a hip joint before anyone knew what was happening.

I wondered about the man sitting beside me in the pickup. He had come for us, which might indicate that he was ready to give up the old way and turn to the starch and antiseptics of a Christian hospital. But, I wondered, had he also, just in case, been careful not to tie the four legs of a sheep together during his wife's pregnancy? Had he guarded himself against watching a calf or horse being branded? If he had refused to observe these precautions, was he sitting here beside me now, worrying for fear his baby would be so coiled in the womb that it couldn't move down properly?

I wondered about the lady herself. She had, no doubt, been willing for her husband to come for us. But had she also, just in case, been careful not to put one sack inside another during her pregnancy for fear of having twins? Had she refused to make the face on a doll for the past nine months because any bobbles in her art might mark the child being formed within her?

If we were really too late, she would, I knew, grip the belt above her and hang on for dear life until the baby came down. Her mother or sister would grasp the infant, cut the cord and tie it, and put the baby on a clean sheep pelt. They would be particularly careful to carry the placenta outside, and bury it, or dispose of it in a prudent place. They would take no chances on any member of the family inadvertently coming in contact with the placenta or any of the blood of childbirth. Even after they had washed the mother, her bath water with the mashed cedar buds in it would be conscientiously poured in the middle of a cluster of trees where no one could possibly pass with a herd of sheep and so become crippled in the back from touching the highly dangerous, female blood.

I had convinced myself by now that if we ever got to the man's hogan, we'd find a scraggly-mustached old "singer," with his corn pollen and his "medicine bundle" all packed up neatly beside him, waiting for the father of the baby to come home and pay for his services.

When we were finally greeted by four barking dogs and had maneuvered our way safely through them toward the shadowy hogan ahead, our headlights shone into a neat brush shelter with an iron stove in the middle and three or four nail-keg seats around it.

On one keg, sat a lady wrapped in a green and purple shawl. She obviously had not given birth to her baby.

I was in no mood to wait in the pickup until all danger of attracting *tchindees* was past. I reached across our passenger and opened the door. I'm afraid I shoved him a little in my rush to get out and get the lady on her way to the hospital. I hurried across to her and asked how she felt. She tucked her small pointed chin into the folds of her shawl, and demurely fixed her eyes on the toes of the saddle oxfords showing beneath her green satin skirt.

Her husband wandered over with his saddle across his arm, and spoke to her in Navaho.

She murmured a one-word answer.

He turned to me. "I liked eat supper before going to hospital."

I knew he'd ridden for hours and must be hungry, but I weighed his hunger against my inexperience, and told him I'd find him something to eat after we arrived at Ganado.

"Do we go back to the road the way we came?" Don asked him.

The man shook his head and flapped his arm toward the south-east. "Go out other way," he said. "Coming to big road after soon."

We never learned to stop asking, "How far?"

The man shrugged. "Maybe mile."

A mile of horse or sheep trail and then the big road sounded promising, but now it started to sprinkle.

We hurried the man and his wife into the front seat beside Don. I climbed into the back. All Navaho ladies pick the front seat, if at all possible, and something about the way they make their choice seems to be in the nature of exercising their prerogatives. Anyway, when I'm the only obstetrician along, I insist that expectant ladies sit in the least bumpy quarters of the conveyance.

Our man's "maybe mile" to the road turned out to be a mile and a half of one-track trail, over hummocks of sand drifted over sagebrush and Mormon tea. Then "the road" proved to be wagon tracks again—cut too sharp and deep to accommodate inflated pickup tires at places, running up an incline now and then and jumping off into space, plowing through a sand wallow that had to be gunned through at top speed, and on and on and on.

Rain came pattering down, and I had to unroll the canvas cover of the truck bed all around. By standing on my knees, I could see through the cab's rear window and the windshield that the rain was slanting across the headlight beams like a twill curtain between us and the wagon tracks. I sat down with my back braced against our tool box.

I expected every jolt to bring our Navaho lady to the end of her waiting. I hesitated even to cushion myself against the bumps. Somehow I had the notion that if I took them at full strength, I'd know better what our patient was going through and be prepared for what was sure to happen. Rigid as a fossil, I sat watching the wet, black wagon tracks scoot away from us behind the truck. We passed no landmarks that I knew. We never seemed to get any nearer to what we would call a road. We bumped and dropped and slithered and twisted. We rocketed over obstacles. We made hairpin loops around obstructions. We leaped a few ditches, and came down on all fours with a thud.

When I looked through the window into the cab, I could see nothing but the straight line of Don's jaw as he plugged doggedly ahead, and the black ellipse that was our Navaho man's roll-brimmed hat. I would have given a great deal to know whether or not the lady was perspiring on her face. All I could see of her, sitting over by the door, was the cowl of her green and purple shawl, standing high and cupping her hair knot, and her man's arm, encircling her shoulders.

Not until we came out on the washboarded but graded Reservation road, did I even dare hope that we might possibly make it to the hospital in time. Then, just as I drew my first deep breath and stuck a blanket behind me to cushion my backbone, we made a turn that I recognized and I got my bearings. We were still thirty miles from the hospital!

Mile by slippery mile, Don managed to keep the pickup moving forward more than sideways. I grew more grateful and a little more hopeful with each minute that we kept moving. I kept peering out for landmarks, but it is difficult to distinguish one yucca from another in the dark.

We had, I was convinced, been on the road long enough to drive all the way across the Reservation. I began to tell myself that we must be at least within racing distance of the hospital. Then I saw, moving away from me on the right, the unmistakable ten-foot-high "wish pile" overlooking Beautiful Valley. We were still twelve or thirteen miles from Ganado.

That shadowy pile of rocks and juniper twigs looked good to me in spite of the set-back it had given my calculations. It was something definite that I knew for sure on a night filled with uncertainties. For a moment I actually considered banging on the back of the cab and asking Don to stop while I broke off a green branch and added it with a rock to the "wish pile." Then I decided that I could make my wish anyway, without the time-consuming formality. After all, I'd been keeping my fingers crossed for hours. Surely a white person's crossed fingers plus a wish tossed in passing toward a Navaho "wish pile" could work together as an effective talisman to help us win our race.

Who can prove that they didn't work together? We did arrive in time.

We got the lady entered at the hospital and put to bed in the labor room. We found a friend who could supply sandwiches and a carton of milk for our hungry man. He took them and actually mumbled, "Thanks," before he ambled across the road toward the community house. We arranged for beds for ourselves in a guest cottage.

Before we started back to Tselani early the next morning, we stopped at the hospital to inquire about our patient.

"Not yet," the nurse told us.

We went on home.

We heard nothing more of our friends until Saturday morning, soon after sunrise. We had no way of knowing then that the handsome, gentle-eyed, elderly man at our back steps had anything to do with our couple of the Sunday before.

This man belongs in a gallery dedicated to human relations. He is an immediately recognizable embodiment of all that is best in Navaho history and tradition.

Navahos are like the rest of us, in that we have one or two good physical features, and one or two characteristics of which our race might be proud. Few of us are tall, dark, and handsome; and very few who are, become also wise, good, and noble. We should be hard pressed to pick a sample white man to send to a world's fair, for instance. A sample Navaho, however, stood shuffling his moccasins on the bulge of sandstone beyond our back steps.

We had no idea how long he'd been there, before we finally heard him and went out.

He stood with his broad shoulders set squarely on his straight body, but he had to dip his head in order to avoid the overhanging branches of our juniper tree. His face was square. Its lines were gentled beneath firm flesh, fine-textured as a baby's and the color of the bark on a cherry tree. Two strands of iron-gray hair had escaped from the red bandana folded and tied around his forehead. One strand lay soft against his slightly hollowed cheek; the other curved behind his ear and curled up in front to frame his turquoise nugget earrings. His long hair had been freshly combed and looped and wrapped with nubby homespun yarn. His Levis were clean, faded to gray at the knees. His shirt, unlike the shirts of the young men who came to shoot baskets or play records, fitted him loosely, blousing a little at his waist. It might have been blue or purple or even brown at one time; now it was the gray produced by repeated washings. Its colorlessness lent added depth to the real blue of his heavy turquoise nugget necklace, and to the silver and turquoise bracelets on his wrists.

He was standing, when we went out, toying with a sprig of juniper broken from our tree.

Don asked, "Can we help you?"

He looked up then, and in his eyes was the whole story of his people. This seems a lot to claim for one look in a man's eyes, and yet there it all was—fear, defiance, submission, suffering, sorrow, cynicism, dignity, and pride. Something more was there, too, that we sensed but couldn't understand until later.

His two hands, holding the sprig of juniper, lifted and fell. His eyes pleaded for help and at the same time denied that he was asking.

We attributed the kind of withdrawal we sensed in him to his reluctance to depart from the traditional Navaho way to accept assistance from *belliganos*.

"We'll have to find an interpreter," Don said. "I'll go to the store and see whether I can locate one."

154

The man he brought back was only barely of help. We had to read between his words far more than he could put into English. We did learn that the older man had come about his daughter. In time, we learned further that his daughter had given birth to a son.

"At the hospital?"

"No."

"Where do they live?" we asked.

Our volunteer interpreter waved off toward the northeast.

"Is the baby sick?" I asked, grasping at straws in my effort to find out what was expected of us. Normally, if a baby is born in a hogan, the mother has chosen the old way in preference to going to the hospital, and that is that.

"Mother sick," our interpreter discovered through a long, murmured interchange.

Don and I conferred and decided to telephone the nurse at Black Mountain. She knew at once from my description who the man was and where he lived. More than that, she knew that we had taken his daughter to the hospital the previous Sunday night. She herself had driven the daughter home from the hospital at this man's insistence, late Wednesday afternoon.

"I begged her to wait for her baby to be born at the hospital," the nurse said, "but she wouldn't. Her father was there insisting that his grandson should be born at home in the old way." A long sigh came through the receiver. "Well, I have another call over beyond their place," the nurse went on. "I was out the door when you rang. Tell him I'll be at his hogan before he can get home."

The next time we were at the hospital, we saw the new grandson of our "sample man," and learned, in a glance, the reason for his holding back when he came to us for help. The baby had been born in the hogan, as he wished it, but with a cleft lip and palate.

Deformity among the Navahos is at least open to the suspicion of having been caused by witchcraft. The baby's strikingly handsome grandfather must have been in torment for long hours before he came to us. He must have weighed the chances of repairing the baby's mouth by means of a "sing," and decided against all that he'd been taught by his father and his grandfathers. Then he must have bolstered his courage to its highest pitch before daring to call on strange white people for help.

Strangers would come to see the mark of an enemy upon his grandson, he must have worried. Would they laugh to see a baby's tongue come out through his upper lip? Would they shrug and say, "A witch has done this, and we do not choose to get involved?" Or, would they have to say, "White men know nothing to do for this; your grandson will have to go through life in this condition"?

We stood looking down on the baby, perfect in every way except that he'd been born with a fissure in the roof of his mouth and a slit in his upper lip. We listened to the nurse's account of all that would be involved in the necessary repair. The lip was to receive surgery that day. A wait of fourteen months was required before the palate could be closed at a distant hospital.

We could think only of the baby's grandfather. We wished that we had known what it had cost him to come to us that early morning. That he had spent the night before in agony, we were certain now. Until this time—his long hair, his turquoise earrings, everything about him testified—the old way had been adequate for his needs. In this emergency, his reason must have told him, the old way would not suffice.

His people are finding themselves confronted by many emergencies for which the old tribal customs and beliefs provide no incantation. In anguish, they are turning their backs on much that they have been taught to believe and practice. They are now right up against the question, "Where do we go from here?"

All too often, they seek answers from persons who are, as we were, indifferent to the price they've paid in coming, and are not equipped to take their problems upon themselves. All we could do was to point the way to help. Perhaps that is all that should be done by us for the Navahos. Robbing them of responsibility for their own actions may have been our greatest sin against The People.

Many of them are turning from the ways of their fathers with a great emotional wrench. Their young people are taking a leap in the dark that tears them from their moral moorings.

The old ones say, "Do this."

The young ones say, "We won't."

Those caught between two cultures are saying, "We must!"

The Navaho tribe is in labor. Soon a new life will emerge. It is to be hoped that when it appears it will be fully formed, without the gaps in moral responsibility that will deform it and deprive The People for an additional hundred years of their birthright.

CHAPTER TWELVE

Social Events of the Summer Season

DIDIBAH HADN'T MENTIONED IT by the time she left for home on Thursday evening. She had washed her hair that day, though, and she had chattered incessantly. Twice I'd found her, without a listener, gabbing away to herself. We should have suspected that something was in store.

By wagon, by horseback, by pickup, by foot people began to arrive at Tselani soon after dawn the next morning. I don't mean that they poured in as people pour toward a stadium just before time for a ball game. Instead, they sort of drifted within range of the trading post and then just happened to hesitate round about somewhere. No one appeared to have come on purpose for anything in particular.

By the time our breakfast coffee had percolated, however, every juniper tree within sight from our table had at least one saddle horse tethered to it. Near the nose of each horse, at least two Navahos squatted on their heels, one knee up and one knee down, their broad-brimmed hats shoved back and resting on their necks.

When we looked out of our bedroom window where we frequently saw one or two wagons, each with a water barrel, we saw nine wagons and three pickups. More striking than the number of vehicles was the fact that only three were carrying water barrels. This clearly augured a social event.

Clumps of women sat, wrapped in their bright Pendleton shawls, in the beds of the wagons. Every other one held a cradle board at that clumsy-appearing forty-five degree angle, which had turned out to be the only feasible position when we'd tried it ourselves. Among them and over them and beneath their shawls, squirmed an assortment of children who had graduated from their cradle boards.

As we peeked from behind our curtains (in Navaholand it isn't polite to let someone see that you are watching him, but not watching is no virtue), more wagons and pickups arrived, and just happened to stop in among the others. Two more horsemen jogged past the window and around to the back of our house.

A gathering at a crossroads store in Kansas or in Oregon would provide itself with a noisy accompaniment of squawling babies, of laughter, and of greetings called from group to group. Here a kind of companionable silence hung on the morning.

We managed, between excursions to various windows, to get through our breakfast. When Didi arrived, she answered our questions in an offhand manner, but a little sparkle of excitement in her eyes belied her calm.

"They just branding, maybe operating on some horses over in that corral." She shrugged. "They always do that way—every year, 'bout now."

"Will it be all right if we go over to see it after while?" one of us asked.

"Sure," she said in the tone one might use with a child who was asking questions just to be asking questions. But Didi was never impatient with us for long. She quickly added, "Everybody come to watch. You two might as well watching."

I can remember Circus Day from my childhood. It was something we woke up with in our throats. It was colored balloons against a shimmering blue sky. It was the unfamiliar smell of popcorn on all outdoors. It was the tingle of promise in barkers' voices. It was the chill of fear inspired by a lion's roar and then by an elephant's trumpeting. (This was the kind of fear that we could really enjoy—all excitement and shivers, with no dread of consequences. After all, there were the iron bars!)

Circus Day was red-and-white striped canvas and pink cotton candy and daddy deciding, "We'd better get the reserved seats. Now that we're here, we want to see what there is to see." Most of all, it was three rings all whirling at once and no possibility of taking everything in. It was band music and spotlights and sequins and prodigality.

Allowing for the fact that I am no longer a child, I don't believe that Circus Day is or can be the same any more. Today most children live in the midst of a prodigality of action, color, and music. At best, the circus can be no more than a small climax for them. They have compensations, but they can never have a Circus Day such as millions of less privileged children knew in the nineteenteens and 'twenties. Those who were children then, if they wish to recapture that rib-thumping elation, can do no better than to go to Tselani at the end of July for the two-day social event staged there in the corral.

This is a social event in the sense that an old-time quilting bee or house-raising was for purposes of entertainment as well as for getting the work done. The work to be done at Tselani on these two days was branding cattle and horses, castrating cattle and horses, and breaking horses. If this sounds like all work and no play, so does building a house or making a quilt. In actual practice, compare the real enjoyment of women sitting shoulder to shoulder around a quilting frame, pricking the skin on their index fingers with every stitch, talking as fast as the needles weave in and out; and the real enjoyment of idle men and women standing around a hotel parlor, sipping cocktails, trying to think what to say next. Some of our famous party-givers might do well to learn the lesson from our pioneer forefathers or from the Navahos, that a little work can provide an unrivaled hook to hang a party on.

We tried to pursue our usual house-cleaning and nursing chores that first morning. We kept interrupting ourselves with, "Come see the wagons arriving," or "Hurry! They're driving in a band of horses."

Our small adhesive bandage business flourished. Everyone was here, so this was the logical time to come to us and get a patch on last week's burn—the blister had broken three days ago—or to cover the slash on a lady's leg where her axe had slipped while she was chopping wood last Monday.

Didi had found half a dozen excuses for going to the store before ten o'clock. We were not supposed to notice that in order to get to the store she had to pass the corral. Actually, the fact that she stayed on the job at all is a monument to her equanimity. Whoever heard of working within sauntering distance of a circus?

When we were finally able to get away to stroll across the road, the corral fence was decorated with rear views of Pendleton blankets and satin skirts of every intense color and of every size. Ladies clung to the rails of the corral like grace notes to a staff of music. Here and there a quarter note in skin-tight Levis stressed the end of a purple cadence or perched in a whole-tone orb on the top rail.

Every precarious ledge of the second mesa that provided a view into the corral held one or two or as many spectators as could edge in and cling there.

None of this reserved-seat audience was static. Up and down the rails of the corral and around the feet of the grownups swarmed a bevy of children and of goers and comers. Back in the schoolyard and in the road leading to the trading post, huddles of boys conferred and dispersed and congregated again. New arrivals bunched themselves in the road, or on the sunny side of the nearby warehouse, or on the shady side of a de-horsed wagon. In the blob of shade provided by the here-and-there juniper trees, ladies nursed their infants for as long as they could bear to stay away from the goings-on, and then relinquished their shade to the next hungry child and his mother.

No frenzy marked the peregrinations of the people, but the feeling all around us was that of movement. It was as if everyone were in such high spirits that standing still was next to impossible. A whiff of fragrant piñon smoke turned acrid and caustic to our nostrils as it gave way to the scent of burning hair.

Not one person was impolite enough to let us see him watching us, as we sauntered aimlessly toward the corral and jockeyed ourselves into position at the railing close to Didi.

One white man—a government agent, we learned later—worked in the corral along with six to ten Navahos. One Navaho, a man of fifty or fifty-five, held attention on the center ring. He was dressed in Levis and a green-and-brown plaid shirt. He wore his long hair in a hank that hung crosswise on his neck beneath the broad brim of his brown, high-topped Stetson. Nuggets of turquoise dangled from his ear lobes. He stood at a slight forward tilt, knees bowed, his arms hanging loose from his shoulders. In his right hand he held a stubby, wooden-handled knife like a ground-down butcher knife.

At the far side of the corral, the side snuggled into the base of the second mesa, three young Navaho men awkwardly swung lariats over the head of a yearling, mottled-gray horse. When one loop finally fell across the horse's withers and midway down his face, he flicked it off and, nostrils flaring, forced his way through the slit opening of the gate along with a half-dozen newly-branded and castrated calves.

Just outside the corral, a boy of sixteen seizing the moment of opportunity, ran and flung his arms around the horse's neck and swung up, sprawled on his belly along the animal's back. The

Photo by Arthur Dodd

Family outside summer tent home in the mountains
for Christian service in Navaho led by Ganado Mission students

Summer home where Navaho family grazes flocks in the mountains

horse stopped in astonishment for an instant. His head jerked up. He craned around as if he'd see just what kind of new-fangled rope this could be that clasped itself around his neck and gave no chance to throw it off. Then his nose dropped to his fetlock, his haunches tightened, and a gasp of expectancy went up from the crowd.

The boy wove his fingers into the mane and managed to stay through half a dozen hard explosive eruptions of the horse's hind quarters. Then the horse stopped short, head down, and the boy slid neatly down the slide provided by his neck. The crowd burst into laughter and turned about-face, back to the corral and the business at hand.

The men with the ropes managed to throw a horse upon his side. They tied his front feet together, using enough rope to hang themselves. When the horse kicked one foot free of the tangle, the audience laughed. When his front feet were securely tied, and two men were holding his hind legs, the man with the knife wagged his head toward the bonfire. A stocky young Navaho hurried over with a branding iron. He side-stepped around until he could place the glowing red brand right side up on the horse's thigh. Then he pushed his weight against it.

The horse's hind legs jerked. One of the holders lost his balance, but he hung on and finally flung himself across the horse's body. The smell of scorched hair and seared flesh stung through the hovering dust and dung.

The audience giggled.

The man with the ground-down butcher knife caught the blade between his teeth, pushed back his hat, and bent down to prepare his patient for surgery. Then he gave the knife a swipe on the seat of his Levis and made his incision. Blood came slowly at first, and so he lengthened the incision and put the bloody knife back between his teeth while with his bare hands he pulled and jerked at the animal's testacles, and finally completed the job with another slash of the knife. Back into his mouth then went the gory blade.

Quickly he reached down and replenished the blood on his hand. Then he touched the horse's forehead, swiped down his forelegs, marked his hind legs with a smear of blood, and ended with a slap on his thigh that signaled the holders to release him. Stunned, the horse got up, dripping blood, and searched for a way of escape while the boys with the ropes began paging the next patient.

The children and babies among the onlookers drank in the excitement and action with the same leaning-into-it intensity that we often see in children before a TV at five-thirty in the afternoon.

When the second patient had been branded, the man with the knife pulled the bloody blade up along the leg of his Levis to clean it before he made his incision. Then he performed the operation and once more ended it with the same pattern of blood marking the animal—at forehead, along forelegs and hind legs, and a slap on the thigh. I suddenly realized that this final act had a ceremonial quality.

Didi had said nothing, but now I remarked, in her general direction but as if I were talking to myself, "I wonder why he does that."

After the proper interval, while the boys were lassoing the next patient, she asked, "Does what?"

"That business of swiping his bloody hand down the horse's legs," I said.

Didi shrugged. "I don't know," she said. "I don't know" and "Oh yes" were always one word as Didi pronounced them.

I watched the next operation and its attendant finishing ceremony. Again I commented to myself, "That's interesting. I wonder why he does that."

Didi said nothing.

Each operation had its little mishaps, and all mishaps were funny to the audience. They giggled or guffawed, according to the size of the bungle committed and the discomfort of the victim. It was all good-natured and easy. None of the ladies fainted at the sight of the blood. Nobody booed the performers. No one pushed for a better vantage point on the rails of the corral. Everybody took in everything and enjoyed it all.

We stood beside the corral as the ground became more and more spattered with blood and littered with the tossed-aside bloody excisions, and remembered that had this been a certain kind of blood, every Navaho here would have avoided contact with it at any cost. An involuntary contact even would be considered sure to bring on crippling. The unfortunate victim of such contact would be required to submit to a lengthy ceremony involving ashes made from the wood of a lightning-struck tree. Still, in the midst of this gore, children, women in their best clothes and all their jewelry, men in their best carved belts and newest hats were all enjoying the show in the corral and the rare treat of togetherness.

The man with the knife had just stuck the bloody blade between his teeth, and performed his blood-smearing ceremony marking the end of one more operation. I said, "I think I'd better go over home and see whether we have any customers."

Didibah turned to me with a mysterious little smile in her eyes. "The old ones say, 'If he don't doing that with the blood, that horse won't run fast,' " she murmured.

We accepted this belated confidence without comment.

"I'll be coming soon," Didi said as Don and I started off.

The first casualty of the day to come to us was one of the lariat-wielding "boys." Fortunately Didibah had come back across the road before the patient arrived, for he couldn't, or wouldn't, speak English. However, words in any language were more or less unnecessary when the broad-shouldered, six-foot "boy" sat down on our cot and opened his hand. His rope had burned across his palm, which was bad enough, but it had also caught and torn a ragged gash through the fleshy base of his thumb.

A doctor might have stitched the flesh back in place. I don't know. All I could do was to soak the hand in disinfectant and bandage it. I prepared my treatment in a washpan, and eased the bloody, ripped hand into the warm solution.

The "boy" grabbed his forearm with his free hand as a shudder of pain went through him. Tears came to his eyes and escaped down his cheeks, but he grinned up at me through the tears and kept his injured hand in the disinfectant. The first shock of pain passed, and there he sat, obediently soaking his hand for the full twenty minutes that I prescribed.

Soon the injured hand began to look so much cleaner than his other one that he noticed it, and made a joke about it to Didi. She giggled and pointed out the contrast to me.

By the time I was ready to apply a bandage, several ladies had come in and seated themselves on Primary chairs around the room. As each had arrived, I'd asked Didi, "Does she want something?"

After a murmured exchange, Didi had reported, "She's just visiting."

I heard no conversation, but noticed some giggling among our visitors as I applied a gauze bandage to my patient's hand. When the job was finished, Didi explained the charge and collected the full twenty-five cents from him on the spot.

"Ask him whether it feels better," I suggested.

She put my question into Navaho and the "boy" grinned at me while he answered her.

"He says, 'Yes,' " she reported.

Still grinning, our patient left to return to the corral. The ladies sat on, silently visiting. I went into the next room to the desk, to write up our record.

Within the hour, our patient was back. Didi called me into the community room. There he stood in the doorway, and just behind him were three of his rope-twirling friends.

"The same one again?" I asked when I saw him. "What is it this time?"

He didn't wait for me to tell him where to sit. He knew all the ropes here as well as in the corral. He came on in and sat on the end of the cot again. His friends stepped inside the door and stood, arms crossed on their chests, watching.

My "boy" merely sat with a kind of foolish grin on his face.

I turned to Didi. "What's the matter with him?"

She asked him in Navaho.

He ducked his head and murmured something in answer. His tall friends giggled.

Then, peeking up at me to watch my reaction, he held out his left hand. There by looking closely I could see a quarter-inch-long slice on his middle finger. It was the kind of nick I frequently have on one of my fingers from peeling vegetables. This cut appeared to be at least two days old. It was beginning to heal, in spite of the crust of dirt on his hand.

I said, "This!"

The "boy" ducked his head and giggled.

So this was a joke—the sort of joke a young man could get courage enough to play, provided a holiday spirit pervaded the air and provided his friends stayed nearby to lend him their collective boldness.

I said to Didi, "Well, either he wants this hand soaked clean to match the other one, or else he just likes to have me hold his hand. Ask him which it is."

When she asked, his friends allowed their held-back laughter to escape in little spurts between their teeth. The ladies on the Primary chairs clapped their hands over their mouths and giggled through their fingers. The joke became funnier and funnier to my audience as I made a swab on a toothpick and soaked it in alcohol. I cleaned a bare half-inch circle around the wound and applied a baby-size adhesive bandage to the accompaniment of easy laughter. Nobody was laughing at anyone else. We were all laughing together and playing little jokes out of sheer high spirits.

For two days we had jokes and work and companionship and

blood and laughter and accidents all scrambled together like the ingredients of a complicated recipe for a dish called Fun. For two days the ladies gloried in showing off their finest satin skirts and their velvet blouses with silver collar-corners and silver buttons running down each shoulder seam from neck to wrist, and silver bowknot buttons down the front from their chins to their waist-bands. In addition, most of them wore valuable squash-blossom necklaces.

The men strode about in their newest, unsweated felt hats with silver (sometimes silver-and-turquoise) hatbands. Or they stood with their thumbs hooked inside their hand-carved belts, their bowed elbows making a nice frame for their savings accounts, which they wore around their necks and on their wrists and fingers in the form of silver-and-turquoise jewelry with accents here and there of coral and of shell wampum.

For days and weeks and months many of these people live five or even ten miles from their nearest neighbors. At their family "camps," live the old folks and their married daughters with their numerous children. For most of the winter, their social life is centered in each "camp," and it consists of herding sheep all day and sitting around an iron or tin-can stove at night while the elders instruct the children in tribal folklore and proper behavior.

They have no clubhouses, no churches, no golf clubs, no hotels, no artificial gathering places of any kind other than the trading posts and, very recently, some schools. An occasion for gathering is an Occasion, and the Navahos make the most of it. A horse and cattle bee such as we had at Tselani is a kind of opener for the social season.

The so-called Squaw Dances (more properly called Girls' or War Dances) start in late spring and are held all through the summer. Even these, which are more nearly social in character than any of the other ceremonials, have a practical purpose at their center. They revolve around the healing of one or more sick persons.

The special brush shelter, prepared for the patient or patients, is the hub of the occasion. Around it whirls a ring of fun and sensual indulgence. To a casual visitor, it appears to be all fun of a carnival sort—with booths set up selling "fry bread" and coffee and warm pop, girls smelling of yucca suds and wearing their most elaborate dresses and jewelry, and a mountainous bonfire throwing up stars to rival the low-hanging Arizona sky. Over it all fans the odor of piñon smoke. The falsetto voices of men singing to the accompaniment of a small thumped drum stir the blood and endue the entire proceeding with an air of eeriness.

The sounds and odors are different from those at a country fair or a carnival in Missouri. The booths selling food and drink, the noise, the bright clothes, the gaiety, and the sensual indulgence are about the same.

Illnesses occur and taboos are broken during the winter, of course, and some ceremonials are held then. However, the weather on the Reservation discourages travel during much of the winter, so summer really becomes the gay season. While ceremonials are held for purposes of "restoring everything to harmony," they are also social events for people winter-starved for conversation, for showing off, and for laughter.

Ladies in New York spend months and fortunes preparing their costumes for attending opening night at the "Met." Ladies on the Navaho Reservation spend the winter months and their fortunes preparing their costumes for attending the Inter-Tribal Indian Ceremonial at Gallup in August. Those who are able to follow the season (as New Yorkers drift to Florida, Havana, or Paris) go to the Phoenix Ceremonial, to the Wickenburg Roundup, and to Santa Fe for Fiesta. Some go to Hopiland as tourists to see the Snake Dances.

Most Navahos, however, the same as many of the rest of us, must stay on the job for the most part in order to make a living. Many Navahos, we found, are in a class with those who own a home in

Kansas City and a summer cottage in Colorado, or those who winter in a New York apartment but summer at Newport. Navahos even have a slight edge on most of these, for when a Navaho moves from his winter home to his summer place, his work goes with him. He is not required to spend hours commuting to the seashore, or sweltering in town while his family swims and golfs, using the summer home as a base.

When grass and forage are exhausted near a Navaho's winter home, he padlocks his hogan and moves higher up to his summer "camp." His work and that of his family continues to be that of herding sheep, and keeping a household running. Here, however, everything is done in vacation style. The cookstove is set up in a brush shelter and all meals are cooked and eaten outdoors. The ladies' looms are strung up outdoors between two trees, and they work in the open air all day with their youngest children safe nearby on their cradle boards.

Those Navahos who are "singers" spend their days in gathering and spreading to dry in the sun the herbs they will use in conducting ceremonies during the coming months.

Boys chase rabbits and prairie dogs and play with their puppies. Little girls make mud pies and play "dress up" and pretend keeping house with their pet lambs for their children.

All too soon, the time arrives when the government inspectors will be waiting at the sheep dips. Then the family must close its summer home, and lead the sheep and goats down from the mountains.

Sheepdipping time is work, and the rotten, sulphurous stench of the dip. It is also the fragrance of piñon smoke and bubbling mutton stew and coffee. It is jokes, and the hilarious accidents involved in tossing a big ram into the narrow ditch filled with dip. It is conversation, and silent visiting, and showing off. It is a music festival with a clunking symphony of sheep bells accompanying a hundred vocal groups, incessantly singing, "Baa-a-a, baa-a-a-a, baa-a-a-a," on every note in the scale. Sheepdipping time, like Easter in Bermuda or Labor Day at Bar Harbor, marks the climax of the social season.

Down from the mountains, from far and near within the dip's district, flocks come wagging their herders and their herders' families behind them. It is "first come, first served," but running each family's flocks separately through the dip, counting, and collecting by the head make slow business. In every direction from the dip, banners of dust signal the approach of more flocks. Soon sheep are bunched in woolly, dust-beige polka dots on the dull green slopes. Now a ten-ring circus is spread over the countryside.

Someone—often a lady wearing a heavy wool shawl and carrying an umbrella to ward off the sun—must keep each flock collected and be ready to herd her charges into the pen when her turn comes. In the large pen, with its single-file lane leading into the dip, men are yelling to make themselves heard above the din of bleating. They thrash their arms around. Still, the sheep are wary and dip-shy. They are full of slithers and dodges for avoiding that dreaded, stinking swim.

The men are in holiday mood, however. Their boots are slathered with fresh dung. Their lungs are heavy with dust. The work is hard. The sheep are cantankerous. The noise is deafening. Everyone in the pen is having a wonderful time, laughing at foul-ups, cavorting, and showing off.

Out away from the center of the hubbub, ladies and children traipse through the rabbitbrush and greasewood. They spot friends they haven't seen since spring. They exchange the summer's news.

"May I take your picture?" I asked two small girls who were wandering, hand-in-hand, toward the pen.

Since this was sheepdip time, they forgot to answer, but they stopped obligingly, and stared at me with solemn eyes long enough for me to click my shutter.

"Take my picture, too," I heard from some distance behind me. I turned and faced a broad grin across a plump, dark face beneath a roll-brimmed hat.

"O. K.," I called, and cocked my camera. "Are you ready?"

The man shoved his hat back and posed with one fist propped on his hip, his arm akimbo; the other daintily balanced atop the stick he'd been using for driving sheep. It was a nice clowning pose, and I snapped his picture.

"Lots of excitement," the man commented, coming up as I stood winding my film. "I wouldn't miss it. Came all the way from Montana this year."

"You did?" I studied his happy, easy grin. He looked like a Navaho to me, but I'd been living deep on the Reservation. I found it hard to believe that a Navaho would call out to me as this man had done, and then take the initiative in carrying on a conversation. No amount of excitement due to Circus Day or sheepdip time would free a person from the Tselani area for this kind of direct, unself-conscious interchange. Somehow I, too, felt free—free enough to ask, "Are you Navaho?"

"Sure," he answered, "but I live in Montana now. I fix it so I come back to visit at sheepdip time. Don't want to miss the fun." He waved, grinned again, and strolled off toward the pen.

There, I thought, is the way it will be with all The People, in time. The constraint, due so largely to uncertainty as to how a white person will or won't respond, will melt away. A camera will come to be an instrument that can be legitimately aimed in two directions. It will no longer be a pointing finger, saying to the Navaho, "You are a curiosity." Little jokes can then be jokes and nothing more. They will cease to be, as we found them repeatedly, a Navaho's respectable means of putting us in our place.

CHAPTER THIRTEEN

Small Victories over a Large Enemy

AT QUITTING TIME ONE EVENING, Didibah came to our house and said, "My daddy planning go to Phoenix. I putting his suitcase behind cot." She waved toward the community room. "When he's leaving, he will coming here. Will say, *'tsits'aa'.'* "

"That will mean that he's ready to go and wants his suitcase?" I asked.

"Yes,"

Don and I both practiced the word, *"tsits'aa',"* struggling with the rising inflection on the last syllable. (If your Navaho word doesn't go up or down at the proper time, it may betray you into an indiscretion.)

Didi listened and corrected us and stayed with us until she decided that we had it "near enough." After all, we shouldn't need to say it, merely to understand what her daddy wanted when he said it.

We rehearsed each other occasionally as we sat in our living room, waiting up for Didi's father to appear. We kept ourselves awake an hour later than usual, and still no one came. Finally we went to bed.

We were wakened at six o'clock the next morning by noises at our back door. We heard no knocks on the door, but we did hear feet shuffling on the cement porch, lumps of sandstone thrown against our piñon tree—those kinds of noises.

"Oh-oh," I said, "one of our ladies! I hope the stork isn't any wider awake than I am."

We both pulled on our robes and hurried to the kitchen.

There stood Didibah's father.

He is tall and lean. His face could pass, in both color and contour, for that of a well-tanned Caucasian. His inclinations and practices, however, are Navaho. Didi had told us that he'd worked enough among English-speaking people that he could understand English "just find." "He could speaking English, too, but he won't," she had added.

We opened the door and said, "Good morning."

He gazed at his feet and said, "Suitcase," in a loud voice.

"You mean *tsits'aa'* ?" Don asked.

Didi's father glanced up long enough to catch the flicker of amusement on our faces, then he laughed.

We laughed with him.

Together we enjoyed the small joke of Didi's teaching him the English word at the same time that she taught us the Navaho word.

Didi's father was still laughing as, *tsits'aa'* in hand, he swung through our gate and crossed the road to the truck that would take him to Phoenix. After all, he was entitled to the last laugh. He had jumped the gun on us, and had actually used the English word without giving us a chance to practice our Navaho on him. All such coups that the Navahos can bring off are dear to their hearts. Their laughter on such occasions tastes sweet on their tongues.

"Small joke," did I say? To Didi's father it was not small. It was, symbolically, a tribal victory over the enemy. It was a kind of blood-less coup, proving that The People are quicker and smarter than *belliganos*. This is something that Navahos, particularly those over thirty, keep proving whenever an opportunity presents itself. Even our "boys" were not above proving it.

174

When we were ready to run down to Ganado one morning to shop at the commissary there, our pickup refused to start.

Didi said, "Johnnie Nez can fixing it maybe. He's always fixing cars."

Half a dozen "boys" were more than willing to stop their "game" and toss the basketball aside in order to watch Johnnie Nez tinker with our carburetor. Then they helped push the pickup down the road to get it started. Johnnie Nez had "fixed" it only in the sense that the motor was now running so we could drive to the garage at Ganado.

This small project provided a ten-minute diversion in our "boys'" bootless day. In view of all that we had done for them, we certainly owed them nothing. Don could have given Johnnie Nez a quarter, or fifty cents at the most, and been far more than paid up. Instead, he made the mistake of asking, "How much do I owe you?"

We saw what we learned to call "that look" come into Johnnie Nez's eyes. "That look" has in it a mixture of fun and cunning. It is the here's-my-chance-to-put-one-over-on-a-white-man look. The "boys" saw it, too. We could feel them holding back their giggles waiting for the trap to spring.

Johnnie Nez said, "Two dollar."

Don realized that he had one foot in the trap and couldn't back out.

The "boys" waited, still holding in, until Don pulled his billfold from his pocket. Then their giggles broke through the dam. Even we had to admit that Johnnie Nez had scored a fine coup. Two dollars, you see, was the price the local bootlegger charged for a fifty-cent bottle of Tokay wine.

The ladies, too, are adept at playing this kind of joke, retaliating for the tribe, when they think they can get away with it.

Didi talked with a buxom matron who arrived at the community room one noon, just at store-closing time. I had seen her pad across the road, lugging a carton of groceries. The thing I hadn't seen was that she donned her worried expression as she set her load on the porch and came inside.

Didi turned, from their lengthy conversation in Navaho, to me. "Her husband being very sick," she reported. "She think he ought to going to hospital."

"What's the matter with him?" I asked.

"He's hurting when pass urine," Didi told me. "Passing blood, too."

"Did he come with her?"

"He's staying home," Didi said. "They don't got car. This lady catching ride."

"Where do they live?"

Didi waved toward the west. "Over Piñon way." She no doubt saw me shaping my usual question, and beat me to the draw. "Not far," she assured me. "Ten mile, maybe."

"If we go for him now, will he be ready for us to take him to the hospital?"

A good deal of tongue-clicking Navaho seemed to be required before Didi could tell me that the lady thought her husband would be ready to go, if we went out to pick him up. "This lady riding 'long with you; show the way," Didi added.

Don helped the lady load her purchases into the bed of the truck. She climbed into the front seat and guided us with full-hand gestures (a Navaho doesn't point with one finger because of various bad-luck repercussions) along the road to Piñon for ten miles, and then for eight miles of wagon tracks. When we finally arrived, Don helped the lady unload her groceries, and we asked to see her husband.

She found him, after a bit of search, in the corral with the sheep. She came back to the pickup without him, and now she had acquired a new skill. Suddenly she could speak English. "He feeling

176

find now. Think he not want going to hospital," she said.

We insisted on seeing the patient.

Sheepishly he came ambling over to our pickup. He looked perfectly healthy, and our questioning failed to convince us that he ever had passed blood with his urine. However, his wife had wangled a ride home from the store with her heavy load.

As a tribe, the Navahos were tricked once, and then tricked again and again. They believed the promises of Washington, made through General Carleton in 1864. They straggled out of their canyons. They came down from their shelves of hiding. They agreed to accept Washington's offer of ready-made houses, of handed-out food. They made the long march to Fort Sumner.

There they found no houses, and no trees that could be used for building hogans. In order to provide some kind of shelter for their families, they were forced to dig holes in the ground and roof them over with brush. The wagon freight, carrying food, arrived at haphazard intervals, but always with fewer beans and less bacon than promised; never with mutton or squash that The People could really relish. There the ridiculous white men insisted on their digging up the ground and planting grains of corn. It was true, as the white men predicted, that corn did grow, but then the grasshoppers ate it.

No doubt the white men were laughing in their snug wooden and adobe houses at night at this joke—they had made the Navahos work in the searing sun to dig and plant and pull weeds in order that the grasshoppers might be fed. Well then, the time would come for the Navahos to laugh. They would see to it that the time came. They and their children and their grandchildren would be taught to turn the joke around. In time, these white men must be made to realize that The People would not be slaves to the grasshopper.

Few Navahos are in a position to win battles in the business world against the white man. Most of them, however, have an alert sense of humor and a fine-honed slant on life that enable them to exult in each small outwitting of a white man.

During World War II, Navahos were in a position to carry on one piece of essential work that no one else could do so efficiently.

Landing operations in the South Pacific were frequently spur-of-the-moment, strike-while-the-iron-is-hot affairs. We landed on this island or that, we advanced to the right or left across a bridge or through a jungle according to on-the-spot tactics devised by ear. A handful of advance communications officers could be smuggled into a strategic blind. Their radio messages to stand-by companies of marines were invariably intercepted. Various codes learned at training bases were as transparent as cellophane. In many instances, a sizable landing would have been greeted by an impenetrable wall of gunfire, except for the Navahos fighting side by side with other Americans.

During the old days when the West was the "wild" West, fur trappers and adventurers frequently allowed as how "one white man are equal to ten Injuns any day." During World War II, two Navahos—one at an advance lookout point, and one with the main body of an attacking force awaiting orders to get on with the war— were equal to whole companies of soldiers.

Orders swiftly translated from English and transmitted in Navaho could be instantly translated into English by the Navaho at the advance base. Nothing to it! Nothing, that is, except that the enemy could not decode the Navaho language in time to find out what was happening. Difficult as it proved for the enemy, on the Reservation even the babies speak Navaho. It was fortunate for us that some of those babies grew up to fit a uniform of the United States. The war in the Pacific had been over and done with for three years before the Navaho veterans of Bataan and Corregidor were granted the privilege of voting in Arizona and New Mexico.

The Navahos themselves make little of the unique contribution

178

of their code-talkers to the war in the Pacific. The story of such and such a bridge being blown up as a result of the code-talking of Chiishch'ilí Begay may be seldom mentioned. The suitcase-*tsits'aa'* story, and the tale of how Johnnie Nez worked us to get a bottle of wine will be repeated and repeated on long winter evenings beside the iron stove in dozens of hogans.

Perhaps the fact that thirty-six hundred Navahos willingly served in the armed forces during World War II, and three hundred of them gave their lives for our country and theirs, kept Don and me from keeping our guard up when matters of less than life-and-death significance were at stake. We blithely went right on "playing it straight," and our neighbors, who never in the world would have considered doing us any real harm, continued to look for opportunities to outwit us.

We had been left gasping by two or three near misses in the obstetrical department of our unofficial duties. Learning that a lady can sweat from running as well as from imminent motherhood had been a happy lesson. However, we had qualms about our luck's holding out indefinitely. So at the first opportunity we arranged to stay overnight in the shadow of the Ganado hospital.

"If there's a chance of a delivery tonight," I told one of the nurses, "please call me."

At ten-thirty her call came. "Hurry up," she said. "We're short on nurses tonight. You can help."

My heart wedged itself at the base of my throat. I raced across the Ganado campus and up the steps at the side door of the hospital. At last I was going to see a delivery! I stopped inside the door to pull in a deep breath. The air was so laden with ether that my much-needed deep breath threatened to flatten me. It did nothing at all to quell the disturbance in my chest and calm my trembling hands.

My nurse friend met me on the second floor. "You're in luck," she said with a grin. "Here put this on." She slapped a gauze mask across my mouth, hung its top tapes over my ears, and pulled its bottom tapes back to tie them all in a wad at the crown of my head. At first the mask seemed impervious to air, but soon I tasted a kind of fuzzy something that served the same purpose, and I sucked it in as fast as it would filter through.

The nurse flicked a papery, white surgical gown off her arm. "Here," she said. She crackled it open and held it toward me as the Puritans must have invited culprits to thrust their arms into the stocks. I pushed into the starch-pasted sleeves and my friend tied the tapes at the back of my neck.

"We've got one in labor," she said, "and I just heard there's another one being admitted downstairs."

The elevator door clattered, and a pert little aid appeared around the corner of the corridor. Expertly backing and maneuvering, she extracted from the elevator and pushed toward us one of those long-legged stretchers on wheels. On it lay a mound covered by a tan and orange Pendleton blanket. As it came alongside, I peered over my mask and discovered a shyly smiling Navaho lady's round face. Her skin against the white sheet looked as clear and deep as a cup of black coffee.

The aid asked, "Any room in labor?"

The word "labor" as used around a hospital has little to do with management. In fact, labor in the sense of being in the travail of childbirth, defies all efforts at management when the ladies so engaged are Navahos. "Labor," in the little aid's question, referred to the room where ladies in labor await the proper moment for being transferred to the delivery room. If management had anything to do with these arrangements, it could not happen as frequently as it does that for a week no lady will be in labor in the labor room; and then on one night such as this, . . .

"There's one bed free," the nurse told the aid. "Help yourself." She assisted and together they wheeled the Navaho lady through the door into the labor room.

I was trying to scratch my nose and wangle a breath of non-upholstered air when I happened to glance down the corridor. Two Navaho ladies, both draped in Pendleton blankets, padded toward me. One was unmistakably a candidate for a bed in the labor room.

I pushed the door open and beckoned my nurse friend into the corridor.

"Oh-oh," she said. "Here we go again."

The doctor, looking somewhat like a maternity case himself in his loose-hanging white gown, sauntered toward us from the far end of the hall.

The imminent mother standing before me clutched her brown and purple blanket with her left hand. It fell apart below her hand to allow room for the bulge of her abdomen. Her royal blue satin skirt swept the floor at her back. In front it hiked up at least a foot, revealing her rust-colored, buckskin moccasin-boots. The silver buttons in close-set rows, that adorned her maroon velvet tunic were all diverted in their lines of march by the necessity of leaving the tunic unhooked beneath her arm.

She extricated her right arm from her blanket and gathered the sweat from her long upper lip as she might grasp the flowers from a clump of rabbitbrush for dyeing a rug. Her timid, upswept glance at the doctor apologized for this display of weakness. It also admitted her lack of integrity in coming here at all. She was taking the easy way, repudiating the way of her mother, and she was a little ashamed.

Hers was one of the long, thin Navaho faces, suggesting that under other circumstances her body too was long and thin. She would be one who herded sheep, striding tall, paying no attention to the fingers of sagebrush that grasped at her satin skirt as she strode along. Now, she ducked her head and pushed at the sweat-dampened strands of black hair loosened from her knot by the hurry-up wagon ride to the hospital. Yesterday, I was sure, she had tossed her head and allowed the sheep-scented air to blow those strands into place. Out on the range with the sheep, a lady has no need to hide her face. The sheep are hers, and provided she has observed the necessary taboos, she is master of her own soul.

As for her baby, she must, by now, have been filled with gnawing doubts. She would have liked to dream of a girl child growing up to become a fine weaver, one whose rugs would command top price at the store. Still, her grandmother had reminded her before she'd left home tonight, that this must be left to chance, if much of the female infant's umbilical cord is tossed carelessly into a container at the hospital instead of being buried within the hogan. She would have liked to dream of a baby boy growing up to become the owner of many fine horses. To bury his cord in the corral would insure this, naturally. Her grandfather had threatened that poverty would hound her boy through life, if she went through with this soft, new-fangled notion of letting her baby be delivered in the white man's hospital.

She had no doubt argued, pointing out certain compensations, playing them over against possible repercussions caused by taking the pampered, fast-becoming-fashionable way. At the hospital, "they" dispose of the placenta and of all bloodstained cloths. This relieves a lady's mother or sister of having to get rid of these things in secret. It relieves the family of the expense of ceremonies to counteract accidental contact.

"But they charge at the Ganado hospital," some older member of the family had surely countered.

"No more than the 'singer' charges," this lady had snapped back, I'm sure.

Actually, her mother's sister's husband's daughter by his first wife had given birth to a beautiful baby at the Ganado hospital less than a month before, and she said it was wonderful. "They even let you breathe through a little thing that takes all the pain away."

I noticed the veins throb in our lady's temple.

The doctor touched her shoulder to get her attention. "Just a minute and we'll take care of you," he promised. He disappeared through the labor room door. The lady and her companion glanced toward each other, ducked their heads, and giggled.

Soon one of the ladies in the labor room was transferred across the corridor to the delivery room. The little aid made up the vacated bed, and we got our most recent arrival off her feet. Her companion—her mother, aunt, sister, half-sister, or what-have-you —accepted the chair we offered and pulled it tight against her charge's bed. Neither one spoke English, nor did the one already occupying the other bed in the labor room. We had one Navaho nurse on duty that night, but Tóli was consoling a homesick boy in "isolation."

Our section of the hospital was as quiet as the inside of a squash. I'd heard, during visits to and stays in various hospitals around the country, groans and screams that nurses had identified as emanating from "delivery."

The doctor came from the labor room, wandered across the hall to touch the forehead of the lady sitting on her heels on the delivery table, and turned back to the nurse and me with a shrug. "I hope I moved the right one in," he said and sauntered away.

We waited. Nobody spoke. Nobody cried out. Nobody so much as grimaced in pain, and yes, I did say that the lady was "sitting" on the delivery table. What is more, the two ladies in the labor room were sitting in the middle of their beds. Their knees were bent back, their feet were crossed, and they were sitting on their heels.

"Are they in labor?" I asked.

"You bet they are," the nurse told me. "I hope that doctor stays within earshot."

We were both whispering. It is strange that we depend on whispers to keep a person who doesn't understand our language from eavesdropping, but when we're determined that we'll make him understand, we shout English at him under the delusion that if our words are loud enough our meaning will surely break through.

183

"If we had three white women in labor in such close quarters," the nurse whispered, "you could hear them from here to Gallup."

The doctor came back, and to our relief, behind him swung Tólí, our Navaho nurse.

Tólí was a graduate of Ganado High School and of the Ganado School of Nursing. Her short hair, expertly curled, bounced around her beaming dimpled face each time her white, rubber-soled oxfords hit the floor. Her starched, white swatch of a cap clung at a precarious angle above her left eye. Her hands in the pockets of her uniform seemed to serve the same purpose, in propelling her down the hall, that oars perform for a rowboat.

As the doctor turned to the left to examine the lady on the delivery table, Tólí started to swing through the door into the labor room. She'd barely glanced at me in my mask and gown. Now she stopped for a double-take. Her face broke open in a grin of recognition. "Hi!" she said, and went on about her business.

The next instant, her head reappeared through the labor room door. "Doctor!" she called.

The doctor came across, shaking his head. "I must have guessed wrong," he muttered. He held the labor room door open for me. "Come on in," he invited.

The nurses had to use their full powers of persuasion to get the lady to lie down on the bed. The doctor called me over. "You can hold this," he said, and handed me something that looked like a small electric hair dryer. "Just hold it to her mouth," he told me. "She'll push it away, when she's had enough. It's the same as Queen Elizabeth had when Princess Anne was born."

Our dark-skinned queen drew in a deep breath, and almost at once, the greatest drama in the world began. It was a drama in pantomime—no wailing, no dialogue, no gnashing of teeth. Then, within a long minute, a black-haired, rosy-skinned doll lay unmoving on the doctor's large hand. A short minute more, during which the doctor and nurses performed routine rites, and then the doll,

184

dangling by its heels and making the proper response to the doctor's cuing slap, broke the silence. The doll had become a living human being.

"*Ashkíí*," I whispered to the mother.

A smile twitched at her lips before she went to sleep, to dream, I have no doubt, of a small boy, round as a ball of yarn, with a dimple in his left cheek.

"A fine teacher you are," I twitted the doctor. "I came to learn proper procedure for the delivery room."

"This is the way you'll have it to do—on a cot or in the back of a pickup," he reminded me.

"Doctor, hurry!" Tólí had been across to the delivery room.

Soon the drama had been enacted again. This time, at our fingertips were the proper devices for holding the mother in the most helpful position, but it was not until the last minute that we could persuade her to lie down. Once more, the room was silent. With foot rests and arm rests and trick table extensions, our results were the same.

Once more I whispered, "*Ashkíí*," to the mother, and she closed her eyes.

The doctor and nurses were busy with shots of vitamin K and eye drops.

"Maybe I should take a look across the hall," I said.

The doctor glanced up from the infant on his palm and nodded.

I leaned against the door to the labor room, pushing it open just far enough to check what was happening without disturbing our lady.

What was happening was that our lady, without having turned on her service light, was lying on her side delivering herself of her baby. Her sister or aunt or mother was trying to help, but she was convulsed with laughter; and, habitually, when a Navaho lady laughs in the presence of a white person, she covers her mouth, so she pretty well had her hands full.

"Doctor!" I called.

The baby gave two wails that sent the sister or mother or aunt into a ripple of laughter. Then I saw that the mother, too, was giggling. Both ladies sent mischievous sidelong glances at me over the hands that covered their mouths. Those dark eyes flicked little gloating darts at me. These were not malicious darts, in any sense. They were, however, eloquent. We needed no common language.

"You pulled a fast one, didn't you?" I said.

They couldn't understand my words, but they understood that I was laughing with them at this small joke they had perpetrated, not on me, but on all white men.

They had swallowed their scruples, turned their backs on the birthing methods of their forebears, and come to the white man's hospital. And for what? Here in this tall white bed, with no red belt swung from a pole in their hogan and no sheepskin-padded, softened place in the hogan floor, they had brought forth this baby behind the white doctor's back. This was sweet vindication for the qualms they'd suffered in making the decision to come. How the old folks would laugh, when they went home and told of this triumph! How the old ones would use this story to convince the young women of their folly in seeking the easy way!

The Navahos in the armed services fought alongside *belliganos* in the Pacific. The Navahos are no longer at war against *belliganos*. They agreed in 1868 that they would never again go to war against the white man, and (except for random raids by young, uncontrollable hotbloods) they have lived by the letter of the treaty. They did not agree, however, that they would not laugh at the white man and at his incredibly funny ways. They did not agree to accept his self-acclaimed superiority without testing their own ways and wits against his.

A hitchhiker taught us, one rainy day, that a Navaho can also set his jaw as stubbornly as any white man.

CHAPTER FOURTEEN

Full Speed Ahead

THE ROAD between Tselani and Ganado would provide some student of soils and their geologic sources with a fine subject for his doctor's dissertation. During dry times, this road gives the impression of being all sand—rose beige in color and with no properties of cohesion. Each passing wagon or pickup wears the tracks a little softer and deeper, until after a week or so of no rain, driving those thirty-five miles can become a nice present-day substitute for two days' travel on the Oregon Trail a hundred years ago.

Some stretches of the road have a sandstone foundation. When the wind blows—and it does—these stretches get swept clean of loose sand. They lie bare before us, an open study in the cross-bedding characteristically produced by vigorous currents of water. Cross-bedding is one thing to write a doctor's dissertation on, and something else to ride on. Our pickup should have been double-jointed. As it was, we took the layers of these exposed rocks one wheel at a time in a pattern of bias twists. The driver lurched and slid on the slick, plastic-covered seat, and hoped merely to maintain a position within reach of the steering wheel. These exposed rocks compose the all-weather part of the road.

Other stretches of the roadbed have no foundation at all. Crossing these is like driving through a series of sand boxes. As long as any moisture remains in the sand, some traction is possible. Each passing vehicle, however, dries out the tracks as its tires lift the sand to the sun and air. The tracks wear deeper and wider. Then along comes a driver who decides that the tracks are no longer to be trusted, and he guns through on the ridges. If he is lucky and doesn't slide off, he marks a new way, and makes it possible for the next driver to follow his course. After a day or so of this, the new tracks, too, become bottomless. Soon, that entire stretch of road is impassable. Then we become pioneers and explore a new trail.

At almost no point is any of this road so sharply demarcated along the sides as to make leaving it difficult. So, when the way straight ahead looks like something out of *The Desert King*, the knowing traveler turns off to the right or left into the rabbitbrush and tumbleweed, and becomes a new-roadbuilder.

This road is not given to monotony. The rose beige of the sand and stone is striped here and there in black. These stripes, a quarter- or half-mile wide, are in dry weeks black corduroy. The first time we drove this way, we ran at soft-sand speed without warning onto one of these teeth-jarring stripes. We soon learned better. Then when we traveled the road after a rain, we quickly acquired real respect for these black booby traps.

A shower turns these black stretches into something resembling glass well-coated with liquid soap. A soil specialist would undoubtedly read some significance into the fact that the black formations stripe the road at somewhat low elevations. To drain some of these dips, culverts have been found to be desirable. However, when the road-builder came to a small stream bed taking a short cut across his road, instead of constructing a culvert to bridge it, he merely laid in a long, narrow packing box.

These box culverts have no guard rails at the ends, of course, and little or no contiguity with the road. They are none too strong, either. Most of them have at least one collapsed board in one of the tracks. These missing teeth are invisible until the moment before a front wheel drops into the trough. The doctors, the traders, the mail woman—all regular travelers of this road—have the broken boards memorized. They pull to the left or right as they come upon each box culvert. If the road is slick, these maneuvers require brilliant driving and a large helping of luck.

A real honest-to-goodness rain turns the black stretches of the road into bottomless quagmires. Approaching one of these, with a pair of tracks running into it and then waggling from side to side and becoming half a dozen pairs of intertwined tracks before disappearing under standing water, is enough to test the mettle of any driver. Sometimes only fools rush in.

Two or three fair-to-middling rains within a week had kept us close to Tselani. We were aware that some wagons and pickups were coming through on the road, but we were grateful when several days passed and no emergency required us to drive to the hospital. Then, the inevitable day came.

Fortunately, the sun had lain warm on the road all morning. The pretty, sunken-eyed young woman with the suspicious cough had probably delayed coming to see us for weeks or months since her symptoms began, but we didn't feel justified in lengthening the delay before treatment could be started. She agreed to go to the hospital for tests, if we'd take her.

We left Didi in charge at the Health Center with the promise that we'd deliver our patient, do a little shopping at the commissary, and come right back. We were sure we'd be back by two o'clock, or three at the latest.

The sun continued to shine as we made our way along the nicely packed ruts through the sand. The first black stretch of the road looked wet, but not soaked. The pickup slithered a little, but we kept going and that was that. The next black stretch is lower and some water stood in the ruts. However, we made it through, and even managed to miss the broken board in the box culvert. This began to look like our first uneventful trip to the hospital.

We delivered our patient and got her admitted for tests. We bought groceries at the commissary and filled the pickup's tank with gas. Then, we noticed a few sprinkles on our windshield.

"We'd better hurry," one of us said.

"Or else wait and see," the other suggested.

We decided to drive out beyond Hubbel's Trading Post, where we could see toward Tselani. When we got to the rise of land that served us as weather station, the sky to the north and east was blue and beguiling with meringue kisses floating here and there above Beautiful Valley. A blue-black cloud with raveled edges had, it was true, usurped the western half of the sky. The cloud, however, appeared to lie well to the west of our road and to be moving toward us at a lazy pace, if it were actually moving at all. We certainly didn't want to go back to Ganado, and deliberately give the cloud a chance to dump its contents on that already saturated road. We decided to outrun it. Older, more experienced hands might reasonably have made the same decision. The weather on the Reservation seems always perversely able to outguess both greenhorns and oldtimers.

That cloud had been waiting to see what we decided. We had no more than got beyond the last safe place for turning around, than the cloud made a bee line for us. A spatter of rain turned to a downpour.

I was driving—an arrangement that prevails in our family whenever driving conditions become precarious. Don has found that, in such cases, there is less criticism of the driver if I'm behind the wheel.

Neither of us expected too much difficulty any place except through those black stretches. Then we discovered that our sand, which had always behaved like sand and should have packed hard under this drenching, had developed new qualities. It was liberally mixed with fine blond clay. The pickup refused to stay in what appeared to be well-packed ruts.

However, the cloud had moved in on us so fast, and the rain was pelting down so hard, that we expected it to shoot its wad and move on across the road. We kept going for two good reasons—we expected to cut through the storm at any minute, and we couldn't turn back anyway. We took it easy and continued to stay on the road.

We slithered up over the crest of a hill, and saw a tall Navaho man beside the road. He wore no hat, only a red cotton scarf tied in a string around his head. He wore Levis and a purple rayon satin shirt drenched and pasted to his hide. He wagged his thumb at us, an expedient he probably wouldn't have resorted to except for the rain. This point on the road happened to be well enough drained for me to risk stopping.

The man ran up, ducked under the canvas cover on the bed of the pickup, and scrambled over the tail gate. He waved at us through the cab window to indicate that he was settled, and we started up with no trouble.

The rain persisted. We were getting near the first stretch of black roadway. I hoped against hope that the cloud had cut across this side of that hazard. Actually, by now, the cloud seemed to be everywhere. It had swallowed the meringue kisses in the eastern sky, and gone poking in all directions looking for more.

We climbed one of the roller-coaster humps and saw below us, gleaming like a long black mirror, our first ordeal by gumbo.

Our Navaho hitchhiker was up on his knees in the bed of the pickup, peering at the road through the rear window of the cab and the windshield. Don, with lifted hands and eyebrows, asked his opinion of trying to go forward. The Navaho's twitch of a grin warned us that to try it was foolhardy, but he nodded his head and flapped his hand, urging us ahead.

I managed to hold the wheels in the tracks that led into the black, oozing muck. Once we were in, however, the tracks deserted us. We slithered and slid and wallowed, first headed northwest, then northeast. Somehow we managed to miss the broken board in the box culvert. We finally emerged at the far end of the slough.

Our hitchhiker grinned from ear to ear through the window of the cab, and settled down cross-legged to enjoy his ride.

Suddenly the rain stopped. Don and I both drew a deep breath. I put the next black stretch of road out of my mind, and gave my full attention to the business of keeping the front wheels of the truck in those sandy-looking tracks that were proving so traitorously slick.

"We should have the chains on," Don said.

"It surely didn't rain much beyond this," I hoped aloud.

Then, at the bottom of the next depression, we could see the box culvert awash with red-brown water. Beside the black road, the grading ditches were flooded. For a quarter of a mile, our road looked like a shallow, elongated pond around and through which a herd of cattle had been milling.

My foot refused to press the accelerator. Our dying gait brought our passenger to his knees again behind us. He surveyed the situation without even a twitch of a grin this time, but he lost no time in rendering a decision. His hand flapped, ordering us forward, and then flapped sideways, directing us to stay to the right-hand side of the road.

We were beginning to get a little leery of letting this stranger prod us into one situation after another. If it hadn't been for the remembrance of the hog wallow behind us, I would have voted for backing the ten or twelve miles to Ganado, and waiting there for seven years of drought. Don and I discussed backing up, while the truck still rolled slowly forward.

"You made the last one all right," he said. "I guess you might as well stay to the right, the way the man says, and keep going."

On the right, muddy water swirled and boiled, gouging away at the side of the road, wherever the side was. I guessed where the edge might be, and pulled as far to the right as my conscience would allow. We mired down, but the truck growled and plowed relatively forward at various angles.

Then I spied the broken board at the right-hand side of the culvert. To go beyond it would have been to court disaster. I had no intention of trying to hold the soap-caked right wheel on the six-inch end of that box. Beyond the end of the box, the muddy, churning pool of water must have been at least three feet deep. My foot on the accelerator was eavesdropping on my indecision. Before I'd attempted to turn the wheels in order to pull to the left of the broken board, we started sliding. We slid to the far side of the road, graceful as a crab, and settled softly into the muck and running water. My unhopeful attempt to back out settled us a little deeper, and there we sat.

It should be said here, to the credit of all white and Navaho men, that no one in our party made any remark, even in sign language, about women drivers.

Don and I opened the cab doors, looked out, and simultaneously began taking off our shoes. When I stepped off the running board, water came to my kneecaps. My feet and ankles sank into cold, slimy mud that gave way like sand at the beach in the wake of a receding wave. I clung to the truck, and hoisted my corduroy skirt into a flora-dora apron effect, tucking the surplus into my belt. By pulling myself along the side of the truck, I made it to the back and shallower water and mud, but still treacherous footing.

From under the canvas truck-bed cover, slid a long bare foot, and then another. Our hitchhiker, Levis rolled to his knees, joined us in the road.

The first one to loosen his hold on the truck discovered that it was harder to remain upright than it had been to hold the pickup to a predetermined course. Our feet persisted in moving in an opposite direction from our intentions. We had to make all our movements like tightrope walkers.

I began trying to remember how many days it had taken the roads to dry out after our last big rain. I was considering sitting in the pickup for three days or so. Then I began figuring how long it would take us to walk, slipping and sliding, to Tselani.

Our hitchhiker, though, made a deliberate, squatting inspection of the three wheels that were available for inspection. The front left wheel was in a hole that had kept us from sliding into the left-hand grading ditch. The rear left wheel was buried halfway to the hub. The right rear rim was well below the top of the rut but the mud at this spot had enough gumption to hold its shape instead of closing in around our tire. The front right wheel stood high and dry, comparatively, in a shallow rut.

Our Navaho man stood up, balanced himself with his arms extended, and asked in sign language—lifting with his left arm, pumping with his right—whether we had a jack. Fortunately for us, our tool box had been stocked by an experienced hand. We found that we were carrying two jacks, a great many short lengths of two-by-fours, and a good set of chains.

For the driver who has been through it, an account of how we dug, laid a foundation, jacked, propped, and re-jacked in that slithering mass of supersaturated goo would serve as nothing more than a painful reminder. For the average driver of today, it would sound like a made-up tale, with mud layered on for effect.

The fact is, that for two hours and ten minutes, we dug, shoved, hoisted, pushed, and heaved. We tore our hands, yanking and twisting off branches of sagebrush for filling ruts. The men strained their backs, trying from uncertain stances to hoist those jacks. When we finally shoved and coaxed the second chain through the mud beneath the tire and stretched it around until we could link it in place, we had mud in our hair, mud in our ears, and mud in our mouths. We were ready to drop from exhaustion.

194

I stood on the running board and, using a screw driver, scraped as much mud as possible off the bottoms of my feet and from between my toes. Then, not daring to hope, I got behind the steering wheel, started the motor, and shifted into reverse. The wheels argued with the mud for a long moment and then, as if all the perverse gods in the world suddenly decided that we'd been through enough, the pickup shuddered onto our sagebrush mat, and rolled back onto firm footing.

The situation appeared so promising from this vantage point that I had a wild moment of believing that it would be possible to turn around. However, soberness soon returned. A ten-foot gumbo roadway with a small river running down each grading ditch, is not the place for too many acrobatics with a pickup. So we'd back out, I decided. We'd back all the way, if necessary, or at least until we got to a safe place for turning. I tapped the horn to call my passengers to me.

Instead of picking up their jacks and planks and coming sanely along, they stood in the muck at the right-hand side of the road ahead of me. Then, like a scarecrow caught by a south wind, that Navaho started waving me forward, back into that black pit from which I'd just been rescued. When I hesitated—giving Don time to tell him to mind his own business—the Navaho stepped gingerly to the middle of the road, flayed his arms to regain his balance, and motioned again for me to come on in. Don merely stood, arms outstretched, maintaining his balance.

"Of all the fool notions!" I thought, but I put the truck into low. I was too annoyed to care much whether I made it or not.

The pickup slithered and wallowed. The wheel jerked from my stinging hands. But I was tired and disgusted. I kept my muddy bare foot on the accelerator, and kept going. I hit the box culvert on the bias, headed for its abrupt end and certain disaster. At the last possible instant, the truck's nose responded to my pull on the wheel and came around. My right front wheel hit the broken board and dropped out from under me, but somehow it caromed out again and I was still under way. The chains on the rear wheels plowed into the muck for a hundred yards until they found some footing. The truck and I came to a halt only after we had reached the top of the nearest sandy rise of land.

While I waited for the men to collect our scattered belongings and bring them up, I rummaged around and found a box of cleansing tissues. I had dry-cleaned one foot when our Navaho friend arrived with a jack in each hand.

He laid the muddy jacks in the back of the truck.

I held the box of tissues toward him. He looked up and grinned.

With handfuls of tissues, we scrubbed at our legs and feet and finally pulled on our socks and shoes.

Don made two trips from the mudhole to the truck, salvaging planks. I knew he must be ready to drop, but I also knew that we had two more strips of black gumbo ahead of us, now that the die was cast and we were, regardless of our own wishes, headed for Tselani instead of back to Ganado.

When Don got some of the mud off his feet and we were loaded in the pickup again, I asked why on earth he'd ever let that Navaho talk him out of going back.

"He'd worked so hard, I didn't have the heart to tell him we weren't going to take him on home," he said. "Besides, he didn't seem to understand my signs for 'No'."

I remembered that the Navaho people had consistently refused to understand all signs meaning "No," from the time they entered the Southwest—possibly as early as 1100 A. D., perhaps in the sixteenth century—until President Lincoln's Secretary of War, Stanton, had sent Kit Carson, a pretty stubborn fellow himself, to interpret the signs.

Persistence can be an admirable trait when it is pointed in the right direction. Now that the Navahos have pointed themselves toward living with white men instead of against them, they can be expected to keep going forward, no matter what the odds.

We fought mud and slickness all the way, but an hour before dark we arrived at Tselani.

Our passenger ducked his mud-caked head from under the canvas, and climbed over the truck's tail gate. His grin seemed more clearly to say, "I told you so," than "Thank you." However, we felt that we were the ones to say, "Thank you," anyway, so we did. He grinned again, and strode off toward the trading post.

Thanks to him, we were home. Thanks to him, too, we were exhausted. As for that pickup, we were ready to leave it tethered to the juniper tree at our back door until the roads turned to dust again. We needed food and about twelve hours in bed.

That night, a seven-year-old girl took us on a snipe hunt.

CHAPTER FIFTEEN

Snipe Hunt

DIDI AND KEE had gone home some time before we got in from our trial by mud and Navaho persistence. Didi had left a note stuck in our screen door. I stopped on my way to the bathtub to read:

"We going home now. Everything O. K. Bah Billy needing shot penicillin. I catch her ride to Black Mountain. She might catch ride here, then you taking her home."

Don was measuring coffee into the percolator. "Everything all right?" he asked.

"Fine," I assured him. I started peeling off my jacket and skirt, along with large and small cakes of dried mud, as I went down the hall. "Oh, Bah Billy might come in," I called back. "She's the one we hauled to and from the hospital when she broke her arm, you remember. If she's late, we'll have to walk her down to her grandmother's hogan, but that's nothing."

"I might make it that far," Don said, "but not a step farther. If she comes while it's still light, we'll just point her in the right direction. It can't be more than two or three blocks down there to Sadie's hogan."

I hurried through my bath and called, "You're next," to Don. The scent of percolating coffee filled the house. I pulled on a clean denim shirt and skirt, and began to feel revived. "How would you like hamburgers?" I asked Don.

"Big," he answered as he shut the bathroom door.

We had each eaten one hamburger and drunk one mug of coffee when Don remembered that he hadn't turned on the porch light at the community house. We always left that light burning all night in case anyone should come looking for help. We'd been so occupied with our mud-removal projects that it had grown almost dark without our noticing.

"I'll go flick that light on, but I want six more hamburgers," Don warned and dashed out.

He should have been back in two minutes, at the most. I took another hamburger off the grill, and laid it on his plate. I filled his coffee mug. I went to the back door and peered out. Finally, when he didn't come, I ran across the yard to the other house.

I found Don, all right, and Bah Billy.

Bah Billy stood inside the community room door, her back against the wall.

"She was on the porch," Don told me. "She won't talk. I don't know how long she's been here."

"Well, never mind." I asked Bah Billy, "You want us to take you home?"

Her small chin lifted ever so slightly and fell.

"All right, come along. We'll have to go over to the other house to get our jackets."

We considered letting Bah Billy wait a bit longer while we finished our dinner; but we decided that if we hurried we could walk that three-block distance to Sadie's hogan and get back while the western sky still held its translucent green-gold glow. Then we'd be free to eat hamburgers and drink coffee without interruption till morning, if we felt like it.

Bah Billy stopped on our back step while we got our jackets and, as an afterthought, a flashlight. When we started out, she moved as far as our pickup, and there she stopped again.

"We're not going to take the car," I told her. "We've had all we want of it for one day. We'll walk."

Then was the time for Bah Billy to start using her school-learned English. Instead, she struck off ahead of us down the path toward her hogan, a straight little yard-stick of a figure, swinging ruler arms at her sides.

"A walk will do us good, after all that pushing and pulling and bending," one of us said. "Straighten out the kinks."

We lifted our tired shoulders and breathed deeply of the piñon-smoked air. Off to the right and just ahead, I could see the dark-domed outline of a hogan against the lighter sandstone hill behind it. Bah Billy's grandmother's hogan was even closer than I'd remembered.

But Bah Billy paid no attention to this hogan. Without looking to the left or right, she marched straight ahead.

"I guess there is one hogan between our place and Sadie's," I mused. I'm never too observing of landmarks. I followed meekly along behind Bah Billy.

The scent of piñon smoke thinned out, but soon it drifted to us rich and redolent again. Now we were within smelling distance of Sadie's hogan, and none too soon either. The western light had deserted us suddenly. Don, bringing up the rear of this little procession, was throwing the beam from his flashlight on the path at Bah Billy's feet. We had discovered that the beaten path gave fair footing, but each false step to the side proved as slick as the road had been that afternoon.

We were walking through what, in dry weather, we considered sand—it disintegrated like sand, blew in and drifted on our window sills like sand, gritted like sand in our teeth. Now, saturated as it was from the afternoon rain, this soil seemed to have in it about the proper amount of sand for an ultra-rich mixture of cement. When we stepped off the beaten path, our feet slid out from under us. If we took two or three steps in succession off the path, the cement mixture caked up on the bottoms and sides of our shoes. So we made every effort to watch where we stepped, and I was somewhat relieved to hear faint sketches of orchestra music as if from a battery radio or record player. Her grandmother's hogan must be near at hand, and we'd soon deliver Bah Billy and get on home to those hamburgers. The music came more clearly now. We must be nearing the side path that led off at a right angle to the hogan.

Then, in disbelief, I heard the music fray out. We had passed up that hogan!

I knew it was a long way to the next camp along this path. "Bah Billy, isn't that where you live—back there?" I asked.

Our rigid little guide marched straight ahead, without a word and without a break in her stride.

I stopped in the path and trapped Don behind me. "Bah Billy," I demanded, "how far is it to your hogan?"

We had to hurry to catch up. Striding ahead in the dark, the child had not faltered and she made no sound in answer to my question. We had no choice but to tag along, trying to light the path, and hoping that surely the next hogan would be her home.

Waves of piñon-scented air teased us only at long intervals now. A large, lopsided moon floated up behind a small red butte that we recognized. This butte, with one unmistakable, high-standing wind sculpture at its near edge, rose a mile and a half from our gate down the road to Ganado. We were still walking parallel to the road, then, and we'd already walked four times as far as we'd bargained for. The first promise of the moon to help light our way slipped beneath a dense, woolly-bear-shaped cloud.

Bah Billy, like a jointed doll, marched straight ahead.

Our path had been getting softer for some time now. Soon, while it was still a path in the sense that it could be distinguished as a snake-laid route through instead of over the sagebrush, it was not hard-packed. The cement mixture caked on our shoe soles with each step. For five or six steps, we kept getting taller and taller, and then without warning the layers on one foot would drop away and we'd have to scramble to keep from falling.

We'd stop, to try to scrape one shoe on the sagebrush, and the other foot would slide out from under us. By whatever method we managed to free our feet of their uncertain stilts, the layering process began all over again with the next step. When we delayed, we fell so far behind Bah Billy that we had to go loping with first one short leg and then another in order to catch up and keep her within following distance.

At intervals, we begged her to tell us where she lived, how much farther it was, and when she had moved from her grandmother's hogan where we'd taken her when she'd gone home from the hospital. Arms swinging stiffly at her sides, she trudged ahead. We couldn't get her to say one word.

We came at last to a slash in the earth that, when Don tossed his light across it, promised to turn us back. It was fifteen feet across— too far for jumping—and fifteen or twenty feet deep.

"Now what?" we asked each other.

Bah Billy never faltered. She angled slightly to the left and made a hairpin turn back to the right. Then she side-stepped along a reckless little angling ledge that somehow, even soaked as it was, continued to cling to the perpendicular side of the ravine.

We followed along like sheep, slogged through the water running in the bottom of the wash, and made our short-legged, long-legged way up the other side along another inclined shelf that Bah Billy knew how to find.

Then on we went, weaving through sagebrush that scratched my legs and tugged at my skirt, and proved to be no help whatsoever in removing our constantly accumulating mud casts. The

202

casts came off when they chose and always at the most unpredictable times.

The moon rode out from behind a cloud in time to show us another ragged, black cut through the plain before us.

"Oh no, not another one!" I objected.

But Bah Billy headed straight for it and down its side, across its muddy bottom, and up its other side. We were both ready to drop in our tracks. Our legs ached from lifting those loads of mud. We were breathing like fighters in the fourteenth round.

"We're going to stop and rest," I said. If Bah Billy couldn't understand that, let her march on in the dark without benefit of our flashlight!

Then we saw a light dead ahead. The light waggled, then it turned toward us. It was a strong flashlight, far stronger than ours. Still without saying one word, Bah Billy broke into a run toward the light. After a moment, the light turned away.

"Hey! Wait a minute!" I called out. "How can we get to the road from here?"

"How far is it to the road?" Don asked.

We waited for an answer. None came. Slowly, though, the light flashed back toward us and then it wagged up and down, seeming to direct us off at a right angle to our course.

Our questions had been understood, but no voice answered. A word or two, even in Navaho, would have humanized the darkness. We could have understood the word for "Thank you" even in Navaho, if anyone had cared to express appreciation for our returning Bah Billy to her home.

How far? An answer would have done us little good. A Navaho mile, you remember, is notoriously the length of a city block or ten miles. Later, in broad daylight we measured by speedometer the mile from the road to Bah Billy's parents' hogan. That night, with mud gumming up on our shoes at every step, with mud-and-water-filled ravines to cross because we couldn't see to avoid them, with every muscle in our bodies aching, and with the heavy knowledge that we'd been led on a snipe hunt by a seven-year-old girl who could but wouldn't speak English, that mile could have been ten.

The moon had lifted itself beyond reach of the clouds by the time we gained the road. That road four hours before had been slick and precarious beneath the wheels of the pickup. Now it lay before us, pale gold in the moonlight, and more or less solid beneath our feet. By keeping to the ruts, we could step without picking up a weight to carry on to the next step.

Even so, we had four more miles to walk before we reached home.

The odor of stale coffee and soggy hamburgers greeted us when we opened our kitchen door. We slid out of our shoes and headed for bed.

We had been taken for a ride and for a walk that day. We had not been thanked for our efforts. Both of our goaders had accepted as their due whatever they could, by insistence or silence, get us to do for them. True, our hitchhiker of the afternoon had somewhat paid his way in work, but most white men would have done as much, and few would have insisted that we go their way in the teeth of further danger and struggle.

Those *belliganos* who live and work with the Navahos are constantly at the Indians' mercy until they learn to throw up guards to protect themselves. The reasons for this are complex. Solutions to the situation can be as baffling and as elusive as trying to reason with the back of a marching yardstick.

We are avowed foes of generalization. To say that all Navahos are ungrateful for help would be as false as the old stolid, wooden Indian concept. We have been thanked profusely for even small favors. The same Navaho, however, who graciously thanks you for a twenty-cent can of peaches can be expected to urge you to use

your car and your gasoline to haul him fifty miles to town, regardless of whether or not you want to go to town. He will direct you
to the street corner where he wishes to stop, without regard to your
destination. He will get out of your car with no word of thanks and
will tell you when he wishes to be taken back home. He will expect
you to pick him up at the place he designates, and if he isn't there
at the time he has selected, you are supposed to wait. He will arrive
when convenient.

Perhaps the kindest and, at least partially true, explanation of
this almost general Navaho attitude is to be found in a look at family life and patterns on the Reservation. A family is not made up of
a mother and father and the offspring of these two. When a man
marries, he goes to make his home with his wife's relatives. All of
these relatives become his family. The family group, living alone
in its camp, separated normally by miles of grazing land from
neighboring family groups, becomes of necessity a kind of mutual
aid society.

Sheep and goats are usually owned by individuals. When they
are sheared, however, the wool is available to all the women in the
family for spinning yarn. The yarn is then available to all who
wish to weave rugs. When the rugs are taken to the store, the coffee
and flour and canned beans obtained in trade are used to feed the
entire family.

This principle applies within even wider relationships. A family
is always considered to include grandparents, uncles, aunts, fifty-
second cousins, and both the legitimate and illegitimate children
of all these. A Navaho who refuses to render aid to any member of
his family immediately becomes a pariah among members of his
near and extended family group, and among all other Navahos as
well. A common admonition against laziness or any unacceptable
behavior is, "Do you wish to shame your family?"

The house in which we were living on the Reservation had been built for an interpreter, you remember. The purpose of keeping an interpreter on the Health Center grounds was to enable the non-Navaho-speaking nurse to understand and respond, twenty-four hours a day, to calls for help. When the house was finished, an interpreter and her husband moved in. Soon they had a baby. The interpreter needed her mother and sisters to help care for the baby while she worked. The mother and sisters and brothers and uncles and aunts all moved into the house.

If the interpreter had refused to let them move in, everyone would have said that she had turned her back on her family—a disgraceful crime—and that she had turned her back on the ways of her people—a form of treason.

Suppose the nurse had insisted that no one but the interpreter's immediate family (as white men reckon it) was to live in the house. Soon women would have begun talking about the interpreter behind their shawls, saying that she was stuck-up. When she went to the trader's and bought red rayon velvet for a new blouse, someone could have been counted on to mention the fact that she had become exceptionally rich in a short time—didn't she have a white man's house to live in with water running in pipes, and money to buy red velvet?

Next, the word for "witch" would have been passed around at the store and at ceremonials. The nurse would soon have heard rumors that her interpreter was bootlegging Tokay wine to her patients. The Navaho people will not let one of their number suffer without rendering aid, but neither will they let one of their number lift himself too far above the level of the group.

The next logical step to most Navaho minds seems to be: if a white man comes into our Reservation to help us, we'll put up with his help. If he has acquired a good car, he has done so by virtue of the gods' (or witches') smiling on him. We will gladly help him quiet his uneasiness over his luck by riding in his undeserved good fortune with him.

Perhaps, as a nation, we have offered help as a means of easing our consciences for the sins of history. Many of our tribes of Indians have long since stopped expecting our acts of atonement to fall into their laps.

The Navahos, because of their dress and distinctive hair styles, are colorful, and so they have attracted much attention. Then, too, they have also remained through the years self-contained and aloof. No one is quite as intriguing to many do-gooders as the person in need of help who proudly stands on his own two feet, and maintains that he can get along. Those people who sop up sympathy like a sponge and beg for more soon wear out their sympathizers. It is the brave, stout-hearted needy who spur us to incessant efforts on their behalf.

Perhaps the Navahos have learned this lesson in psychology. More likely, as a result of tribal experience, and hence by nature, they are more independent than most peoples. If so, every red-blooded American of pioneer heritage should stand up and cheer. Instead, our efforts to help the Navahos, in spite of our intentions, have resulted in making them dependent.

Sentimentalists are given to attacking the "Indian problem" with handouts of used clothing and sporadic outpourings of pity. Hard-headed realists are inclined to say, "We've done enough for the Indians. Let's leave them on their own."

Some place between these two extremes stand those who know the Navaho people and would like to see them attain standards of living—social, economic, and moral—on a par, at least, with those of Americans generally. They do not wail and bemoan the hardships borne by the Navahos during their four years at Fort Sumner. Conditions there were, indeed, deplorable. General Carlton, however, did what he could with what he had. The Navaho people were nursing a grudge. Because of it, they refused to learn English, they refused to learn farming; they cut off their noses to spite their faces.

Those who know the Navahos and their history are well aware

that the United States promised, by treaty, a schoolhouse and a teacher for every thirty children between the ages of six and sixteen, and that the government made very little effort to meet this obligation. However, they also know that the promise was unrealistic—words written at a desk in Washington by one who knew nothing about distances and water limitations on the Reservation, and nothing about the temper of the Navaho old-timers.

The Navahos themselves know that had the government laid out section lines all over the Reservation and placed a checker-man schoolhouse on every other square, the parents of 1868 and of 1900 and of 1940 would not have sent their children to school. But a horse that wouldn't have drunk anyway can still stir up a lot of sympathy by pointing out that he was led to a dry trough.

Navahos are still being "helped" on this very day by traders who pocket a big bite out of a government check as a fee for running the risk of cashing it. They are being "helped" by the Public Health Service of the Department of Health, Education, and Welfare of the United States government with expensive medical care for which they are charged nothing because the Department doesn't have the staff for figuring out equitable fees.

These extremes of exploitation and mollycoddling affect Navahos the same as they affect a child who knows that his father will spank him for fighting, but that his mother will cuddle him and serve him three kinds of dessert for dinner. He is cantankerous for what he can get out of it, and when he gets a little, he expects a little more.

We have been ridiculously slow to recognize that the Navahos are human beings with innate dignity. Because we have been so slow and so obtuse, the Navahos also are somewhat in need of relearning this fact about themselves.

They will relearn it. They are on their way.

When three thousand Navahos returned from World War II and said, "Our children must be educated, they must learn to speak

English, they must take their place in American life," schools appeared as if by magic on the Reservation. Today, going to school has become socially acceptable and the father or grandfather who turns thumbs down is an oddity.

When Tsosie and Hasbah and Bah Billy are equipped for making their own way in the world, it can be expected that they will no longer find it necessary to impose on white people by way of getting even for wrongs done their grandparents. They will no longer lean on white people by way of getting something for nothing. Then, and only then, can the Navahos' traditional and inherent self-reliance be released to pour its needed stamina into the common stream of American character.

CHAPTER SIXTEEN

Readin', Writin', and Rhythmitic

BILLY JOHN WAS A NATURAL. The nurse had mentioned him to us. She'd said something casual such as, "Some of the boys will come around to play basketball, I'm sure. Billy John will come, I'm positive. He couldn't stand it not to come." Something about the shine in her eyes when she said his name gave us the clue that Billy John was special.

Drop everything and go to your nearest high school. Watch the boys at football skirmish, especially when they're on their own with no coach around. Watch basketball practice, or tennis, or swimming. In any large group of high school boys, it's a fairly sure bet that you'll find one who stands out.

He's a six footer at sixteen. He has outgrown his adolescent awkwardness, if he ever passed through that phase. He has mastered the crawl and is inventing swim strokes with which he is swimming circles around every other boy in the pool. He understands football signals before they're called. He handles a tennis ball as if he were controlling it by radio. Toeing the free throw line and shooting baskets is nothing to him. He has that down pat. Instead, he turns his back to the hoop, and makes baskets by shooting upside down and blind between his legs.

Photo by Arthur Dodd

"The young ones must learn English.
This is a thing we found out when we went to war"
Children leaving home for boarding school

Photo by Arthur Dodd

"The Navahos have been swallowing education in great gulps"
Mother and daughter on graduation day

This boy, in your high school, is in the swing of things. He's always there when the ball is. He's graceful and eager and out ahead of the pack. He adds sport to every sport. He proves with every move he makes that this is the way human beings are intended to function.

This boy, among the troup of young Navahos who hung out at the Health Center, was Billy John. He was good at everything he tackled and proud of it, but he wasn't a show-off. He had found the rhythm of life and swung into it, as when a child he no doubt stood swaying to discover the tempo and then ran in to jump the rope being turned by two of his brothers.

Billy John looks very little different from that boy you can pick as outstanding in your high school. Slender as a yucca stalk, he usually dressed in a tight-fitting sport shirt or T-shirt and Levis that might have been put on with a trowel. He kept his hair—sun-faded from black to brown—cut in a "butch." His skin was the color of any boy's who spends his summer vacation on a farm or tennis court. He had a ready smile and a long-billed blue cap, which he frequently resettled by flipping it up in the back and then scooting it up the ridge of his nose and back along his forehead until his free hand could smooth it down behind. He had quick, good-humored eyes, and that flowing rhythm that made everything come right for him.

Billy John had never been to school.

He could not write his name. He could not pick up a book in English or in Navaho or in anything at all and make sense of even one printed word. He could not read a pay check. He could not read the notice of a public meeting. Billy John was a natural. He could have licked the world with both hands tied behind him, but Billy John was illiterate.

He had not been too shy to come look us over—politely, of course, without our knowing that we were being looked over—our first day at Tselani. He came in, looking a bit pleased with his own bravery, settled his cap just behind his right ear, and picked up a Ping-pong paddle.

Don was free, and he moved to the far end of the table. A game—not a score-keeping game, just batting balls back and forth—began of spontaneous combustion.

Billy John had evidently picked up Ping-pong with no instruction and a rather inept example to follow. He hadn't batted more than a dozen balls to Don until he changed his grip on the paddle. After a dozen more practice shots, he got the "feel" of the new grip, loosened up his swing, and was soon giving back all he was taking.

Shooting baskets from impossible angles, hampered by an incinerator almost on the court area, a gnarled juniper tree, and an intruding spectator's bench, was far too tame a sport for Billy John. He loved to ride through our gate on his dappled gray horse when the other boys were shooting baskets. Once more like jumping rope, he'd pull up on the sidelines and sit, getting the "feel." Then he'd ride in, swing down hanging by one stirrup, scoop up the basketball, and gallop to the far hoop to shoot a basket.

He had trained his horse, without having read a book on the subject, to stand ground tied on command, to rear, to buck. But one day the horse was frightened by the uranium ore truck that regularly passed our place. Billy John was drinking at the small miracle beside the community house, a bubbler, and didn't notice until his horse was well on her way across our yard and off into the wide, wide world. Billy John swiped the back of his hand across his dripping mouth, and broke into a gallop. He caught up with his horse just as she started between the rough-hewn posts that marked our gateway. With split-second timing and no more than half-inches to spare, he leaped into the air, landed with his left foot in the near stirrup, and swung into his saddle. It was a performance that a dare-devil rider in a circus would have practiced for months before attempting.

Billy John could beat either of us at checkers and frequently did, but we couldn't talk to him, apart from signs and laughter, except through an interpreter. We would have given anything in the world to be able to wave a wand and make it so that Billy John had been to school for the past ten years, so that he could have the opportunity to develop one or a dozen of his many talents, so that his wonderful ability to swing with the rhythm of the universe could find an outlet that would so surely benefit the entire country. Never before had we felt personally frustrated by a treaty between any tribe of Indians and the United States government. Now we did. We didn't actually expect to set everything right, but in order to understand just why Billy John and thousands of his generation had been cheated out of an education, we started probing.

We found a copy of the treaty signed by Andrew Johnson, President of the United States, and by honored members of the Navaho tribe who were at the time captives held by force at a military fort three hundred miles from their homeland. We had known that in this treaty the government had promised to provide schools for Navaho children. With mounting anger, because of Billy John, we read the words in black and white, "The United States agrees that for every thirty children between said ages, who can be induced or compelled to attend school, a house shall be provided, and a teacher competent to teach the elementary branches of an English education shall be furnished."

"Why hadn't we (meaning our government) done what we'd promised?" we asked each other.

That "why" set us to asking nosier and nosier questions. It finally brought us to a brilliant conclusion that isn't exactly original. Namely, there are two sides to most arguments. The school argument, on the Navaho Reservation, has been debated for close to a hundred years. And, we discovered, one side is fully as responsible as the other for the fact that Billy John got to be sixteen without cracking a book.

The government tried to turn the Navahos' captivity at Fort Sumner into a kind of boarding school experience for the tribe. The food was "foreign" and therefore distasteful to The People. It was also in short supply. Living arrangements were miserable. So, pupils went to their agriculture classes in a disgruntled frame of mind and with empty bellies.

The laboratory equipment provided by the government, iron shovels and plows, should have been a stimulating revelation to The People. They had never seen such tools. But what captives have ever been overcome with admiration for the chains of their captors? The freedom-loving Navahos no doubt leaned on their iron shovels while their eyes gazed into the distance beyond that tiresome, flat land toward their beloved mesas and valleys. Captive children have always gazed through school windows toward freedom, until some spark of fact or vision flared up to light their way to freedom in the opposite direction.

And so the Navahos refused to learn. Not only did they refuse to learn the art of tilling the soil, they refused to learn anything from their captors. They finally added to their non-collaboration program enough nagging to get themselves that treaty duly bearing greetings from President Andrew Johnson. It offered them a chance to go home, and never mind the terms.

Most treaties, and especially those made between the United States government and various tribes of Indians, seem to be punctuated with loopholes instead of periods. The "school article" in this one had a two-way dilly. The words "induced" and "compelled" served the Navahos, who had no intention of sending their children to school; and the same words served the government, which had more to do than act as truant officer to three thousand small but well-indoctrinated sheep herders.

The first time a mother, tightly wrapped in her Pendleton shawl, came to us with a wheezing, under-dressed child, we suggested that since she and her husband were on their way to Gallup they might stop at the Ganado hospital. Tentatively I predicted that the doctor would be able to give little Desbah a shot that would cure what looked and sounded to me like imminent pneumonia. Didi interpreted my suggestion, this mother spoke to four-year-old Desbah, telling her, I discovered later, all that I had said.

Desbah broke into terrified screams.

Her mother giggled and cooed reassuring sounds that I could have interpreted myself even before Didi told me that the child didn't like to get a shot so they wouldn't stop at the hospital.

"But she needs to see a doctor," I objected. "All I can do is give her aspirin."

Didi carried on a brief interchange with the mother, and turned to me. "She say, 'Do that then. She taking the aspirin.' "

I sighed. "It isn't enough. She ought to see a doctor." I did get a box of children's aspirin from the medicine cabinet. "She should take one of these now, before they go on in that old, breezy pickup. But she still should see the doctor when she gets to Ganado." I got a paper cup of water. "Ask whether Desbah can swallow a pill," I told Didi.

"She say, 'No. She don't liked swallow that pill,' " came the roundabout answer.

"All right, get me a spoon and we'll smash it up for her." I was trying to keep the impatience out of my voice. I felt sure that this mother could interpret impatience in my tone as easily as I could interpret indulgence in hers.

Desbah nibbled at a crumb of the aspirin crushed in the spoon, screwed up her face, and pushed the spoon away.

"We must get this down her," I said to Didi. "Suppose you try."

Didi had very little chance to try. The mother cringed as the child whimpered. When Desbah started to wail, her mother gathered her inside her striped brown shawl, and prepared to leave.

"Is she going to the hospital after all?" I asked.

Didi followed her to the door. When they got outside, Desbah's cries came to an abrupt stop.

"She say her little girl don't liked to swallow that medicine," Didi reported, "and she guess she going to be all right."

This was one of many experiences we had with indulgent Navaho parents. The fact is that Navaho children curl their parents around their little fingers. They have done so down through history and they will probably continue to do so far into the future.

Navaho parents, in the summer of The Treaty, did not "induce" or "compel" their children to do anything that the children themselves did not wish to do, with the possible exception of herding sheep. Certainly they would not induce or compel their children to attend school conducted in English, the language of the enemy, when they saw no reason for school, and when they needed the children at home to help make the family's living.

What young Hashké, knowing his parents' hatred for anything having to do with the enemy white man, would hesitate when asked, "Do you want to go to the white man's school?"

Hashké didn't want to go to the enemy school, and neither did Kee nor Willie nor Hasbah nor Nellie.

Naturally, if thirty pupils from one area could not be induced to attend school, the government felt no need to provide a schoolhouse and a teacher competent to teach the elementary branches of an English education.

The Navahos went all-out against schooling.

Three thousand children between six and eighteen played hooky on the Navaho Reservation in the year of The Treaty. Ten years later, with the child population booming, four thousand boys and girls were playing hooky. It took another ten years to induce (I'm sure they were not compelled) thirty-five boys and girls to attend school.

"But this was in the last century," you object. "We were all a little backward in those days."

216

Maybe so, and yet the "brains" at Harvard University in those days might not agree with you. They had celebrated their two hundred and fiftieth anniversary two years before. In any case, the end of World War II is within the memory of many present-day high school pupils. In that year, over twenty thousand school-age Navahos were out of school, while only sixty-five hundred were attending school. It was not until the year 1950, halfway through the present century, that Navaho children became divided almost evenly— half in and half out of school. Since then, however, the out-of-school percentages have been running downhill like spilled milk. By 1957, for every ninety-one boys and girls sitting at shiny new school desks, only nine were out herding sheep.

Don't imagine that World War II suddenly changed all Navahos into stern parents who told their children what they must do. Navaho children still do pretty much as they please, but today most of them please to go to school.

Thinking of Billy John, we were curious as to how this reversal had come about, and still regretful that it hadn't come early enough to include him. We knew that down through the years since The Treaty, various agents and officials had done their best to sell the Navahos on education. We knew that different church groups had succeeded, early in the nineteen hundreds, in establishing a few schools, and the government had managed to round up enough pupils to justify one or two boarding institutions. Dogged, dedicated men and women who saw possibilities in the Navahos drove in the entering wedge. In addition, most of those who attended these first schools probably carried good reports back home. More than likely they at least said, "It is easier than herding sheep all day."

But when young Zonnie came home for school vacation, Hastiin Yazzie regularly went to his favorite "singer" of Blessing Way, arranged to pay in sheep and velvet material the price of the "sing," and notified his relatives that he would like to have them come help purify his daughter after her long contact with the enemy.

Going to school, therefore, didn't really catch on in a large-scale way until Navahos in uniform returned to the Reservation from the South Pacific and from the European Theater, until Navahos drove home from Los Angeles and Phoenix and Albuquerque in brand-new pickups and first-hand leather jackets and twenty-dollar Stetsons.

Those who had stayed on the Reservation—herding sheep, planting little patches of corn and melons, harvesting their peaches, gathering herbs—said, "Our young people are going to the coyotes. They are a disgrace to our old ones. They have dipped into the pot of the white man's civilization, and now they no longer relish mutton stew."

The young men squatted by a hogan fire, one knee up and one knee down, and reminded the old men, sitting cross-legged on their sheepskins, of the story passed down from the time of Kit Carson's ruthless roundup.

"You remember," they said, "how the leaders among our old ones tied a goat to a tree, and made the people walk by to watch it butting itself to death. 'It is just as crazy as this for the Navahos to hold out against the white man,' they said."

Little by little, as the Navahos heard it in their own language, from the mouths of their own young men, schools began to be talked around bubbling, fat-fragrant pots of mutton and corn. Schools were talked in the Tribal Council. Schools were talked at the windmills and beside corrals. It was like a revival meeting. Navahos by the thousands were getting converted to schools. These were going out, converting others. The Navaho people themselves were taking the responsibility. Schools were no longer something that Washington wanted them to have. Now schools were something they wanted on their own, and meant to get.

Miles from a real road, at a hogan remote from everything, a Navaho friend interpreted for us the words of a four-year-old with laughing black eyes and cheeks he could barely see over. "When I get two-more-year big," he said, "I going school and buy my mama big blue pickup."

Perhaps it is the four-year-olds, wide-eyed and on tiptoe, who have given schools their social standing among many peoples down through the ages. Or possibly credit goes to adults who look back with longing on their school days.

We attended a high school basketball game at Ganado and saw one way in which this looking back can affect adults who have never been to school. Spectators began arriving that night by foot, by wagon, by pickup, by horseback an hour before the starting whistle. Boys in the dorm started nagging their house mother: "Mom, my folks outside. May I going now?"

By game time, excitement on the campus had reached the boiling point. Parents and friends and relatives of pupils couldn't possibly resist it. They ate it with the popcorn they bought at the door of the gym. They drank it down with their bottle of room-temperature pop.

When the whistle blew, the teams gave their all. On the sidelines, grown-ups who had never been permitted a chance to knock themselves out for their school, made up for lost time.

On several previous silent meetings we had been intrigued by one man, who frequented the Ganado campus. His tall, lean figure, his imperturbable bearing, every smooth, deliberate move that he made told us that here was a man who wore with pride the heritage of his tribe. He kept his hair long, always freshly hanked and wrapped with yarn, but it took a bit of doing to see it. He invariably wore a soft, buff-colored, broad-brimmed hat with a higher-than-usual crown adorned with a silver band and a turquoise buckle. The heavy nuggets of turquoise that dangled from his ear lobes were easier to see beneath his hat brim. If molten copper had been cast sparingly over his handsome bone contours, he could not have looked more like a statue of the "old way" Navaho. We had asked about him, and learned that he was actually "old way" to the core. Still, his son attended Ganado High School and played basketball on the first team.

Watching this father that night, we saw him break out of his cast. He gobbled down popcorn in his nervousness when the opposing team pulled out in front. He jerked off his beautiful hat and beat it on his knees. He yelled and urged his favorites on. He stood up, holding his breath, when his son tried a free throw. He laughed. He sighed. He moaned. He flung his hat in the air.

Forty-five years earlier he would have made an unbeatable player. That night, he played with the same heart as the boys on the team. He couldn't have helped looking back, wondering what might have been, if he had gone to school, if he had played this game, if he had learned to speak the foreign words that his son now tripped off the tip of his tongue as if talking English were nothing at all.

The younger boys' house mother with whom we sat ran our handsome Navaho, and every other Navaho in the gym, a close second in her sideline enjoyment of the game. She was born and reared a down-Easterner with an accent straight out of Bar Harbor. She has a heart that crowds an ample, motherly bosom, and a sense of humor that frequently overrides her inbred sense of propriety. Her boys adore her. They call her "Mom." They borrow money from her, call on her to intercede for them with the principal, weedle her into doing their mending, send for her—no matter how many years after they have left school—when they get in jail, or want a witness for their weddings or a godmother for their children, or when they need a reference in order to get a job.

At basketball games her boys watch for her approval and listen for her shouts of warning or encouragement. She stews herself into a lather every time the ball is worked down the floor. She dies with every missed goal, and revives with a squeal of joy at every brilliant play.

220

When the Ganado boys finally won the game, Mom stood up and stretched her wings. In her best broad-*a*, down-East accent she said, "Oh, for the land sakes, I'm going right home and give every boy on the team a vitamin pill." She took two steps toward the door, and stopped. "On second thought, I guess I'd better take one myself, too." She turned to us. "Come on over. It's time for the boys to go to bed. I'll just have to read a story to the little ones, and then we can visit. That dorm gets quiet as a tomb after nine o'clock."

We climbed the steps in Mom's wake. She led us through the boys' parlor, deserted now, along the hall, and into her apartment.

We could hear the usual boy noises in the two big sleeping rooms opening on the hall, but the fever-pitch excitement of the game had died out quickly. Water ran in the bathrooms, a titter of laughter came through the walls, sneakers whispered and scuffed on bare wooden floors—these were the sounds of fifty boys getting ready for bed.

A youngster with touseled, curly hair and a turned-up nose brought in a left-over nickel for Mom to bank. A tall Freshman with an elaborate, drake-tailed hair arrangement came to the door and, seeing us there on Mom's sofa, began shifting his weight from one foot to the other. Finally, he found the courage to stammer, "Mom, I ran out of pomade. Could you . . . ?" An eight-year-old ran in, clutching his unbuttoned Levis, and blurted, "Mom, did you fixing my pajamas yet?"

Mom introduced each boy to us as he appeared at the door, and then took care of his problem. As soon as possible, she went to her refrigerator for her vitamin bottle and came out, gulping down a capsule as she headed for the boys' sleeping rooms. "I won't be ten minutes," she promised. "The little tykes think they can't go to sleep 'thout I read, but I'll cut it short tonight."

Don and I sat comparing this peace and quiet with the tales we'd heard of rowdy, boarding school boys.

221

"It would take an hour to calm down a bunch of white boys after a game like that," Don commented.

Mom reappeared in no time flat, and dumped herself into her wide-lapped rocker. "Well, that's that," she sighed. "What a game! Wasn't my little Winfield terrific? I gave him two vitamin pills."

"You're sure they weren't sleeping pills?" Don asked. "Or do you just go around and bop each boy on the head at bedtime?"

"They're good boys," Mom said, with just the kind of indulgent smile on her face that we'd seen on the faces of mothers, both white and Navaho, all our lives.

Her words had barely escaped when we heard a sound that could have been caused by the wind, or by the moving of a dresser. We froze and listened. A dull thud came next.

Mom toed around, searching for her kicked-off loafers and frowning toward the door. "What in the world?"

The next thud came, unmistakably, from one of the sleeping rooms.

Mom couldn't wait to get into her second shoe. One on and one off, she tore down the hall and flung open the door on the right. We were at her heels.

The boys' room was in an uproar. Two mattresses were on the floor. When we appeared, boys scattered from a giggling huddle and made long dives for their individual beds. The few who were caught in incriminating immobility, no longer needed to cover their mouths with their hands to muffle their laughter. They went suddenly sober.

"Well, I never!" Mom commented.

Then, at the end of her pointing finger, the boys restored the room to order. Finally, with each boy's frightened eyes peering up at her over his sheet drawn high beneath his chin, she said, "To-morrow, instead of play period after school, you are all to come in and write fifty words on 'Why I was out of bed after lights out.'"

We retreated to Mom's apartment before we dared enjoy a laugh.

But we left soon with the promise that we'd be back the next night to read those papers.

We discovered the next night that Navaho boys at boarding school are boys at boarding school. The only differences between these and any other boys arise from complications due to language mishaps and from the unfamiliar taboos of the white man, especially of white house mothers.

Mom patted a stack of yellow pages on her desk. "I've waited to read them until you got here," she said.

We each took half a dozen sheets and settled down to read.

"Listen to this," I said, and read aloud:

" 'After the light turn off I should not go any of the bed or not talk. Last night I was talk and laughing and took off the mattress from a boy bed. After I run to the bath room and wet towel and clouth and throw them to the boys. And jump on the bed and jump from the table to my bed. When Mom back we were still laughing and talk.' "

"Jumped from the table to his bed?" Mom exclaimed. "Whose paper is that? Why I had no idea they'd tried that. Somebody will get hurt." She rocked back with her hands folded on the sheaf of papers in her lap. "That's the trouble. Every time I punish them by having them write on what they've done, I find out all these other things they're doing that I didn't know anything about. Jump from the table to his bed, indeed!" She started to read again, but Don stopped her.

" 'I should do after nine o'clock is go to sleep and no talk or running around,' " he read. " 'After the lights go off we should keep quiet and nobody should go into the wash room. And nobody should throw things around to each other. Nobody should turn the bed over or pull the mattress down on floor. And nobody should throw the blanket around too.' "

"Turn the bed over, of all things!" Mom muttered, but her eyes were fixed on the paper in her hand, and her face was crinkling in laughter. She had to keep wiping laugher tears from her eyes as she read: " 'I was out of bed because it tickle between my toes, so I started to get up, then I went to the washroom to wash my feet. At the same time Lee went in to. When I was washing my feet Lee started to wash his feet too. So we wash our feet and went out. Next time I will go to bed after the light out. I will don't run round to people bed. I will don't throw bed round. I will be behave at night. I will don't turn on the light.' "

Aside from variations in spelling (and I have no doubt that boys at the Lawrenceville Prep School have variations of their own), these could have been the excuses and reasons and promises of any boys anywhere. One of us made some such comment.

Mom reached over and picked another punishment assignment off her desk. "I'll say they're like boys anywhere. I've been saving this one from my last batch to read to you." She adjusted her spectacles. "They were running in the dorm this time when I caught them."

She read: " 'I will not run in here because I don't do it at home that is because we don't have enough boys to play with. Here at school we have enough boys to play with that is why we do it, it's a rule not to do it too. At home I am always tired that is why I don't run but here I don't get tired excepted on Sat. and Sun.' "

Mom interrupted herself to remind us that Saturday and Sunday are work days, when chores are performed by the boys in part payment of their board and room, and then read on:

" 'I don't run at home because we don't have as many beds in one big room but here we have it liked that, that is why we liked to run and have fun instead of doing something else. I should not run in the dormatory because it disturds people who are studling. I will not run anymore and I will try and do other things than running.' "

A scream from somewhere down the hall brought Mom to her feet. "What in the world?"

Then a door banged, and on another scream, Mom's apartment

224

door burst open. Four feet of blazing-eyed indignation stood before us. "Mom! Tsosie Joe almost nearly threw me right into the piss bowl!"

Mom's mouth fell open and it took her a long moment to locate her voice. "McKinley!" she finally gasped in horror.

"Yes'm," McKinley answered, and flicked a quick, worried glance over his shoulder.

Mom drew a deep breath. "McKinley, I want you to watch your language," she said.

"Yes'm." McKinley continued to stand in the doorway.

We knew that Mom was smothering in held-back laughter.

She managed to say, "You may go now."

Still the boy stood. "Yes'm," he said.

"Well!"

"But, Mom! Tsosie Joe did almost nearly—"

"McKinley! Go!"

"But he's still in there—in the washroom—and I got to—"

"McKinley!" Mom turned him around and propelled him from the room. She got her apartment door shut before we all exploded. When she could speak again, she was once more the indulgent mother. "The way they live in their hogans it's no wonder that a spade comes out an unvarnished spade now and then. At home their humor, and believe me there's plenty of it, is largely what we'd call obscene. On the whole, my boys do mighty well."

Excuses, promises, forbidden words slipping out, and a house mother taking your side, making excuses for you that you can't think of yourself—these are the fun and the worry and the privileges of boarding school whether at Staunton or Ganado Mission. These are the experiences that our Billy John had never known. Private schools are expensive, depending on how much a dad can raise, whether it's three thousand or a hundred dollars a year.

Billy John's dad could not afford private school, and although Bureau of Indian Affairs boarding schools are free, Billy John could not be spared from home all the time. He was needed evenings and weekends to help with the sheep and horses. But if he'd been born just ten years later, he could have gone, would almost inevitably have gone, to day school.

Once the Navahos themselves took on responsibility for the situation, they got twenty-five million dollars appropriated for educational purposes. Since 1950 this money has bought light, airy, wide-winged school buildings with big, modern kitchens serving hot lunches, with pianos and the latest style school desks and play equipment and libraries. It has bought big yellow school buses that somehow manage to make impossibly long, treacherous rounds over everything from paved highways to sheep trails. The money has built attractive, modern apartments for teachers. It has converted Quonset huts into school dining rooms and classrooms. It has brought in trailers equipped with blackboards and desks and ruffled curtains. It has brought in trailers equipped with toilet and shower facilities, and dug wells in order that toilets and showers might be used. It has brought in trailers for teachers' homes.

The Navahos themselves have provided the magic that has turned seventy-five thousand "No's" into a loud, concerted "Yes." From the four-year-olds on remote corners of the Reservation, to the most venerable delegates to the Tribal Council, Navahos have gone "whole-hog" for education. The children are taking to school as a coyote takes to prairie dogs. If only Billy John had waited to be born!

We visited the new public school at Ganado the week it opened. We saw a class of non-English-speaking five-year-olds getting their first language lessons under a teacher who has lived on the Reservation, as teacher and trader's wife, for years. She began with sign language—using the signs established and generally accepted for trading Indians out of beaver skins all over the Far West in the early days.

A month later, these children of illiterate parents were reading

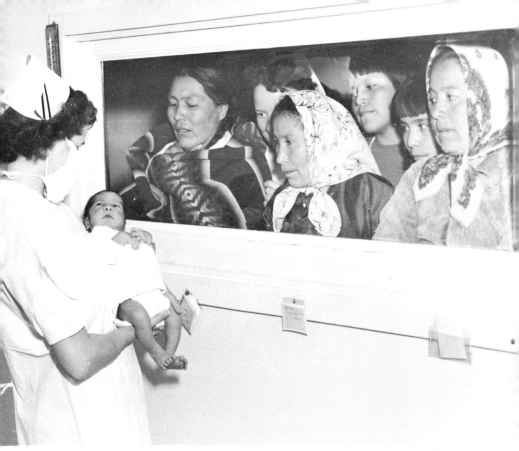

Photo by Arthur Dodd

Still the best news in any language, anywhere: the new generation

Opening the new school at Ganado, later enlarged one-half

words from flash cards and doing simple two-plus-twos. They were saying, " 'Scuse me," when they passed in front of visitors on their way to the drinking fountain, and making up reasons for passing in front of visitors so they'd have the opportunity of saying, " 'Scuse me."

We watched classes arrive in the music room that first day—classes made up of shy youngsters from deep on the Reservation. Within ten minutes, a willow-wand teacher whose heart obviously beats in four-four time had them limbering up their twists and squats on action songs and then softly trying out the strange word sounds on their tongues. Those youngsters were catching rhythm the way children born earlier on the Reservation caught diphtheria.

A month later, we stood in the hall outside the dining room at this school as classes were dismissed, and the children lined up to march by the serving windows for their trays. Singing as they waited, they all but raised the new green roof with:

> *One little, two little, three little Indians,*
> *Four little, five little, six little Indians . . .*

One little, ten little, twenty-five thousand little Indians are going to school. They are going to trailer schools, boarding schools, Bureau-operated reservation day schools, reservation public schools, public schools in towns around the edges of the Reservation, mission schools, and to several off-reservation boarding schools.

Here, at last, is a chance for Billy John!

For adolescent Navahos who were growing up during the days when their people were going all-out against education, a special five-year program has been set up, and Billy John is going to school. He has been taken by bus to Riverside, California, and he is now a Sherman boy. Within five years, he is expected to learn to read and write English. He is expected to learn a vocation. Above all, he is expected to learn how to get along with people off the Reservation.

This is expecting a lot of a strapping young boy whose social

227

habits have long since been formed. But we are betting on Billy John. Other adolescent boys and girls who served as guinea pigs for the Special Program did as much as three years' academic work and achieved over three years' development in personality and social adjustment in one school year. We predict that Billy John will break records at Sherman and, if he chooses, go on to college.

College? For a people who have for only ten years believed wholeheartedly in the first grade?

The Superintendent of Ganado Mission asked for a conference with the Tribal Council's Committee on Education.

"Just what do you want in our high school curriculum?" he asked. "Would you like for us to give more attention to developing vocational skills and practical, everyday work abilities?"

"No, no, no!" the Navahos answered to a man. "We want just what you've been doing, only more so. We want you to prepare our boys and girls for college. Don't waste their time with farm work and work in the shop. Government schools do plenty of that. You teach our boys and girls mathematics and history and science. They must be ready to go on to college."

"You know," one young man said, "Ganado High School is the Groton Prep out here on the Reservation. We want you to keep it that way."

An older man, one still wearing long hair and nugget earrings, spoke up. "You know, Doctor, we just authorized five million dollars of tribal money to set up a scholarship trust fund. We're going to help our young people go to college."

Watch out for the Navahos. Children and adults have swung into the rhythm of school days. Before many years, they will all be able to read. Some will be able to manipulate figures, to develop scientific theories, to solve whatever problems are then baffling mankind. Who can tell? It may be a Navaho who will finally project a fully integrated, truly all-American culture upon the moon. It could be Billy John.

228

CHAPTER SEVENTEEN

The Day We Traveled a Thousand Years

DURING OUR STAY on the Navaho Reservation, we had spent every free minute walking and climbing mesas. Always we were searching for ancient pottery.

Pottery shards lay everywhere. We soon learned that the fragments which all but paved our nearby mesas dated back to the early Pueblo periods, 700–1300 A. D. We also learned that a heavy rain or a persistent blow might uncover a perfectly preserved bowl or pot that had been imprisoned for a thousand years.

We never returned from our walks empty-pocketed, but neither did we return satisfied. We found handles and lips and the smoked sides of cooking pots. We found pieces that were coil-decorated, slip-glazed, or painted in an infinite variety of angular and spiral designs. We never wanted to stop walking. We were teased on and on by a particular shade of slate-blue clay or by a third of a bowl for which we just might find the other two-thirds intact. We fretted through the sandstorm days and the all-day rainstorms because they interrupted our walks.

All too soon the day for our departure came, serene and blue, but our pottery collection still consisted only of shards. We cherished each fragment for its texture, for the piecrust fluting some housewife-manufacturer had pinched into the clay hundreds of

229

years before Columbus got his big idea, or for the hair-line delicacy of its black or red pattern painted on with a yucca-leaf brush. We cherished these bits, too, as reminders of the trails we'd explored where no other white person had walked. Still, we longed for just one whole bowl from which a prehistoric mother had coaxed a child to eat his blue-maize mush.

Didibah arrived early that last morning. Her round, usually smiling face was sober. She wore her newest red print skirt and her entire savings account of turquoise and silver bracelets, but she seemed to have something bothersome on her mind. We almost suspected her of being sorry to have us leave.

She went outside and played basketball with Kee Tso for a few minutes. She came in, unlaced their infant daughter from her cradle board, and changed her diaper. She wandered back to our house to watch us pack.

Finally, well into the morning, she said, "My daddy knows where is a pottery. He says you can have it."

"A whole piece?" we gasped in unison.

"Yes. Only it's one crack in it."

"Where is it?"

Didi's arm flapped toward the northeast. "I don't know." Her smile came back now, full-blown. "Someplace where my grand-mother live."

We remembered the twenty impossible miles we'd driven to take her grandmother and grandfather home from the hospital. Still, the road alone would not have deterred us, but we had to be packed and ready to leave Tselani with the doctor when he finished conducting clinic that afternoon.

"You just might have time to drive up there," Don said, "if you hurry."

"Can you find it, Didi?" I asked.

"Yes. . . . I guess so. . . . My daddy out herding sheep." Her arm

230

flapped again toward the northeast. "We can stopping and ask him where is this pottery."

I climbed into the truck. Don and I instinctively looked at our watches. "You won't have any time to spare," he warned.

Didi slid onto the seat beside me, but when I stepped on the starter, she balked.

"Are you driving?" she objected. "Isn't Don come too?"

"He has to stay and pack so we'll be ready to leave with the doctor," I told her. "I'm driving."

Didi flung open her door and got out. "Wait a minute," she called, and padded off toward the community room.

For five minutes, I fidgeted. When Didi came back, with her came two of our "boys" who had substituted shovels for their Ping-pong paddles. The shovels clattered into the back of the truck. The "boys" came lounging after. Didi climbed into the cab beside me, and slammed the door. "Now," she said. "Might getting stuck."

So, properly equipped for travel on the Reservation, we started.

We descended The Hill—a feat that should be attempted only by suicidal burros—and had gone a mile or so into the valley, when Didi pointed off to the left. "There's my daddy."

Didi's father is a tall, spare man in his fifties. Long creases down each side of his face and across his forehead frame far-seeing eyes, straight, narrow-bridged nose, and a strongly sculptured mouth. He speaks no English, as far as we had ever heard, except the one word, "suitcase." He is one who weighs and accepts only that which he finds good in the white man's culture. In the main, he has retained his Navaho beliefs and practices. He sends his children to school, but he still harbors a distrust of white men in general that was drilled into him by his parents and grandparents. He had sedately ignored us during our stay at Tselani.

Didi giggled. "My daddy seeing us," she said.

When we stopped, Didi's father, flanked by curious sheep, wandered toward us through the sage and salt bushes. He approached smiling, but at the ground. Naturally he would not presume upon our privacy by looking directly into our faces.

Didi giggled. Her father chuckled. Impatiently I waited. Precious minutes ticked away.

Finally, Didi spoke in Navaho.

Her father gazed at his toe, making circles in the dust, and answered in Navaho.

Then, saying nothing, Didi fiddled with the truck's frayed sun visor.

Her father made no move to get on with his herding.

Although they did not look at each other, I had no scruples against studying their faces. Time was slipping away, and Didi appeared completely baffled as to the whereabouts of the piece of pottery with one crack in it.

Prodded by my watch, I finally asked, "Could your father possibly go with us?" I knew I was being most presumptuous to expect this dignified man to leave his work and go off to find a piece of pottery for me.

When Didi had put my question into Navaho, and the usual time-consuming silence had ticked away, her father spoke, then laughed.

Expecting a scornful rebuff, I looked to Didi for an interpretation.

She giggled. "He says, 'Sure, I will go with you girls.' "

We all, including the two shovel "boys" in the bed of the truck, laughed together.

"But we must going to our hogan; bring back my auntie to herd this sheep," Didi added.

More time! I looked at my watch. "Let's hurry then," I said.

We waved and drove on the mile and a half to the hogan for Didi's auntie. I was sure that she, busy with her weaving, would flatly refuse to herd sheep while Didi's father went off on a wild-goose chase with us "girls."

Didi ducked through the door of the large central hogan at the camp, and I waited. Before long she came back, and climbed into the truck. She did not consider it necessary to tell me that her auntie was changing into her sheep-herding clothes.

It took us a full half-hour to make the exchange of sheep herders, and get on our way.

We had tracks of a kind to follow as far as Grandmother's hogan. There after time out for a visit, Didi changed places with her father so he could direct my course. I forced the truck to follow his wag-gles through virgin sage and tumbleweeds half buried in drifted sand. Whenever the truck balked, I fretted over the wasted time, backed up, and explored a less sandy way. We had gone three or four miles when my guide stopped me with a vigorous flapping of his hand.

"*Sái! Sái!*" he warned.

"Sand too deep. Now we walking," Didi called out.

We all climbed down, and Didi's father led the way, off to the north at a right angle to our course in the truck. The two "boys" left their shovels and tagged along. We walked toward a series of red sandstone hills, their tops rounded by the incessant wear of wind and grinding grit, their valleys half filled with flour-fine, red sand.

We waded through sand that sucked at our feet and held us back as if we were plodding through wet snow. I frowned at my watch. The farther we went, the heavier grew my disappointment. If a piece of pottery had been left out in the sandstorms of the past two weeks, it might as well have been buried for centuries. There'd be no possible way for us to locate it in the few minutes I could spare before I must start back.

Still, Didi's father strode on, leading us around the end of the near sandstone ridge and behind, into a kind of mountain-rimmed bowl. The bowl was too large, however, to provide barriers against blowing sand. If anything, sand had drifted deeper inside the enclosure than out on the open range where it could move on and on with nothing higher than sagebrush and tumbleweeds to catch and hold it.

Didi's father stopped. Slowly he turned, studying the top of each red hill surrounding us. To me, they looked identical.

He and Didi exchanged a few staccato words and a long conversational silence.

"He was herding sheep when he finding that pottery," Didi explained to me. "He putting it under a tumbleweed."

The only evidences of tumbleweeds anywhere in this drifted basin were dry sprigs, none more than an inch in length, prickling up through the sand. These were everywhere.

With a kind of resigned sigh, Didi's father poked at a sand drift with his toe. Then he went down on his knees and started pawing a hole.

I could see none of the fabled Indian's sureness of instinct in the manner of his digging or on his face. I thought, "He doesn't have any idea of where it is, but he's going to put on a show of searching for my benefit." I looked around at the infinite number of places within that vast bowl where a few sprigs of tumbleweed broke the sand. "I'm afraid the wind's been blowing too hard lately," I said.

Didi's father stood up.

I abandoned all hope of finding anything. I thought, "He doesn't expect to find it. Maybe he wanted to visit Grandmother and decided to work me for a ride." I wished I'd stayed at Tselani to welcome the nurse when she drove in.

Didi's father took three steps to his left, and dropped again to his knees. A subtle change came over his face. Something about his manner now made me go down on my knees beside him, and start

234

pawing at the sand. Soon he gave a whoop. The sound had in it all the elation and frenzy that his grandfather would have poured into a war cry.

Together we gently eased the sand aside, and he lifted from its bed beneath the skeleton of tumbleweed a large cooking pot, fragile as eggshell and almost as thin. The spirit of a peaceful people haunted its utilitarian design. The smoke of campfires lighted with a fire-stick a thousand years ago blackened its bottom. Fingerprints of a housewife, concerned with feeding her family, decorated the outward-curving rim. Did I only imagine that I could smell boiled corn?

We got to our feet and Didibah's father thrust the pot toward me. I held a thousand years in my trembling hands. Awed, I looked up. He gazed directly into my eyes. Then his face broke open in a delighted smile.

Didi said softly, making nothing of it, "It been four years since he was putting that pottery under that tumbleweed."

Four years! A thousand years! A half-day for doing a near-stranger a favor! Time suddenly assumed a new grandeur for me. Never again would it submit to being ticked off in little minutes by a nagging watch.

I knew only one appropriate word of Navaho. Fortunately, I had learned early the word that I need most frequently when I am among The People. It is the word for "Thank you."

"*Ake'he*," I said, giving it my best guttural. "*Ake'he*."

Didibah's father kept his eyes on his outspread fingers as he nodded. I remembered another word of Navaho, *bila' 'ashdla'ii*—human being. Then he threw back his head and laughed. He, too, was making nothing of this thing he had done, but I had accepted his time and his gift and had thanked him in his own language. We were, after a thousand years, on an equal footing. Beginning there, we could become friends.

Bibliography

BOOKS

Adair, John. *The Navaho and Pueblo Silversmiths*. Norman, University of Oklahoma Press, 1945.

Amsden, Charles A. *Navajo Weaving*. Santa Ana, California, Fine Arts Press, 1934.

Bancroft, Hubert Howe. *History of Arizona and New Mexico, 1530–1888*. San Francisco, The History Company, 1874–89.

Browne, J. Ross. *Adventures in the Apache Country*. New York, Harper and Brothers, 1869.

Cremony, John C. *Life among the Apaches*. San Francisco, A. Roman and Company, 1868.

Curtis, E. S. *The North American Indian*. 20 vols. Cambridge, Harvard University Press, 1907–30.

Dale, Edward Everett. *The Indians of the Southwest*. Norman, University of Oklahoma Press, 1949.

Dyk, Walter. *Son of Old Man Hat*. New York, Harcourt, Brace, and Company, 1938.

Elmore, Francis H. *Ethnobotany of the Navajo*. Albuquerque, University of New Mexico and School of American Research, 1944.

Franciscan Fathers. *An Ethnologic Dictionary of the Navaho Language*. St. Michaels, Arizona, St. Michaels Press, 1910, 1929.

———. *A Vocabulary of the Navaho Language*. St. Michaels, Arizona, St. Michaels Press, 1912.

236

Haile, Berard. *Navaho Sacrificial Figurines.* Chicago, University of Chicago Press, 1947.

——. *Navajo War Dance.* St. Michaels, Arizona, St. Michaels Press, 1946.

——. *The Navajo Fire Dance.* St. Michaels, Arizona, St. Michaels Press, 1946.

——. *Prayer Stick Cutting.* Chicago, University of Chicago Press, 1947.

Haile, Berard, and Leland C. Wyman. *Beautyway: A Navaho Ceremonial,* Bollingen Series LIII. New York, Pantheon Books, Inc., 1957.

Kluckhohn, Clyde, and Dorothea Leighton. *The Navaho.* Cambridge, Harvard University Press, 1946.

——. *Children of the People.* Cambridge, Harvard University Press, 1947.

Kluckhohn, Clyde, and Katherine Spencer. *A Bibliography of the Navaho Indians.* New York, J. J. Augustin, 1940.

Leupp, Francis E. *The Indian and His Problem.* New York, C. Scribner's Sons, 1910.

Newcomb, Franc J. *Navajo Omens and Taboos.* Santa Fe, The Rydal Press, 1940.

Newcomb, Franc J., and Gladys Reichard. *Sandpaintings of the Navajo Shooting Chant.* New York, J. J. Augustin, 1937.

Oakes, Maud. *A Navaho War Ceremonial,* Bollingen Series I. New York, Pantheon Books, Inc., 1943.

Reichard, Gladys A. *Dezba: Woman of the Desert.* New York, J. J. Augustin, 1939.

——. *Navajo Medicine Man.* New York, J. J. Augustin, 1939.

——. *Navajo Religion,* Bollingen Series XVIII. 2 vols. New York, Pantheon Books, Inc., 1950.

——. *Navajo Shepherd and Weaver.* New York, J. J. Augustin, 1936.

——. *Prayer: The Compulsive Word.* New York, J. J. Augustin, 1944.

——. *Spider Woman.* New York, Macmillan, 1934.

Sabin, Edwin L. *Kit Carson Days, 1809–1869.* 2 vols. New York, Press of the Pioneers, 1935.

Sapir, Edward, and Harry Hoijer. *Navaho Texts.* Iowa City, Iowa, Linguistic Society of America, 1942.

237

Seymour, Flora Warren. *The Story of the Red Man*. New York, Longmans, Green and Company, 1929.

Thomas, Alfred Barnaby. *Forgotten Frontiers*. Norman, University of Oklahoma Press, 1932.

———. *The Plains Indians of New Mexico, 1751–1778*. Albuquerque, University of New Mexico Press, 1940.

Twitchell, Ralph E. *The History of the Occupation of New Mexico*. Denver, Smith-Brooks Company, 1909.

———. *The Leading Facts of New Mexican History*. 5 vols. Cedar Rapids, Iowa, Torch Press, 1911–17.

Underhill, Ruth M. *The Navajos*. Norman, University of Oklahoma Press, 1956.

———. *Red Man's America*. Chicago, University of Chicago Press, 1953.

Vestal, Stanley. *Kit Carson: A Happy Warrior of the Old West*. Cambridge, Massachusetts, Riverside Press, 1928.

ARTICLES AND MONOGRAPHS

Amsden, Charles A. "Navajo Exile at Bosque Redondo," *New Mexico Historical Review*, Vol. VIII.

Bailey, Flora. "Navajo Foods and Cooking Methods," *American Anthropologist*, Vol. XLII, No. 2, Pt. 1.

———. *Some Sex Beliefs and Practices in a Navaho Community*. Peabody Museum Papers. Cambridge, Massachusetts, 1950.

Blumenthal, E. H. "An Introduction to Gallina Archaeology," *New Mexico Anthropologist*, Vol. IV, No. 1.

Brewer, Sally Pierce. *The Long Walk to Bosque Redondo*. Vol. IX, No. 11 in Museum of Northern Arizona, *Museum Notes*. Flagstaff, 1937.

Haile, Berard. "Navaho Chantways and Ceremonials," *American Anthropologist*, Vol. XL (1938).

———. *Origin Legend of the Navaho Enemy Way*. No. 17 in *Yale University Publications in Anthropology*. New Haven, 1938.

———. *Origin Legend of the Navaho Flintway*. In *University of Chicago Publications in Anthropology*. Chicago, 1943.

———. *Starlore among the Navajo*. Santa Fe, Museum of Navajo Ceremonial Art, 1947.

Hill, W. W. *The Agricultural and Hunting Methods of the Navaho Indians.* No. 18 in *Yale University Publications in Anthropology.* New Haven, 1938.

———. "The Hand Trembling Ceremony of the Navajo," *El Palacio,* Vol. XXXVIII (1935).

———. *Navaho Humor.* No. 9 in *General Series in Anthropology.* Menasha, George Banta Publishing Co., 1943.

———. *Navajo Pottery Manufacture,* University of New Mexico *Bulletin* (Anthropological Series), Vol. II, No. 3 (1937).

———. *Navaho Warfare.* No. 5 in *Yale University Publications in Anthropology.* New Haven, 1936.

———. *Some Navaho Culture Changes during Two Centuries.* No. 100 in Smithsonian Institution, *Miscellaneous Collections.* Washington, 1940.

———. "The Status of the Hermaphrodite and Transvestite in Navaho Culture," *American Anthropologist,* Vol. XXXVII (1935).

Hill, W. W. and Dorothy W. "Navaho Coyote Tales and Their Position in the Southern Athabaskan Group," *Journal of American Folk-Lore,* Vol. LVIII (1945).

Kluckhohn, Clyde. *Navaho Witchcraft.* Peabody Museum Papers. Cambridge, Massachusetts, 1944.

Kluckhohn, Clyde, and Leland A. Wyman. *An Introduction to Navaho Chant Practice.* American Anthropological Association, *Memoirs,* No. 53, 1940.

Leighton, Alexander. *Gregorio, the Handtrembler.* Peabody Museum Papers. Cambridge, Massachusetts, 1949.

Matthews, Washington. *The Mountain Chant.* Washington, Bureau of American Ethnology, 1887.

———. "Navajo Gambling Songs," *American Anthropologist,* Vol. II (1889).

———. "Navaho Legends," *Memoirs of the American Folk-Lore Society,* Vol. V (1897).

———. *Navaho Myths, Prayers, and Songs.* Vol. V in *University of California Publications in American Archaeology and Ethnology.* Berkeley, 1907.

——. *Navajo Silversmiths*. Washington, Bureau of American Ethnology, 1883.

——. *Navaho Weavers*. Washington, Bureau of American Ethnology, 1884.

——. "The Night Chant," *Memoirs of the American Museum of Natural History*, Vol. VI (1902).

——. "The Prayer of a Navajo Shaman," *American Anthropologist*, Vol. I (1888).

——. "A Study in Butts and Tips," *American Anthropologist*, Vol. V (1892).

Mera, H. P. *Navajo Textile Arts*. Santa Fe, Laboratory of Anthropology, 1947.

Morgan, William. *Human Wolves among the Navaho*. No. 11 in *Yale University Publications in Anthropology*. New Haven, 1936.

——. "Navaho Dreams," *American Anthropologist*, Vol. XXXIV (1932).

——. "Navaho Treatment of Sickness: Diagnosticians," *American Anthropologist*, Vol. XXXIII (1931).

Reichard, Gladys A. "Human Nature as Conceived by the Navajo Indians," *Review of Religion*, Vol. VII (1943).

——. "Review: Father Berard Haile's, *Origin Legend of the Navaho Flintway*," *Review of Religion*, Vol. VIII (1944).

——. *Social Life of the Navajo Indians*, No. 7 in Columbia University, *Contributions to Anthropology*.

——. "The Story of the Big Star Chant"; "The Story of the Male Shooting Chant Evil"; "The Story of the Male Shooting Chant Holy, by Grayeyes"; "The Story of the Navajo Hail Chant." Privately printed or in manuscript form.

——. "Two Navaho Chant Words," *American Anthropologist*, Vol. XLIV (1942).

Stallings, W. S. *Dating Prehistoric Ruins by Tree Rings*. Laboratory of Anthropology, *Bulletin* No. 8. Santa Fe, 1939.

Steward, Omer. "Navaho Basketry as Made by Ute and Paiute," *American Anthropologist*, Vol. XL (1938), No. 4.

Tschopik, Harry, Jr. "Taboo as a Possible Factor Involved in the Obsolescence of Navaho Pottery and Basketry," *American Anthropologist,* Vol. XL (1938).

Wheelwright, Mary. *Hail Chant and Water Chant.* Santa Fe, Museum of Navajo Ceremonial Art, 1946.

———. *Navajo Creation Myth.* Santa Fe, Museum of Navajo Ceremonial Art, 1942.

Woodward, Arthur. *A Brief History of Navajo Silversmithing.* Museum of Northern Arizona, *Bulletin,* No. 14. Flagstaff, 1938.

Wyman, Leland, and Flora L. Bailey. "Navaho Girl's Puberty Rite," *New Mexico Anthropologist,* Vol. VI (1943).

———. *Navaho Upward-Reaching Way.* University of New Mexico *Bulletin* No. 389. Albuquerque, 1943.

———. "Two Examples of Navaho Physiotherapy," *American Anthropologist,* Vol. XLVI (1946).

Wyman, Leland, and S. K. Harris. *Navajo Indian Medical Ethnobotany.* University of New Mexico, *Bulletin,* No. 366. Albuquerque, 1941.

Wyman, Leland, and Clyde Kluckhohn. *Navaho Classification of Their Song Ceremonials.* American Anthropological Association, *Memoirs,* No. 50, 1938.

PUBLICATIONS OF THE UNITED STATES INDIAN SERVICE

Boyce, George A. "A Primer of Navajo Economic Problems" (mimeographed). Window Rock, Arizona, Department of the Interior, Navajo Service, 1942.

Underhill, Ruth M. *Here Come the Navaho.* Lawrence, Kansas, Haskell Institute, 1953.

Van Valkenburgh, Richard. *A Short History of the Navajo People.* Window Rock, Arizona, United States Indian Service, 1938.

Young, Robert W., ed. *The Navajo Yearbook.* Window Rock, Arizona, United States Indian Service.

Young, Robert W., and William Morgan. *The Navaho Language.* Phoenix, Arizona, Education Division, 1943.

———. *A Vocabulary of Colloquial Navaho.* Phoenix, Arizona, Education Division, 1951.

Index

Index

Clothing: 49, 52, 63, 71–72, 77ff., 88, 94ff., 106, 110, 136, 145, 154, 159, 162, 168f., 211, 219–20
Cradle board: 16, 70f., 79, 159

"Davy Crockett": 30ff., 93
Death: 48, 56f., 59, 122, 140f.
Diarrhea: xii, 15, 24, 62–74
Doctor: 11, 34, 42, 97–104, 139ff.

Education: 9f., 210–228; trailer schools, 9, 34, 74, 75–92; schools promised, 9, 85, 208, 213f.; boarding schools, government, 9, 86, 88, 105, 225ff., 227f.; criticism of, 79–92
Enemy Way chant: 141
Erosion: 108, 114
Evil Spirits (*tchindees*): 13, 26, 58f., 150
Evil Way chant: 141

Five fingers, meaning: 4
Fort Defiance: 6, 15, 98
Fort Sumner: 5, 8, 22f., 90, 132, 177, 207, 213f.
Funeral expenses: 56–58

Gallup, New Mexico: 4, 18, 100, 129, 169, 215
Ganado Mission (Arizona): xiii, 10, 18; superintendent, xii, 11f., 15, 228; high school, xiii, 88, 184, 219f., 228; boys' housemother, xiii, 219ff.; hospital (Sage Memorial), xiii, 17, 24, 45, 48, 51, 54ff., 98, 100, 129, 141, 145, 150, 153ff., 179–86, 190, 215
Ganado public school: 226–27
Girls' dance: 35, 38, 168–69

Hand-trembler (diagnostician): 46
Health, Education, and Welfare, Department of: 208
Hill, The: 17, 19, 22, 38, 145–47, 231
Hogan: 13, 17, 28, 69, 83–92, 179, 201, 218, 232f.
Hopi: 6f., 128ff.
Hubbel's Trading Post: 126, 190

Interpreters: 78ff., 145, 154f.; Tselani Health Center, xiv, 16, 62, 64, 121ff., 206; World War II, 178–79

Jewelry: 106, 126–27
Jokes: 166f., 172, 175, 186

243

Navahos Have Five Fingers has been printed on paper designed for an effective life of not less than three hundred years. The text has been set on the Linotype in twelve-point Granjon, a type design of this century which has grown to be one of our most popular book faces. Like most useful types, Granjon has its origins in type designs of years before, having been derived from the French Garamond face of the sixteenth century.

UNIVERSITY OF OKLAHOMA PRESS

Norman

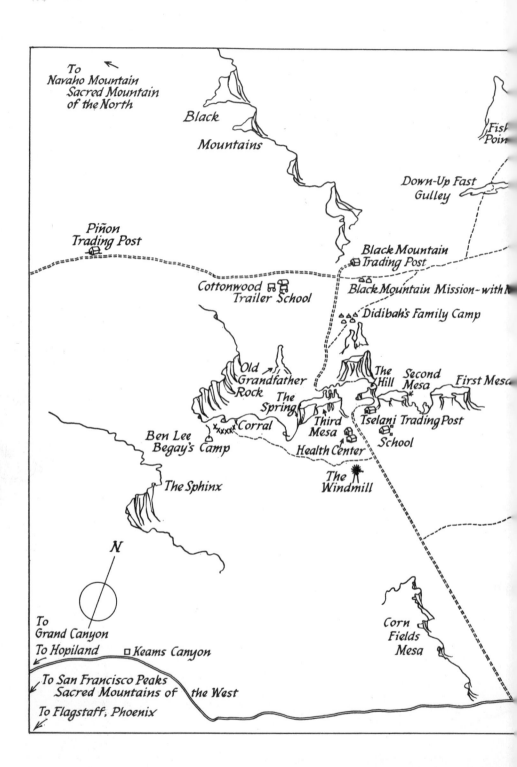

To
Navaho Mountain
Sacred Mountain
of the North

Black

Mountains

Fish
Point

Down-Up Fast
Gulley

Piñon
Trading Post

Black Mountain
Trading Post

Cottonwood
Trailer School

Black Mountain Mission–with M

Didibah's Family Camp

Old
Grandfather
Rock

The
Spring

The
Hill

Second
Mesa

First Mesa

Corral

Third
Mesa

Tselani Trading Post

Ben Lee
Begay's Camp

Health Center

School

The Sphinx

The
Windmill

N

To
Grand Canyon
To Hopiland

Keams Canyon

Corn
Fields
Mesa

To San Francisco Peaks
Sacred Mountains of the West

To Flagstaff, Phoenix